SECOND EDITION

◆

TCP/IP
and
ONC/NFS™

**Internetworking
in a UNIX™ Environment**

◆

Data Communications and Networks Series

Consulting Editor: Dr C. Smythe, University of Sheffield

Selected titles

NetWare Lite
  S. Broadhead

Running a Low Cost Network
  T. Dennis

PC-Host Communications: Strategies for Implementation
  H.-G. Göhring and E. Jasper

Token Ring: Principles, Perspectives and Strategies
  H.-G. Göhring and F.-J. Kauffels

Ethernet LANs
  H.G. Hegering

Local Area Networks: Making the Right Choices
  P. Hunter

Network Management: Problems, Standards and Strategies
  F.-J. Kauffels

Distributed Systems Management
  A. Langsford and J.D. Moffett

Managing NetWare
  F. Nowshadi

X400 Message Handling: Standards, Interworking, Applications
  B. Plattner, C. Lanz, H. Lubich, M. Müller and T. Walter

Systems Network Architecture
  W. Schäfer and H. an de Meulen

Frame Relay: Principles and Applications
  P. Smith

TCP/IP: Running a Successful Network
  K. Washburn and J.T. Evans

SECOND EDITION

◆

TCP/IP
and
ONC/NFS™

Internetworking
in a UNIX™ Environment

◆

Michael Santifaller

Santix Software GmbH

Translated by Stephen S. Wilson

ADDISON-WESLEY
PUBLISHING
COMPANY

Wokingham, England · Reading, Massachusetts · Menlo Park, California · New York
Don Mills, Ontario · Amsterdam · Bonn · Sydney · Singapore
Tokyo · Madrid · San Juan · Milan · Paris · Mexico City · Seoul · Taipei

Cover designed by Chris Eley and
printed by The Riverside Printing Co. (Reading) Ltd.
Printed in Great Britain by the University Press, Cambridge.

First printed 1991. Reprinted 1991 (twice).
Second edition printed 1994.

British Library Cataloguing in Publication Data
A catalogue record for this book is available from the British Library.

Library of Congress Cataloging-in-Publication Data
Santifaller, Michael.
    [TCP/IP und ONC/NFS in Theorie und Praxis. English]
    TCP/IP and NFS : internetworking in a UNIX environment / Michael
Santifaller ; translated by Stephen S. Wilson. -- 2nd ed.
       p. cm.
    Translation of: TCP/IP und ONC/NFS in Theorie und Praxis.
    Includes bibliographical references and index.
    ISBN 0-201-42275-1
    1. Local area networks (Computer networks)   2. UNIX (Computer
file)   3. TCP/IP (Computer network protocol)   I. Title.
TK5105.7.S2713   1994
004.6'2--dc20
                                                94-14981
                                                CIP

Preface

I first heard about NFS in 1984 when I began working with 4.2BSD and TCP/IP. At the same time, I was a witness to the intensive OSI discussions which were then under way. In common with many other UNIX developers who, like myself, were convinced from year to year that the next year would bring the breakthrough for UNIX, I then believed that, after a brief blossoming, TCP/IP and NFS would generally be replaced by the corresponding protocols from the ISO world.

Thus, I am even more surprised today to find that interest in these three technologies by the commercial data-processing world is in fact only now appearing. While this is very regrettable (in fact, it has often caused me great frustration over recent years), I am today convinced that the age of PCs and of MS-DOS was important and necessary. Through their experiences with the PC, users have learnt to apply the computer as a tool, and to understand the software that runs on it, despite its partial inadequacy. In addition, today the user is willing to accept a system with the complexity of UNIX, since he must perceive that performance exacts its price, as can be seen from the example of OS/2 with its storage requirements and its use of processor cycles. On the other hand, in recent years the ranks of UNIX gurus have been augmented by people for whom the operation of a computer is merely a means to an end and not the substance of life, and this has greatly improved the reputation of the UNIX operating system.

Another major change has also taken place in recent years. With the introduction of PCs on users' desks, users have come of age and hardware and software suppliers can no longer palm off products that have no apparent advantage other than their architectural conformity. *De facto* standards are accorded the importance they deserve. Manufacturers have, on the other hand, learnt that open, non-proprietary systems in which components, data and above all the knowledge about software and hardware are themselves portable and interchangeable, bring advantages for all sides. Our three technologies are examples of these principles:

- UNIX for portability to different hardware platforms;
- TCP/IP for reliable exchange of data between heterogeneous systems;
- NFS for transparent integration of heterogeneous computer systems into the network.

If we consider the history of UNIX, TCP/IP and NFS, it is conspicuous that, measured by the rapid pace of the data-processing industry, all three technologies are relatively old soldiers and, in the case of UNIX and TCP/IP, even real veterans. This could lead one to conclude that other technologies, presently being developed or standardized, may have to wait some time before their breakthrough occurs.

It may be that all good things take time to mature. For you, the reader, this will mean that, after reading this book, you will be able to use (exploit) your newly acquired knowledge for quite some time. Have fun!

Acknowledgements

At this point I would like to thank several people who have supported me during the production of this book:

> Hans Strack-Zimmermann, who led me from the back benches to the front line and thus made everything possible in the first place.
>
> Stefan Vogel, who was a great help as a technical conscience and a discussion partner during the correction of the manuscript.
>
> My former colleagues at iXOS, without whose tolerance nothing would have worked out.
>
> Peter Reiser, who was a reliable source of information on ONC.
>
> And, in particular, my wife Frau Christa and my two sons, Christoph and Marvin, who left me in peace, when necessary.

In addition, I heartily thank the Addison-Wesley Publishing Company for its commendable cooperation during the publication of this book.

Michael Santifaller
January 1991

For reasons of simplicity, the pronoun 'he' is used to relate to both male and female throughout the book.

Preface to the second edition

Against all my expectations, this book has been reasonably successful, thanks to the many readers who have bought it and to whom I should like to express my sincerest gratitude at this point. I am particularly pleased to have achieved my aim of writing a book on such an abstract topic as data transmission protocols which is understandable to a broad circle of readers beyond those with an appropriate bias.

This success is also partly a result of the positive development of the two technologies with which the book is concerned, which have spread meteorically since the publication of the first edition of the book. In addition to leading to further important technological developments and raising interesting commercial questions relating to usage, this has also meant that the limits of the current architectures have become apparent. In my role as architect of the OSF/DME I have been able to analyse these themes extensively and concretely in recent years. Naturally, it would be nice to discuss all these themes in a revision of the book; however, for reasons of time, this is only possible to a limited extent.

I have therefore decided that the second edition should focus on the following:

- The treatment of the TCP/IP protocols has been improved and additional figures have been included. Innovations in wide area networking and future developments are discussed.

- Additional examples are given in the area of TCP/IP applications and administration, which, like the TCP/IP protocols themselves, have remained stable.

- As a technology, NFS has not undergone substantial development in recent years, although here too a number of interesting new possibilities have arisen as far as its use and administration are concerned. These possibilities are discussed here.

- The most extensive changes affect the section on RPC, which is shown by the inclusion of the abbreviation ONC, for Open Network Computing, in the title of the book, and the treatment of the programmer interfaces for TCP/IP and RPC. The latter were, unfortunately, dealt with too briefly in the first edition, and I wish to redress that misjudgement here. As far as RPC is concerned, this model of distributed processing has caught on, not least because of the introduction of other technologies such as the OSF/DME, and this fact is taken into account in a more intensive treatment and a critical comparative analysis.

- A number of examples of socket and TLI/XTI programming have been included in the chapter on programmer interfaces (Chapter 13). The new interfaces of ONC/RPC 4.0 are included in the list of RPC interfaces and in the associated examples.

Because brevity is the soul of wit I shall no longer detain you with prefaces and wish you the best of luck in your further reading of this book. It may be, although I cannot know about it yet, that, if these lines have a long and honourable life, the third preface will be lying in wait for you on the next page.

Michael Santifaller
April 1994

Contents

Trademark notice

386/ix^{TM} is a trademark of Interactive Systems Incorporated.

DCE^{TM} and OSF/1^{TM} are trademarks of Open Software Foundation.

DYNIX^{TM} is a trademark of Sequent Computer Systems Incorporated.

Ethernet^{TM} and XNS^{TM} are trademarks of Xerox Corporation.

iXOS^{TM} is a trademark of iXOS Software GmbH.

Macintosh^{TM} and LocalTalk^{TM} are trademarks of Apple Corporation.

MS-DOS^{TM}, MS-OS/2^{TM}, LAN Manager/X^{TM}, Windows^{TM}, Windows NT^{TM} and
XENIX^{TM} are trademarks of MicroSoft Corporation.

NetWare^{TM} is a trademark of Novell.

NFS^{TM}, NIS^{TM}, SPARC^{TM} and SunOS^{TM} are trademarks of Sun Microsystems
Incorporated.

IBM 370^{TM} and OS/2^{TM} are trademarks of International Business Machines Corporation

Prestoserve^{TM} is a trademark of Legato Systems.

RPCTool^{TM} is a trademark of Netwise.

SINIX^{TM} is a trademark of Siemens AG.

UNIX^{TM}, RFS^{TM} and System V^{TM} are trademarks of AT&T.

VAX^{TM}, VMS^{TM}, DECstation^{TM} and Ultrix^{TM} are trademarks of Digital Equipment
Corporation.

Introduction

About this book

This book was developed from course material prepared on the same topic for iXOS Software GmbH. The book is not intended for specialists only. However, anyone who wishes to know even more details of the individual protocols described here or of specific algorithms is referred to the sources listed in the Bibliography. Nor is the book intended as a reference or a replacement for a manual. Whether you are a user, an administrator or a developer, the book should ease your entry into the world of UNIX systems networked with TCP/IP and NFS. It may possibly give you an appetite for networks and it should help you to tackle acute problems.

As far as the choice of topics is concerned, the characteristics of TCP/IP and NFS architectures mean that their protocols appear in various forms and guises on a large variety of computer systems. Every run-time environment has individual features that influence user and programmer interfaces, as well as the nature of available networking options.

A presentation and discussion of this variety would occupy all the space in this book several times over. Thus, we shall restrict ourselves to the operation of TCP/IP and NFS on computers running under the UNIX operating system, and within this topic to those areas that give an understanding of the architecture, of the interfaces and of their uses. Even on UNIX systems there are many differences in comprehensiveness and functionality.

This book is not a guide to the implementation of any of the protocols described; rather the intention is to enable you to understand what is happening in the computer and in the transmission medium when you use a command or programmer interface. This understanding will also help you to diagnose errors more rapidly and to correct any problems.

Some of the themes of this book can only be touched on; thus, the following areas are at best discussed in brief:

- gateway protocols
- routing
- network management
- domain name service, name server and resolver

1

- electronic mail.

Experience shows that most UNIX networks currently used in industry are too small to justify the installation of network management and routing. Electronic mail, and in particular the UNIX program *sendmail*, would fill a book on its own. The reader is referred to the literature available in the product documentation, which is usually sufficiently comprehensive to support the work of the system administrator.

Description of the notation used

As is generally the custom, different typefaces have been used to facilitate understanding and for emphasis:

- New terms are introduced in *italics*. Terms shown in this way are listed in either the Glossary or the Index.
- A `typewriter font` is used for screen output and program listings.
- All user entries in screen dialogues together with program and path names are given in an *`italic typewriter font`*.

Standards

Many readers will immediately ask themselves how they should rate the information from the following pages. Thus, to clarify the situation right from the start, here are a few comments on standards.

Only one of the protocols described in this book is a worldwide standard in the sense of an official norm from ISO, IEEE, DIN or other body; namely, the IEEE 802.3 standard for local area network technology. However, this does not imply that no reference specifications exist for all other protocols in the TCP/IP and NFS world or that implementations are at the discretion of individual manufacturers.

As you will find out in the following chapters, most protocols of the TCP/IP architecture are specified by a so-called *RFC* (Request For Comment). RFCs are publications for the Internet community; namely, those people and institutions who belong to the ARPA-Internet (more about the ARPA-Internet in Chapter 2). RFCs are published by the IAB (Internet Activities Board). They may be obtained either by electronic mail from the *Network Information Centre* (NIC) at the *Stanford Research Institute* (SRI) or in machine-readable form by file transfer from a computer in the NIC. The precise addresses for information about RFCs are given in an appendix.

Both specifications of individual protocols and articles about general problems of network operation are published in the RFCs. Not all the protocols published in RFCs are at the same time also Internet standards. A standard is first declared after verification by the IAB and a six-month transition period (draft standard). In total, approximately 1200 RFCs have now been issued. Relevant RFCs are listed in the Bibliography, and the RFC numbers are given in the discussions of the individual protocols.

Since uniform standards are in the interest of both the user and the manufacturer, the RFC specifications are overwhelmingly adhered to in all TCP/IP and NFS implementations known to the author. Compatibility is increased by the fact that the products of most manufacturers are based on the same source code and are additionally tested against generally recognized reference machines (for example, the Sun workstation for NFS). However, there are some differences in the robustness of the implementations (that is, system failures occur or connections are left hanging).

In addition to being Internet standards, IP, ICMP, TCP, FTP and SMTP have also been declared to be *MIL-STD* (the standard of the US military). These standards are laid down in publications of the *Department of Defense* (DOD). Although RFC and MIL-STD specifications are formulated in very different ways, the protocols they specify are largely identical.

In addition to the official and semi-official standards, there are also the much-valued industry standards, developed by copying the interfaces and functions of the product of a market-leading competitor, which cannot be the worst for the user. This category includes the NFS protocols and the well-known Berkeley utilities, with which we shall become acquainted later.

When talking about standards, we should not omit to mention the validation of implementations in respect of conformance with the standard. Like many other things, this point is handled pragmatically in the TCP/IP and NFS worlds. There are at present no official test specifications for TCP/IP. As previously mentioned, individual implementations are tested against a generally complete and seemingly robust implementation from another manufacturer. For NFS, a package of test programs is available for the licensee of the reference implementation source code, which may be used to test various aspects of the operation of NFS. But this proof can scarcely be termed validation. Sun Microsystems organizes an annual meeting on this topic (so-called *connectathon*) in California, at which manufacturers can test their NFS implementations against each other. This means that problems with the implementation of NFS or with the underlying protocols are as a rule soon recognized. Other test venues include the so-called *multivendor shows* at computer fairs, when, even here in Europe, computers from different manufacturers intercommunicate on a single network for demonstration purposes. If you are looking for a form of seal of approval for UNIX networking, you will be disappointed, since there is no such thing at present.

1

Protocols

- Why do we need protocols?

- The Open Systems Interconnection reference model

- Tasks of a protocol

- Connection-oriented and connectionless protocols

In this book, we shall talk a great deal about protocols. Therefore, before we begin the discussion of TCP/IP and NFS, it is sensible to reiterate briefly certain fundamental things about protocols.

Why do we need protocols?

Computer applications communicate with one another by so-called *protocols*. Protocols are rules that coordinate the exchange of messages between partners and thus make this exchange efficient, much as a certain formalism is required for understanding between people. An example of a protocol in the human world is the use of 'Roger' and 'Over' in radio traffic: both communication partners acknowledge that they have understood the message with 'Roger' and signal a change in the direction of speech with 'Over'.

Data exchange between data-processing systems naturally involves similar but also more extensive requirements, as we shall see in the next section. Because of the complexity of communication between data-processing systems, it is not sensible to execute all the necessary tasks in a single protocol. Thus, it is usual to apply several data-communication protocols simultaneously which, in the form of several overlaid protocol layers with different functions, cooperate and together provide a service for the user.

The Open Systems Interconnection reference model

In order to provide a uniform way of viewing the functions to be executed at each level, the *International Standardization Organization* (ISO) has proposed a protocol-layering model ('architecture model'), the so-called *Open Systems Interconnection* (OSI) seven-layer reference model (OSI, 1984).

This model, shown in Figure 1.1, is at present generally used as a framework in which to describe protocol characteristics and functions. In addition, it forms the basis for the development and standardization of ISO's own standard protocol layers. As a rule, every collection of protocols (including TCP/IP) has its own architecture, whose layers incorporate the individual protocols and their functions. Although in the following pages we discuss the TCP/IP architecture model in detail, we still use the ISO nomenclature, since this is generally known and recognized.

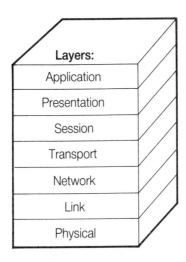

Figure 1.1   OSI reference model.

The layering is based on the principle that any layer (for example, the network layer) may use the services of the layer below it (in this case the link layer) without knowing how the latter provides these services. The layer above (in this case the transport layer) is offered a specific service of its own. The effect of this is to distribute the work across the layers. The major tasks of the protocol layers in the OSI model, as far as our consideration of the TCP/IP architecture is concerned, may be defined as follows.

Physical layer

This controls, among other things, the exchange of individual information bits (relating to transmission rate, bit coding, connection, and so on) over a transmission medium. Usually, the function of this layer is closely related to that of the overlying link layer. *X.21* and *RS232*, among other things, also specify characteristics of the physical layer.

Link layer

The task of this layer is to ensure the reliable transmission of information units (packets or blocks) and to address stations connected to the transmission medium. *HDLC* and *CSMA/CD* are examples of protocols here (see Chapter 3).

Network layer

The main task of this layer is to establish virtual paths between stations in the network, for example, by transmitting packets via switching nodes. IP is resident in this layer. Another well-known protocol is *X.25*.

Transport layer

This layer is responsible for transporting messages between communication partners; it usually controls the data flow and ensures that the data is not corrupted. TCP and UDP are transport protocols (see Chapter 3).

Session layer

This layer controls the exchange of messages in the transport connection (for example, change of transfer direction, session restart after interruption of a connection, and so on). One very well-known protocol of this class is *LU6.2*. In the chapter on ONC protocols (Chapter 9), we shall also consider the RPC protocol in more detail.

Presentation layer

Computer systems sometimes use different methods of encoding text, numbers, and so on. In this layer, it is determined how data types are to be encoded so that they may be exchanged between different systems. Examples here are *ASN.1* and *XDR*.

Application layer

The protocols that run in the application layer are defined by the task-specific programs (for example, for file transfer, database queries, and so on).

Tasks of a protocol

In addition to the addressing of the communication end points, the control of data flow and many other things, one of the main tasks of protocols is usually to provide reliable data-transmission services. Table 1.1 lists some of the most important tasks of protocols and examples of how they are implemented.

Table 1.1 Tasks of protocols.

Task	How implemented
Error detection	Checksums, sequence numbers, acknowledgements, watchdog timers
Error elimination	Retransmission of packets, correction methods (for example, *Hamming codes*)
Addressing	Address fields
Flow control	Receive windows, acknowledgements

Networks, computers and data lines are in no way reliable against the corruption of transmitted data or against a system failure. Since a user of a network service, whether an end user at a terminal or a protocol in a higher-ranking layer, expects error-free data, data-transmission problems must be first identified and then, if possible, resolved.

Data corruption during transmission, together with data loss, are among the most frequent problems. In large networks, a message may also be jumbled, for example, when a node sends the individual component packets of a message over several paths in the network. Here, we must ensure that the data is forwarded to the destination in the same order in which it was sent by the source (*sequencing*). Another common problem in data communication is that, usually, the sender sends the data more rapidly than the recipient is able to accept it and process it further. In order to prevent loss of data, the sender must, if necessary, be slowed down. This process is known as *sequencing* or *flow control*. We shall learn more about some methods of handling this problem in our discussion of TCP/IP.

Connection-oriented and connectionless protocols

In data communications, we distinguish between two different types of protocol, the so-called *connection-oriented* and *connectionless* protocols. In the former case, a connection with the communication partner is generated before the data is exchanged, while in the latter case only individual messages are sent. Without going into further details of their advantages and disadvantages here (which are sometimes discussed with religious fervour by experts), the two types of protocol may usually be distinguished by the volume of their reliability functions (which in turn affects their efficiency). A connection-oriented protocol with many reliability functions usually has a higher computational processing requirement than a connectionless protocol. Table 1.2 lists the characteristics of both types of protocol.

Table **1.2**   Types of protocol.

Type	Mode of operation	Application areas
Connection-oriented	Three phases: connection set-up, data transfer, connection shutdown	Terminal sessions, bulk data transfer
Connectionless	Transport of self-contained messages, stateless	Directory services, databases, transaction systems

The execution of message exchange in a connection-oriented protocol is similar to a telephone conversation. The data exchange only begins after the call partners have been introduced to each other and several formal exchanges have taken place. The connection is only broken off when both parties have agreed that the exchanged data is intelligible. Thus, connection-oriented protocols are also said to form *virtual circuits*. Virtual circuits, which from a UNIX programmer's view behave like a bidirectional pipe, are used when, in the context of the message exchange, it is important to maintain a connection over a relatively long period of time, or where data-transmission reliability plays a role. Several virtual (logical) connections may usually be maintained over a physical (real) line.

Information units in connectionless protocols are similar to telegrams, in that they usually form self-contained messages. Thus, these information units are also called *datagrams*. Connectionless protocols come to the fore in the transaction mode, for example, for database queries.

Because reliability functions such as flow control and packet repetition are incompatible with the stateless nature of connectionless protocols, it is sometimes necessary to define a superordinate layer which contains appropriate mechanisms and thus guarantees a reliable data transfer. Examples of such combinations include TCP as a superordinate layer for IP and RPC over UDP.

The transport layer of the TCP/IP architecture involves both types of protocol, with TCP as a connection-oriented protocol and UDP as a connectionless protocol (see Chapter 3). As we shall see later, IP is a connectionless protocol of the network layer.

2

Genesis of the TCP/IP architecture

- The beginnings of ARPANET

- Goals of the TCP/IP architecture

- Comparison of OSI and TCP/IP architecture

- Importance of the Berkeley UNIX implementation

The TCP/IP architecture (sometimes also called Internet architecture) has, over recent years, moved from a shadowy presence in the world of established proprietary protocols to the centre of heterogeneous networking. Before going into the technical details of the associated protocols, let us take a brief look at the historical background of the overall TCP/IP architecture.

The beginnings of ARPANET

At the end of the 1960s, there was great demand at various US universities and research centres for a network to permit nationwide utilization of their existing computer resources. In addition, it was also felt desirable to provide the researchers with a facility for data exchange. There was particular interest in practical experience of the design, implementation and use of network technology in general and of packet-switched networks in particular. To this end, the *Advanced Research Project Agency* (ARPA), a US government organization which later (from 1972) promoted primarily projects of military interest (and was thus renamed DARPA), formed the *ARPANET,* or the *DARPA Internet* as it is now known. In 1985, the Internet project was wound down.

Initially, ARPANET was a network of leased lines connected by special switching nodes, the so-called *Internet Message Processors* (IMPs). A host computer accessed ARPANET via connection to an IMP using the *1822* protocol; 1822 was the number of the *Internet Engineering Note* (IEN) in which the protocol was specified. Today, ARPANET is a subnetwork of the worldwide TCP/IP Internet; meanwhile, in research and industry there exist hundreds of other large TCP/IP networks, which are connected to one another.

The first proposal for ARPANET in Summer 1968 was initially for four IMPs at the University of California in Los Angeles (UCLA) and Santa Barbara (UCSB), the Stanford Research Institute (SRI) and the University of Utah. The contract was won in December 1968 by the company *Bolt, Beranek & Newman* (BBN). Over the following years, this company was to have a strong influence on the development of the TCP/IP architecture. Designs for the individual protocols and specific notions of what the ARPANET should achieve were developed, gradually at first. Demands existed for remote logins and file transfer (these two services came on top of the *Network Control Program* (NCP), the predecessor of TCP/IP). The TCP/IP collection of protocols was only developed later. ARPANET entered into regular use in 1971. In summary, it may be said that the success of ARPANET was determined by the uniform allocation of three services to all connected computers:

- remote login
- file transfer
- electronic mail.

At first, electronic mail was still integrated in FTP (see Chapter 4) and was thus a variant of file transfer. Only later was an individual protocol provided for this service (SMTP, see Chapter 4). Today, most of the Internet traffic is mail-oriented.

Goals of the TCP/IP architecture

In 1973, it was clear that the protocols then used in the lower layers were functionally inadequate. Consequently, a project was initiated to propose a new protocol basis. The main features of TCP/IP and the gateway architecture were first laid down in an article by Cerf and Kahn in 1974. The goals of the architecture were then defined to be:

- independence from the underlying network technology and from the architecture of the host computer;
- universal connectivity throughout the network;
- end-to-end acknowledgements;
- standardized application protocols.

Of these goals, at least the first two (namely, the requirement for heterogeneity on the host computer side and for the applicability of very different communication media or subnetworks) were unusual (in a world in which predominantly proprietary protocols were used). These properties are the reason why now, in the 1990s, TCP/IP can establish itself as an OSI technology.

As previously mentioned, in the years 1983 to 1984, the US Department of Defense had already declared certain protocols of the TCP/IP architecture to be MIL-STDs and introduced them as criteria in tenders. Version 4 of TCP/IP, as found on UNIX computers, was standardized in 1981 in ARPANET through RFCs. The full transition from NCP to TCP/IP throughout ARPANET only occurred in 1982.

The main characteristics of the TCP/IP architecture that directly implement the above goals are:

- connectionless protocols in the network layer;

- nodes as packet-switching computers;

- transport protocols with reliability functions;
- a common set of application programs;
- dynamic routing.

Comparison of OSI and TCP/IP architecture

The OSI reference model was introduced in the last chapter. There is also a reference model for the TCP/IP architecture. Since experiences of TCP/IP projects have influenced OSI standardization, it is not surprising that the two models are in part quite similar. The model shown in Figure 2.1 is intended to provide an insight into the thought processes of the TCP/IP developers.

The differences between the OSI and the TCP/IP architectures relate primarily to the philosophy in the layers above the transport level. Here, the OSI model has two additional layers, the session layer and the presentation layer. TCP/IP architects, on the other hand, viewed the functions of the presentation and session layers as part of the application layer.

The requirement for independence from the transmission medium also resulted in the decision to combine the later OSI physical and link layers at the network level of TCP/IP. In TCP/IP jargon, the elements of the

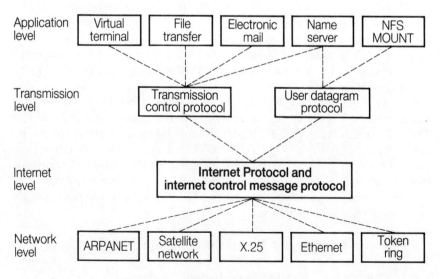

Figure 2.1 TCP/IP architecture model.

network level are termed subnetworks. In practice, the architectural solution is at this point thoroughly pragmatic, since the functions of the two lowest OSI layers will largely be implemented in a closed manner on intelligent (for example, Ethernet) controllers. In addition, the construction permits a self-contained network with its own nodes, protocol layers, gateways, and so on to be used as a subnetwork. Thus, for example, it is possible to operate TCP/IP over X.25 or any other network.

The requirement for universal connectivity is supported by the *Internet Protocol* (IP): at the network level of TCP/IP there is *only one* protocol which all participating hosts and nodes can understand. The *Internet Control Message Protocol* (ICMP), a component of every IP implementation, transports error and diagnostic information for IP.

At the transport level, in addition to the *Transmission Control Protocol* (TCP) and the *User Datagram Protocol* (UDP), other protocols are also operated in the Internet, mostly for research purposes. However, TCP and UDP are the two most common protocols.

Importance of the Berkeley UNIX implementation

The success of TCP/IP in the UNIX world was largely a result of the fact that the University of California in Berkeley undertook an implementation of TCP/IP on behalf of DARPA for its UNIX systems – namely, the famous 4.2BSD (*Berkeley System Distribution*) – and that the source code of this implementation was made available as *public domain software* in September 1983. Legally, research results and developments of American universities belong to the American people: they are available to anyone for a nominal fee, provided that the originator's copyright is recognized. For this reason, practically all TCP/IP implementations under UNIX are based on the Berkeley code. Moreover, many manufacturers of non-UNIX systems and intelligent peripherals have also referred back to the Berkeley basis. Since this results in the use of only one interpretation of the specifications, there are no problems associated with the use of systems from different manufacturers.

Meanwhile, there are new versions of the BSD system in which the implementation of the TCP/IP architecture is both corrected and improved: most of the TCP/IP implementations available today contain, in some form, either the modifications or the whole code of 4.3BSD as released in April 1986. Further optimizations of the TCP implementation were released in the so-called 4.3BSD/Tahoe version in June 1988.

3

TCP/IP – layers 1 to 4

- General specifications

- Internet Protocol

- Transmission Control Protocol

- User Datagram Protocol

- Internet Control Message Protocol

- Subnetworks

In this chapter, we are concerned with the protocols of the TCP/IP architecture in the lower layers, up to and including the transport layer.

In Figure 3.1, these layers are marked in the OSI reference model. We begin with the Internet Protocol (IP), since it is the central protocol in the architecture. From here, we move a layer upwards to the transport protocols, the Transmission Control Protocol (TCP) and the User Datagram Protocol (UDP), which together with the Internet Protocol exist in all systems and are independent of the transmission medium. Finally, a short section is devoted to the Internet Control Message Protocol (ICMP). Equipped with the necessary tools, we then consider the most commonly used transmission media in UNIX systems and their associated protocols.

In the discussion of protocol attributes, we shall describe the construction of protocol headers and the addressing in the different layers. Then we shall consider several algorithms that may be used to increase the efficiency of the implementation.

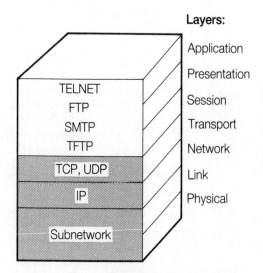

Figure 3.1   The lower protocol layers of the TCP/IP architecture.

General specifications

Not all computer architectures encode data in the same way; thus, the exchange of packets with protocol fields between such systems necessitates the determination of a uniform format for these fields. The same is true of user data; however, this problem is described in full in the section on the XDR protocol in the chapter on ONC protocols (Chapter 9). For the moment, we shall restrict ourselves to the protocol headers:

- Since TCP/IP protocol fields contain both single bits and integers, the bit and byte order is defined to be *big-endian*, with the element of lowest order at the lowest order position.

- An integer consisting of several bytes is sent with the highest-order byte first (see Figure 3.2).

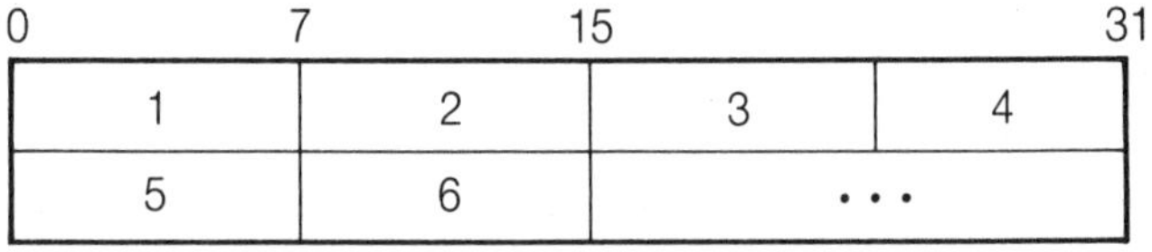

Figure 3.2 Byte sequence in protocol headers.

Internet Protocol

The Internet Protocol (IP) is the cornerstone of the TCP/IP architecture and is specified in both RFC 791 (Postel, 1981a) and MIL-STD 1777 (DOD, 1983a). All computers in Internet understand IP. The main tasks of IP are the addressing of the computers and the fragmentation of packets; it contains no functions for end-to-end message reliability or for flow control. IP makes the 'best effort' to forward packets to the next destination, although this forwarding is not guaranteed. Before we begin our discussion of the protocol header, here is a brief summary of the main attributes of IP:

- connectionless protocol;
- fragments (divides) packets if necessary;
- addressing via 32-bit Internet addresses;

- 8-bit transport protocol addresses;
- maximum packet size of 65 535 bytes;
- contains only a header checksum, no data checksum;
- protocol fields that are not always required are optional;
- finite packet lifetime;
- 'best-effort' delivery.

The fields in the protocol header shown in Figure 3.3 have the following meaning:

Version number

This 4-bit field contains the version number of IP, the current version number being 4.

Length

This specifies the length of the IP protocol header in 32-bit words. The shortest IP protocol header contains five words, since, as is normally the case, almost all TCP/IP packets begin with $45_{(16)}$. The length of the protocol header may be increased by the addition of optional fields, whence, for the purposes of interpretation, the exact length must be known.

0 3	7	15	18	23	31
Version number	Length	Service type		Packet length	
Identification			D F	M F	Fragment offset
Time to live		Transport		Header checksum	
Source address					
Destination address					
Options				Padding	

Figure 3.3   IP protocol header.

Type of service

This field contains entries for IP protocol devices to process the message according to set criteria. Figure 3.4 shows the detailed structure of this field. In practice, the value 0 is almost always used since qualitatively different paths between two computers seldom exist. Moreover, as far as is known, no UNIX IP implementation evaluates entries in this field (this may be because there is no program interface to fill the field).

Bits	If 0	If 1
0–2	Precedence	
3	Normal delay	Low delay
4	Normal throughput	High throughput
5	Normal reliability	High reliability
6–7	Reserved	

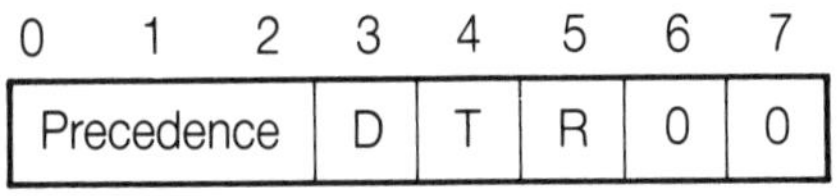

```
 0   1   2   3   4   5   6   7
+-----------+---+---+---+---+---+
| Precedence| D | T | R | 0 | 0 |
+-----------+---+---+---+---+---+
```

Figure 3.4   Structure of the service type field.

Packet length

This contains the length of the packet including the protocol header. This entry is used to establish the data length and is later passed to the transport protocol in the so-called pseudo header. Since this is only a 16-bit field, an IP packet (including the header) may have a maximum length of 65 535 bytes ($2^{16} - 1$). The IP specification states that any host must be capable of receiving and reassembling (that is, putting together again) packets of up to 576 bytes in length, which corresponds to 512 data bytes plus additional protocol headers. As a rule, computers are able to process much larger packets, at least up to the maximum size for the networks to which they are attached (for example, an Ethernet packet).

Identification

This is a unique identifier (for example, a counter) which is created by the sending host. This field is used in the reassembly of fragments to identify all the pieces of a fragment chain.

Flags

Two bits, DF (Don't Fragment) and MF (More Fragments), control the handling of packets in the case of fragmentation. If the DF bit is set, the IP packet is not to be fragmented under any circumstances, even if it can no longer be forwarded and must be discarded. The MF bit shows whether or not the IP packet is followed by more subpackets. The first bit of this field is unused. The fragmentation algorithm is described in more detail later in the chapter.

Fragment offset

If the MF bit is set, the fragment offset contains the position of the submessage contained in this packet, relative to the beginning of the whole message. The receiving host can use this entry to reassemble the original packet correctly. Since, because of the flags described above, this is only a 13-bit field, the offset must be counted in units of 8 bytes and the maximum length of an IP packet is thus $(8 * 2^{13}) - 1 = 65\,535$.

Time to live

Here, the sending host specifies how long the packet may remain in the network before it must be discarded. RFC 791 (Postel, 1981a) specifies the units used in this field, in seconds, and dictates that every node must decrease this field by at least 1 even if the processing time is less than one second. Thus, the time to live (TTL) is usually equal to the maximum number of nodes that a packet may pass through. If this field contains 0, the packet must be discarded by the current processor: this prevents a packet from circulating endlessly in the network. In this case, the sender of the packet receives an ICMP message about this event. As a rule, UNIX machines set this field to a value between 15 (4.2BSD) and 30 (4.3BSD). Old 4.2BSD-based IP implementations reduce the field by 5, while new versions reduce it by 1 only.

Transport protocol

This contains the ID of the transport protocol to which the packet has to be handed over. For example, for TCP, this number is 6, for UDP the number is 17 and for ICMP the number is 1. These numbers are determined by the NIC in regular RFCs (Reynolds and Postel, 1992). Currently, there are approximately 50 official higher protocols. In Table 3.1 a number of examples of transport protocol numbers that are currently assigned are listed; some of these relate to experimental protocols that will never be used in a commercial environment.

Table 3.1 Extract from the official list of transport protocol numbers.

Number	Abbreviation	Name
1	ICMP	Internet Control Message
2	IGMP	Internet Group Management
3	GGP	Gateway-to-Gateway
6	TCP	Transmission Control
8	EGP	Exterior Gateway
17	UDP	User Datagram
20	HMP	Host Monitoring
22	XNS IDP	Xerox NS IDP
27	RDP	Reliable Data
28	IRTP	Internet Reliable Transaction
29	ISO TP4	ISO Transport Protocol Class 4
30	NETBLT	Bulk Data Transfer
80	ISO IP	ISO Internet
86	DGP	Dissimilar Gateway
87	TCF	Transparent Computing Facility
89	OSPF	Open Shortest Path First

Header checksum

This field contains the checksum for the protocol header fields. Control checks prevent nodes or hosts from working with false data. For efficiency, user data in the IP packet is not checked; this check is carried out by the recipient within the transport protocol. Since the IP packet is altered at every node by a decrease in the TTL field, it is important that the checksum is created very efficiently. The so-called *Internet checksum*, for all protocols in the TCP/IP architecture in which checksums are used, is given by *the 1s complement of the 16-bit sum of all 16-bit words of the data to be checked.*

This algorithm is simple and fast; it is a prerequisite for the efficient operation of nodes. The error-detection ability of the Internet checksum is limited however: since it only involves simple addition, it would not, for example, detect missing 16-bit words that only contain zeros. However, the data checksums of TCP and UDP cover other entries (length, sender, and so on) in addition to the data, so that undetected data loss is practically ruled out.

Source and destination addresses

The 32-bit Internet addresses, whose structure will be described in detail in the following pages, are entered here.

Options and padding

For special tasks (network management, security), the IP protocol header is extended to include options that we shall consider later. So that the number of 16-bit words in the IP protocol header is always a multiple of 4 (we recall the header-length field), padding characters must be inserted, if necessary.

Addressing at the IP level

The addressing of a communication partner, such as an application program, requires four different addresses when passing through the first four protocol layers:

(1) a subnetwork address (for example, an Ethernet address);

(2) an Internet address;

(3) a transport protocol address;

(4) a port number.

Two of these addresses, the Internet address and the transport protocol address, are given in fields in the IP protocol header. The more important of these two addresses is the *Internet address*, which is a 32-bit field. It is more important because every Internet node has one or more unique addresses of this type and part of the packet-forwarding service provided by IP involves the use of fields in the Internet address.

As shown in Figure 3.5, there are three address classes with *network* and *host computer identifiers* of different lengths. The network ID defines the network in which a computer is situated: all computers in the same network have the same network ID. The host ID identifies a specific computer within this network. Host IDs with all bits set to 0 or 1 are reserved for special functions and should not be assigned.

Why are there three types of Internet address? The explanation is simple: when ARPANET began there were only *class A* addresses, since it was assumed that there would only be a few large networks. With the introduction of local area networks in many organizations, it was soon clear that this assumption was no longer tenable and it was decided to introduce two further types, namely, class B and class C addresses: *class C* for small networks with few hosts and *class B* for medium-sized networks. For several years, experiments have been carried out with so-called *multicast addresses*, in which IP packets with a *class D* address are simultaneously distributed to a group of hosts. Because, among other things, this mechanism requires an additional protocol which may be used to determine whether a host is a member of a specific group, it is only supported by a few systems. A detailed description is given in RFC 1112 (Deering, 1989). *Class E* addresses are currently reserved for research purposes.

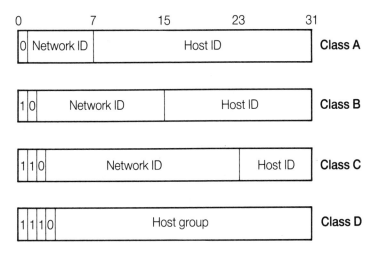

Figure 3.5 Internet address types.

However, there are advantages and disadvantages in the fact that the Internet address consists of a host ID and a network ID:

- The Internet address provides an unambiguous description of the access to a host in the network; thus, the gateways do not need to manage a host–network assignment table. Consequently, given the Internet address, the nodes can immediately make their routing decisions without first having to take time to determine the network number of a host.
- If a host is connected to another network, its Internet address is different.
- If a host is connected to several networks (so-called *multi-homing host*), it has several Internet addresses and thus several names, as shown in Figure 3.6.

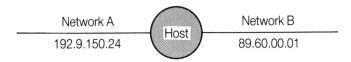

Figure 3.6 Schematic example of a multi-homing host.

- If only one of several connections fails, the host cannot be reached at this address, even though access via intact connections may still be possible.

Subnetwork routing

RFC 950 (Mogul and Postel, 1985) introduced a convention to facilitate routing in large subnetworks. In this convention, the host ID part of the Internet address is further subdivided into a subnetwork number and the station number proper. The subnetwork number may be used to branch into internal subordinate networks within the subnetwork; outwardly the whole network appears as a unit.

Figure 3.7 gives an example of a class B address with an 8-bit field for the subnetwork ID. The size and position of the subnetwork ID are not fixed, the size depending on the number of addressable subnetworks and the number of hosts per subnetwork. Both must be fixed for the whole network by the network administrator. Readers are strongly recommended to adopt the position between the network and host IDs as shown in Figure 3.7 and the ordering as for a single field. As a rule, UNIX hosts support subnetwork routing, at least all TCP/IP implementations based on 4.3BSD. The TCP/IP system must be told which bits of the Internet address form the network address; this is done using a network mask via the command *ifconfig*, which executes a logical AND operation with this mask and compares the result with the remaining bits of the original address. For example, for the address shown in Figure 3.7, the network mask would be FF.FF.FF.00$_{(16)}$, whereas without a subnetwork it would be FF.FF.00.00$_{(16)}$.

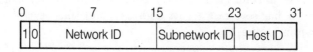

0	7	15	23	31
1 0	Network ID	Subnetwork ID	Host ID	

Figure 3.7   Class B address with field for subnetwork ID.

Internet addresses in practice

In practice, only addresses of classes A to C are used. Figure 3.8 shows examples of various address types, again as used in actual networks. The network ID is in **bold** type; the remaining bytes contain the host ID.

Class A
$10.0.0.32_{(10)}$ = **00001010**.00000000.00000000.00010000$_{(2)}$

Class B
$128.14.58.60_{(10)}$ = **10000000.00001110**.00111010.00111100$_{(2)}$

Class C
$192.9.150.202_{(10)}$ = **11000000.00001001.10010110**.11001010$_{(2)}$

Figure 3.8 Examples of Internet addresses.

When a host is connected to a network, the network and the host IDs must be assigned. If the host is to be integrated into a network that already exists, the complete new Internet address of this computer should be allocated by a network administrator, to avoid overlap with other hosts. If a new network is to be constructed, prior consideration should be given to whether it will be possible to operate later in association with other networks in the Internet. In this case, it is advisable to choose a suitable, non-colliding network ID immediately, since later changes are always very expensive. For this, you should apply to companies that provide access to the Internet as a service; these companies will then allocate an appropriate Internet address from their quota. A number of contact addresses are given in the relevant Appendix.

Inasmuch as network IDs are not prescribed externally, each of the three classes A to C may be used. The only point to note here is the maximum number of addressable hosts per class: 255 for class C against up to 16 million for class A. If a very large network is planned, the address should be chosen so that subnetwork addressing is possible.

If you allocate Internet addresses yourself you should also bear in mind that:

- network and host IDs with all bits set to 0 or 1, in other words, the addresses 0.0.0.0 and 255.255.255.255, are reserved for broadcasts and other purposes and therefore should not be allocated;
- the network ID 127 is reserved for the internal loopback network (see Chapter 6);
- host IDs equal to 0 or 255, for example, 192.9.200.0 or 192.9.200.255, are also reserved.

Fragmentation

In order to transmit packets over any type of network, IP must be capable of adapting the sizes of its datagrams to each network. Thus, for example, *CCITT X.25* packets should not be larger than 128 bytes, while an Ethernet packet may transport up to 1526 bytes of data. It goes without saying that data transport in the subnetwork should also be efficient.

To achieve this, it is not sufficient that the transport protocols, such as TCP or UDP, are themselves only able to generate small packets. Since a packet, *en route* from the source to the destination, may, in certain cases, pass through several different networks with different maximum packet sizes and since, moreover, this route may vary from packet to packet within a TCP connection, a flexible procedure must be applied: *fragmentation.*

Fragmentation means that the IP of each node in the network should be capable of dividing a received packet, in order to transmit it over a subnetwork to the next node or host. Every destination IP should be capable of reassembling fragmented messages.

Fragmentation process

Every fragment of a message contains its own complete IP protocol header together with the identification field for the initial message, which may be used to recognize all the fragments of a message. Individual fragments of a message may reach their destination over different routes. The position of the data of a fragment within the whole message is communicated using the fragment offset field.

Figure 3.9 shows a schematic representation of a fragmented IP packet. If a recipient has to forward a message fragment further, it may either forward the individual fragments unaltered or reassemble the whole message. (Of course, the second course is only possible if a recipient can be certain that it has received all the fragments, for example, in the case of a point-to-point link.) Thus, in certain cases, another, possibly optimal,

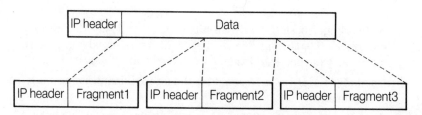

Figure 3.9   Fragmentation of an IP packet.

packet size may be provided for the next network. If the source processor wishes to prevent the packet from being fragmented, possibly because the destination is not capable of reassembling it, it may set the DF bit in the IP protocol header.

The following example shows the contents of various IP protocol header fields during the course of fragmentation. Note that the fragment offset is measured in units of 8 bytes; thus, all packets except the final packet must have a length divisible by 8 (in our case, 104 bytes). The whole of the data and the IP protocol header of length 20 bytes give a total length of 124 bytes.

Initial situation:

- Network maximum packet length: 128 bytes.
- Number of data bytes to be sent: 300 bytes.
- Packet identification: 2354.
- DF bit not set.
- No options.

Result after fragmentation:

- Fragment 1: length 124, offset 0, MF bit = 1, ID = 2354.
- Fragment 2: length 124, offset 13, MF bit = 1, ID = 2354.
- Fragment 3: length 112, offset 26, MF bit = 0, ID = 2354.

When the first fragment of a message reaches the destination, a watchdog timer is set. If the watchdog timer terminates before the remaining fragments arrive, the incomplete message is discarded. This prevents incomplete messages from reserving unnecessary buffer storage when fragments have been lost. If the sender is nonetheless interested in the delivery of the message, it will usually repeat it after a certain time (for example, for TCP after the termination of the acknowledgement timer). The reassembly timer in IP on UNIX systems is usually set to 30 seconds.

Options

In IP datagrams the so-called *IP options* are also sent as an extension to the IP protocol header. This optional extension was chosen so that it is not always necessary to reserve space for rarely used fields and so that the IP protocol header is kept as small as possible. The list of the available IP options is as follows:

Source route

The IP protocol header is followed by a list of Internet addresses through which the datagram must pass. Thus, a specific route may be prescribed. Here, we differentiate between a *strict source and record route* and a *loose source and record route*. In the first case, the nodes must follow the given path exactly, while in the second case any intermediate stations may be used.

Record route

The nodes through which the datagram passes are instructed to return their Internet addresses. Thus, we may determine the route taken by a datagram.

Time stamp

The time of passage through the nodes is returned, so that, for example, delays on sections may be measured. If at the same time a list of Internet addresses is requested, a specific route can then also be preset.

Security

Here, directions for handling the packets according to security requirements are laid down. This option was included in IP for military purposes and is only supported by a few commercial implementations. The most recent specification of this option may be found in RFC 1038 (St Johns, 1988).

Stream identifier

This is an outdated option, which should be ignored.

End-of-option list

This indicates the end of the list of options.

No operation

This may be used to pad out the option list.

Options consist of either a single byte with the option identifier or a combination of identifier, length field and data. Should entries in the options be recorded by nodes, the sender must reserve sufficient room for the option data in the IP protocol header. This prevents the IP protocol header from expanding and avoids data being copied from one area to another to make room for option data. In this case, a pointer points to the next available space in the options. Further details may be found in RFC 791 (Postel, 1981a).

Usually, UNIX implementations support all the above options with the exception of security and stream identifier.

RFC 1063 (Mogul *et al.*, 1988) proposes a *probe MTU option* to determine the least *Maximum Transfer Unit* (MTU) on a route. This information enables a transport protocol to generate an optimal packet length and thus prevent additional fragmentation. Suppose that an IP datagram with this option is sent. The nodes passed through by the IP packet enter the MTU of the next subnetwork in a field provided for this purpose, whenever the MTU is less than the value already contained in that field. The recipient generates and returns a response datagram. This option is expected to be supported by UNIX systems in the future.

Transmission Control Protocol

The Transmission Control Protocol (TCP) is a protocol of the transport layer, and thus lies above IP. Its main task is the reliable transportation of data through the network. TCP is specified in RFC 793 (Postel, 1981c) and in MIL-STD 1778 (DOD, 1983b). Its transport address in the IP protocol header is 6. Briefly, the main attributes of TCP are:

- Provides a fully duplex bidirectional virtual circuit.
- As seen by the user, data is transmitted as a data stream (not in blocks).
- Reliable data transmission using:
  - sequence numbers
  - the formation of checksums with acknowledgements of receipt
  - acknowledgements with timeout
  - segment retransmission after acknowledgement timeout.
- Sliding-window principle for greater efficiency.
- Urgent data and push function.
- Transport-user addressing using 16-bit port number.
- Graceful connection shutdown.

The functionality of TCP is not very different from other complicated transport protocols (such as ISO-TP4) except for the fact that block boundaries are not preserved. The reason for this difference in behaviour is the byte-oriented nature of TCP: nearly all the fields used in the protocol

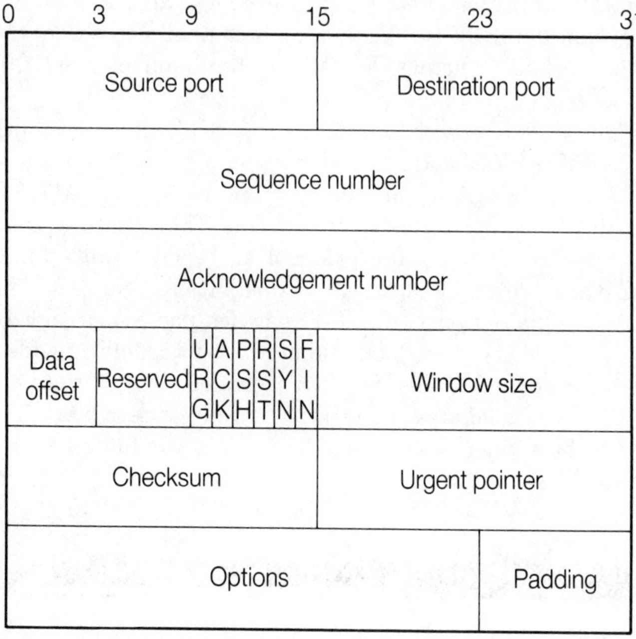

Figure 3.10 TCP protocol header.

header are calculated in bytes and not in blocks. This allows a flexible dimensioning of blocks. Data is transmitted in the form of blocks (in TCP jargon: segments); however, the size of the segment in the network is determined by parameters such as network load, window size or the resources of one of the partners. Thus, given these variable segments, it would be very expensive to preserve the distribution over blocks as generated originally by the user (or in some cases randomly). Experience also shows that it is not absolutely necessary to preserve block boundaries in the transport layer and that this may be undertaken by functions in other layers (for example, in the session layer).

Figure 3.10 shows the structure of the TCP protocol header. The fields included have the following significance:

Source and destination port numbers

These are two 16-bit fields that denote the end points at both ends of a virtual circuit. We shall discuss the significance of the port number in more detail later in the chapter.

Sequence and acknowledgement numbers

Each of these is a 32-bit word that gives the position of the data within the data stream exchanged during the connection. The sequence number refers to the send direction and the acknowledgement number applies to the number of bytes received by the other end. On connection set-up, each partner of a TCP connection generates an initial sequence number whose most important property is that it is not repeated within the period during which a packet may remain in the network (IP time to live). These numbers are exchanged and acknowledged on connection set-up. On data transfer, the sender increases the sequence number by the number of bytes already sent. In the acknowledgement number, the recipient states how many bytes of the message have been correctly received. The large numerical range of 2^{32} provides sufficient protection against duplication and overlap, since on overflow sequence numbers start again at 0.

Data offset

This entry contains the length of the TCP protocol header in 32-bit words and is used to determine the start of the data.

Flags

These bits are used to trigger actions in TCP. If they are set to 1, their meaning is shown in Table 3.2.

Table 3.2   Meaning of the TCP flags.

Name	Explanation
URG	Pointer in *Urgent* field is valid.
ACK	Acknowledgement number is valid.
PSH	Data in this segment should be passed immediately to the application: an acknowledgement for this segment means that all data up to this acknowledgement number has reached the communication partner. UNIX implementations always send PSH when they send all the remaining data in the send buffer with the segment.
RST	Resetting of the connection or response to an invalid segment.
SYN	Connection set-up request, must be acknowledged.
FIN	One-sided connection shutdown and end of the data flow from this direction, must be acknowledged.

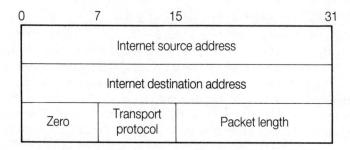

Figure 3.11 TCP and UDP pseudo header.

Window size

This contains the number of bytes that the recipient can receive in its data buffers for this connection (*receive window*). The destination TCP uses this entry to control the data flow: a window size of 0 would, for example, effectively stop the source TCP. The data flow is restarted by gradually increasing the window size. The maximum window size is 2048 bytes in 4.2BSD and 4096 bytes in 4.3BSD. Optimal determination of the window size during data transfer is one of the most complicated algorithms of a TCP implementation.

Checksum

The checksum is applied to the protocol header, the data and the *pseudo header*. As in all other protocols described here, the same algorithm as used to generate the IP checksum is used to generate the TCP checksum.

In the pseudo header shown in Figure 3.11, a number of fields from the IP protocol header are delivered to the transport protocol together with the data segment. These are included in the TCP checksum calculation for the segment and should, in addition to providing the information contained, prevent packets from being incorrectly forwarded by IP. Moreover, a check for undetected data loss is also possible, using the length entry (see the description of the IP checksum).

On the sender side, a pseudo header is also generated on creation of the TCP checksum and is included in the checksum. The data in the pseudo header is however not transferred in this form in the segment.

Urgent pointer

Together with the sequence number, this is a pointer to a data byte. This data byte is the end of a message section where the following data is identified as being important. This function is termed *urgent data*. Since this mechanism is somewhat unusual and complicated, a separate section has been devoted to it in the following pages, so as to provide more details of the function and its application.

Options

TCP has only three options: End-of-Option List, No Operation and Maximum Segment Size. The latter is sent on connection set-up to indicate readiness to receive segments larger than 536 bytes. As a rule, UNIX systems cater for segment sizes between 1024 bytes (4.2BSD) and the maximum network packet length (4.3BSD).

Port numbers

As already noted, port numbers are used for addressing at the transport level. Since port numbers are 16-bit fields, a host computer may theoretically establish up to 65 535 different TCP connections concurrently.

UDP also uses port numbers for addressing. Note however that TCP and UDP each have their own address space; thus, port number 511 in TCP is not identical to port number 511 in UDP. The range of validity of a port number is restricted to a host. Together the network number, the host ID and the port number determine a communication end point (or socket), similar to an extension of a telephone installation, as shown in Table 3.3.

Connection establishment over TCP proceeds as for the telephone; here too there is a passive partner (the person being called) and an active partner (the caller). Before two programs can communicate with one another, both must initialize communication end points, whose addresses are used in the protocol headers of the individual layers. So that they may be indeed connected together, the address of the passive partner must be known to the active partner; thus, both parties must have previously agreed upon a port number at which the passive partner (or *server*) should await the connection. The port number of the active partner (or *client*) is irrelevant, unless the server prescribes a special port number for the client.

Like the service department or the speaking clock in the telephone

Table 3.3 Analogy between Internet addresses and phone numbers.

Internet socket	*Telephone*
Network number	Area code
Host ID	Phone number
Port number	Extension

Table 3.4   Extract from the list of fixed port numbers.

Service	Port number	Protocol
echo	7	UDP
echo	7	TCP
discard	9	UDP
discard	9	TCP
daytime	13	UDP
daytime	13	TCP
quote	17	UDP
quote	17	TCP
chargen	19	UDP
chargen	19	TCP
ftp-data	20	TCP
ftp	21	TCP
telnet	23	TCP
smtp	25	TCP
time	37	UDP
time	37	TCP
tftp	69	UDP
finger	79	TCP
portmap	111	TCP
portmap	111	UDP
exec	512	TCP
login	513	TCP
shell	514	TCP
printer	515	TCP
who	513	UDP
syslog	514	UDP
talk	517	UDP
ntalk	518	UDP
route	520	UDP
Xserver	6000	TCP

system, TCP/IP applications, such as, for example, *TELNET* or *FTP*, could be regarded as fixed services, which are available at a given, well-known number. In the TCP/IP world, such a number is called a *well-known port number*. Then we may say that: *every service must have its own fixed port number. The client addresses the server, which provides the service at this port number.*

Table 3.4 contains examples of some of the services available on UNIX machines, together with their port numbers and the protocol used for these services. These and other details are found in the file /etc/services. As you will see, rlogin and rwhod use the same port number; but they do so without colliding, since one service is executed over TCP and the other over UDP. On the other hand, in the case of the NFS portmap program, the same service is offered over both protocols and for simplicity the same port number is used for both. The operation of several protocols is actually implemented in the server itself, since the latter opens a communication end point for each protocol used.

Sliding window

TCP works on the *sliding-window* principle (Figure 3.12): each party to a connection may send the number of bytes specified in the window, without having to wait for an acknowledgement from the other party. During the send process, acknowledgements of receipt of the data by the other party (which may again simultaneously set new window sizes) may be simultaneously received. This means that the sender does not have to wait for the corresponding acknowledgement after each segment.

Simple protocols without a window mechanism send (for example) a data block at any given time and then wait for an acknowledgement before

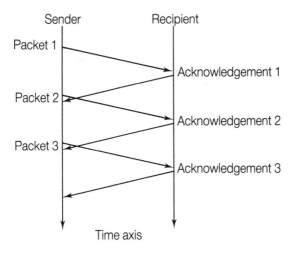

Figure 3.12   Schematic representation of the sliding-window principle.

sending another block. It is clear that this cannot provide a satisfactory data throughput rate, for example, on a satellite circuit with several seconds, elapsed time, and that valuable transmission bandwidth is lost. Simultaneous send-and-acknowledge achieves a parallelism that produces an optimal throughput rate even on subnetworks with a higher elapsed time.

Urgent data

Other protocols, such as the ISO transport protocols, contain a feature called *expedited data*. This provides the possibility of sending urgent messages (usually of restricted length) to the communication partner over and above the normal data stream ('*out-band*'). This function is generally used to signal an unusual state: for example, program abortion or the like.

Urgent data (Figure 3.13) is a different mechanism, which is often wrongly compared with expedited data. Unlike expedited data, in this case the message is not preferentially transported; instead TCP signals to the receiving application that important data, which should be read immediately, is to be found at a certain point in the data stream ('*in-band*'). The urgent pointer points to the last byte of the previous data, and the next byte is the start of the urgent message. It now falls to the receiving application to read the data at the position following the urgent pointer.

In UNIX systems, a signal may be sent to notify an application of the receipt of urgent data.

The urgent-data mechanism was specially conceived for TELNET: the TELNET client uses it to send *synchc* events, upon which the TELNET server is instructed to discard all data queuing in the circuit and to look

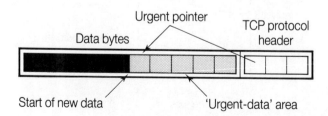

Figure 3.13 Schematic representation of the urgent-data mechanism.

for TELNET protocol statements. In this way, for example, an urgent statement can be forcibly processed, even though the TELNET server has not processed all the input data prior to this statement.

TCP scenarios

In this section, we shall show in three stages how TCP uses the fields of the TCP protocol header in the most important phases of a connection, namely, *connection establishment, data exchange* and *connection shutdown*. In the diagrams, the arrows always indicate the segment send direction. The fields of the TCP protocol header are given in brackets.

Figure 3.14 shows a connection. Here, there is a so-called *three-way handshake* in which each party, activated by the SYN flag, must acknowledge the other party's sequence number by increasing it by 1. The sequence number (SEQ = 100) of TCP A is found in the response of TCP B in the acknowledgement field (ACK = 101), and vice versa. The ACK flag indicates that the value in the acknowledgement field is valid.

Figure 3.15 shows a data exchange that is taking place in both directions simultaneously. Note how the destination always acknowledges by entering the sequence number in the SEQ field (SEQ = 101) increased by the number of data bytes received (DATA = 5) in the ACK field (ACK = 106). Data is sent in the opposite direction together with the acknowledgement and is acknowledged in the same way.

TCP A   **TCP B**

→   (SEQ = 100),(FLAGS = SYN)

                    (SEQ = 300),(ACK = 101),(FLAGS = SYN,ACK)   ←

→   (SEQ = 101),(ACK = 301),(FLAGS = ACK)

Figure 3.14   Connection in TCP.

TCP A   **TCP B**

→   (SEQ = 101),(ACK = 301),(FLAGS = ACK),(DATA = 5)

              (SEQ = 301),(ACK = 106),(FLAGS = ACK),(DATA = 10)   ←

→   (SEQ = 106),(ACK = 311),(FLAGS = ACK)

Figure 3.15   Data exchange in TCP.

TCP A		TCP B
→	(SEQ = 106),(FLAGS = FIN,ACK)	
	(SEQ = 311),(ACK = 107),(FLAGS = ACK)	←
	(SEQ = 311),(ACK = 107),(FLAGS = ACK),(DATA = 5)	←
→	(SEQ = 107),(ACK = 316),(FLAGS = ACK)	
	(SEQ = 316),(ACK = 107),(FLAGS = FIN,ACK)	←
→	(SEQ = 107),(ACK = 317),(FLAGS = ACK)	

Figure 3.16   Connection shutdown in TCP.

Figure 3.16 shows how the connection is shut down on one side when TCP A sends a FIN flag. TCP B acknowledges the FIN flag by increasing the sequence number (SEQ = 106) in the response segment by 1 (ACK = 107). This acknowledges the receipt of all data sent by TCP A up to that time. After that, no more data should be sent by TCP A. However, TCP B may continue to send until it itself sends a FIN flag.

While during connection establishment one party is active and the other passive, during data exchange and connection shutdown initiatives both partners have equal rights.

Timers

In all protocols, a great deal of consideration is given not only to the protocol elements but also to the algorithms and the associated operations. Thus, in all protocol implementations timers are used to monitor the different operations. In this section, we shall consider the functions of these timers in TCP implementations in more detail.

Retransmission timeout

The *Retransmission Timeout* (RTO) is set off when the prescribed time interval between the sending of a TCP packet and the receipt of the corresponding acknowledgement is exceeded. In this case, the packet must be resent. In fact, the time interval should not be fixed, since otherwise TCP could not be operated over networks with different elapsed times. If, for example, we compare Ethernet with a serial connection via several gateways, the transmission rates differ by a factor of a thousand. Thus, for every packet in TCP, the time between transmission and receipt of an acknowledgement (the so-called *Round Trip Time* (RTT)) is measured. This measurement is fed into a formula that filters out peaks and troughs but also gradually adjusts to an extended or reduced elapsed time. The result is the *Smoothed Round Trip Time* (SRTT), which is the mean elapsed time for

---

$$\text{SRTT: } S = \alpha S + (1 - \alpha)R$$
$$\text{RTO: } T = \min(U, \max(L, \beta S))$$

Key
$S \equiv$ Smoothed round trip time
$R \equiv$ Round trip time
$T \equiv$ Retransmission timeout (for example, 30 seconds)
$U \equiv$ Maximum time limit (for example, 1 second)
$\alpha \equiv$ Smoothing factor (for example, 0.9)
$\beta \equiv$ Scaling factor (for example, 2.0)

Figure 3.17   Calculation of SRTT.

segment exchange. This time is again scaled to allow for unforeseen delays.

Figure 3.17 shows both formulae specified by RFC 793: firstly, the SRTT filter, then the calculation of the RTO. If, after the retransmission of a segment, the retransmission timer again goes off, the RTO is usually increased exponentially up to 12 times. The connection is only deemed to be disrupted when this increase has no effect.

Persistence timer

In data exchange over TCP, it is in principle possible for the receive window to be exactly 0 and for a segment intended to reopen the window to be lost at that exact same instant. As a result, both TCPs then go into an infinite wait for each other. A countermeasure against this is the persistence timer, which sends small TCP segments (1 byte) at set time intervals to check whether the receiving party is ready again. If, as before, the window size is 0, a negative acknowledgement is returned; if the window size is larger, further data may be sent after the positive acknowledgement.

Quiet timer

The designers of TCP were very careful people who wished to prevent any possible confusion of connections because of out-of-date TCP segments wandering about in the network (this possibility was distinctly possible in a network of the scale planned). Thus, after TCP connection shutdown, port numbers are only released after a fixed time interval of twice the *Maximum Segment Lifetime* (MSL) has elapsed. The MSL corresponds to the time in the TTL field used by IP.

UNIX users notice this waiting time when they reopen a connection between the same two partners (same port numbers) immediately after a

Table 3.5   TCP timer settings (implementation-dependent).

Timer	Setting (seconds)
Retransmission timeout	Dynamic
Persistence timer	5
Quiet timer	30
Keep-alive timer	45
Idle timer	360

shutdown. The system tells them that the port number used is still busy. A new connection set-up is only possible after approximately 30 seconds.

Keep-alive timer and idle timer

Here, we are concerned with two timers which were not foreseen in the original TCP specification, but which are implemented in UNIX systems. Both are related. The keep-alive timer has the effect that an empty packet is sent at regular intervals to check that the connection to the other TCP still exists. If the partner TCP does not reply, the connection is broken off after expiry of the idle timer. An application activates this timer with the KEEP_ALIVE option via the socket interface.

The values of the timers are given in Table 3.5. Note that the duration of the timer is implementation-dependent and need not always be set to the values given. The values given here are from UNIX implementations up to and including 4.3BSD.

Algorithms to increase efficiency

A TCP implementation 'according to the specification' and a high-grade optimized TCP subsystem, as found in UNIX systems, are very different. Countless improvements have been made to UNIX TCP implementations over recent years and many new algorithms have been integrated into 4.2BSD, 4.3BSD and subsequent versions, as described briefly here.

Acknowledgement delay

This is a veteran that was already present in 4.2BSD. Normally, the destination TCP immediately sends a response segment, which reduces the window size and acknowledges the data, after a segment is received. After the data is copied to the receiving process, the system data buffers are freed, with the result that a segment to increase the window size is sent. When the program has processed the data, usually a response follows shortly; thus, one transaction requires three segments.

It has been shown that in many cases, for example, in TELNET operation, it is advantageous to delay the acknowledgement segment by two tenths of a second. After this brief period, all three items of information (window size, acknowledgement and response) may be sent in a single segment. So as not to slow down data transfers requiring a high throughput rate, the delay is omitted when a receive window is changed by at least 35% or two maximum segments.

Silly window syndrome avoidance

In certain circumstances, the receive-window entries sent are so small that the network and the computer are overloaded with the many acknowledgement segments. To prevent this, the receive window is only expanded when sufficient space is available (more than a quarter of the data buffer or a maximum segment). Conversely, the sender TCP behaves in a conservative way and only sends if the window provided is sufficiently large.

Nagle algorithm or small packet avoidance

Named after its inventor John Nagle, this algorithm attempts to prevent the sending of small TCP segments. In this case, it is a question, on the sender side, of preventing data presented to TCP in small units by the application from being forwarded in this form. A first segment is sent immediately, while further data on the sender side is buffered until either a full maximum segment can be sent or an acknowledgement for the first segment is received. There are problems with this algorithm for applications that send many small messages (such as the X window system) without receiving a response. In this case, the Nagle algorithm can be deactivated in a connection-dependent way.

Slow start with congestion avoidance

These related algorithms, sometimes also called the Jacobson algorithms, have only recently become known and are mainly important for slow networks and for the operation of networks with gateways.

Over recent years, it had been noticed that as its load increased the Internet delivered an increasingly lower throughput and indeed, to some extent, more or less broke down. When the processes were considered in more detail, it was established that more than half the packets in the network were retransmissions of lost TCP segments. What had happened? A network path (here from the sender's data buffer, possibly via gateways, to the destination) can only carry a finite amount of data. When a gateway or a host is heavily loaded with traffic, it may happen that there is insufficient buffer space available in which to enter segments. In this case, the segments are discarded by the gateway, whereupon the sender of the packet decides to send a retransmission after the RTO has elapsed, and consequently the total network load again increases unnecessarily. The slow-start algorithm now attempts to determine how much data may be *en route* to a destination at a given time without losses occurring. This is done by gradually increasing the transmitted data set until a point is reached at which there is an equal flow of data without retransmissions. Where previously the data set to be transmitted was determined by the size, now the storage capacity of the network path, the so-called *congestion window*, is the determining factor, where the congestion window is always smaller than or equal to the receive window. Once the congestion window has evened out, it is only altered again when the occurrence of retransmissions signals an increase in the network load; in this case, congestion avoidance comes into play. At the same time, attempts are made to use any resources that may be released by constant, careful expansion of the congestion window. Because of the conservative behaviour, the throughput may be increased by up to 30% and the number of retransmitted segments decreased by more than 50%.

In association with these two algorithms, the determination of the retransmission timeout is also improved. The new algorithm produces even faster changes in the round-trip time; thus, additional packet retransmissions are avoided.

User Datagram Protocol

The User Datagram Protocol (UDP) is a connectionless transport protocol. It is specified in RFC 768 (Postel, 1980) and its transport address is 17. Unlike TCP, UDP is a real lightweight. Its attributes are:

- connectionless
- addressing via port numbers
- data checksums
- very simple
- 'best-effort' forwarding.

The fields of the UDP protocol header as shown in Figure 3.18 are as follows:

Source and destination port numbers

As in TCP, port numbers are the reference to the transport protocol users.

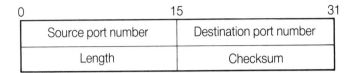

Figure 3.18 UDP protocol header.

Length

This is the length of the whole datagram, including the protocol header.

Checksum

The Internet checksum involves the data, the protocol header and the pseudo header. If this field contains the value 0, the sender has not entered a checksum and the UDP recipient does not carry out a check. In the first versions of the 4.2BSD system, the UDP code contained an error that led to the generation of an incorrect UDP checksum. (Since this checksum was not checked on the receiving side, the bug went undetected for some time.) In later versions, this fault has been eliminated. Normally, no UDP checksums are created in SunOS and SunOS-based systems, since it is assumed that the underlying network (usually Ethernet) guarantees data integrity. Checksums may be switched on by altering an operating system variable (*udpcksum*).

Over and above the work performed by IP, UDP only provides a port number and a data checksum. Unlike TCP, in this case there are no transport acknowledgements or other reliability measures; however, the lack of these additions makes UDP particularly efficient and thus suitable for high-speed applications (for example, distributed file systems (NFS) or the like) which are, anyway, only suitable for installation on fast, reliable transmission media as, for example, in *Local Area Networks* (LANs).

Internet Control Message Protocol

Errors occur from time to time in all networks and nodes. These must be notified to those responsible or to those concerned. The notification is the responsibility of the Internet Control Message Protocol (ICMP,) which is specified in RFC 792 (Postel, 1981b). ICMP is a component part of every IP implementation and in its role as a transport protocol its only tasks are

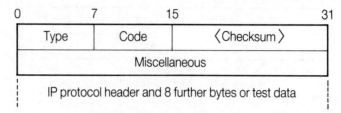

Figure 3.19 ICMP protocol header.

to transport error and diagnostic data for IP. Its transport protocol address in the IP protocol header is 1.

Since ICMP has to transport various information, only the basic structure of the ICMP protocol header is fixed, the meaning of the individual fields being variable.

The structure shown in Figure 3.19, which is common to all ICMP messages, contains the following fields:

Type

This specifies the type of the ICMP message. Table 3.6 gives a list of types.

Code

This is a further code that indicates subfunctions within a type.

Table 3.6 ICMP packet types.

Type field	Function
0	Echo reply
3	Destination unreachable
4	Source quench
5	Redirect
8	Echo request
11	Time exceeded for a datagram
12	Parameter problem on a datagram
13	Time stamp request
14	Time stamp reply

Checksum

This contains the Internet checksum for the complete ICMP message.

Miscellaneous

This is a 32-bit field that contains information for miscellaneous purposes (sequence number, Internet addresses, and so on).

IP protocol header

This contains the triggering IP datagram and the first eight bits of the message transported in it. If the ICMP message is triggered by a message from TCP or UDP, the application program can be determined from the first eight bytes of the TCP or UDP protocol header and an error message sent (for example, that the server port number specified in the connection request is not active in the target processor). This field may also be used to contain test data (for example, in echo request).

ICMP messages are initiated and processed internally by both IP and TCP and UDP. They should never be generated in response to another ICMP message or a broadcast, otherwise an endless loop might arise.

ICMP packet types

Since the following ICMP packet types are implemented on all UNIX systems, we shall consider them in detail.

Destination unreachable

This forwards a message reporting the following errors:

(1) Network, host, protocol or port unobtainable. The user program is sent a corresponding error message.

(2) Fragmentation required, but the DF bit was set.

(3) Source route option unsuccessful (see IP options).

Source quench

If a gateway does not have the capacity to buffer a message, it may send this ICMP message to the responsible host. The transmitting host must then reduce the rate at which subsequent messages are sent. From 4.3BSD, TCP reacts to this message; in 4.2BSD it was simply ignored. In systems with congestion avoidance, the congestion window is decreased. UDP also ignores the message, in which case the sender's application program should be informed.

Redirect

This is sent when a gateway recognizes that the sender of an IP packet could send the packet directly to the next gateway (thus an unnecessary detour is being made). The ICMP message contains the Internet address of the next direct gateway, which is entered into the sender's routing table.

Echo reply and echo request

An *echo request* is sent to a computer and an *echo reply* follows as a consequence. The echo request and the echo reply are used to implement such practical functions as verification of operational readiness or measurement of elapsed time. Test data of arbitrary length is sent in the ICMP message in place of an IP protocol header; this data is returned in the echo reply.

Time exceeded

This message is sent to a sender whose IP datagram had to be discarded on expiry of its TTL or for whose message the fragment reassembly timer has terminated.

Parameter problem

The sender of an IP datagram is informed that, owing to faulty entries in the IP protocol header, the packet has had to be discarded.

In RFC 950 (Mogul and Postel, 1985), two new ICMP packet types, *Address Mask Request* and *Address Mask Reply*, are proposed for the determination of the subnetwork ID address mask (see section 'Addressing at the IP level'). They have not been implemented on any UNIX system known of to date.

Subnetworks

Ethernet and IEEE 802.3

Ethernet is a LAN technology that was developed at the beginning of the 1970s by the Xerox company. Version 2, which is predominantly used today, was standardized in 1978 by Xerox, Digital Equipment Corporation and Intel (DEC, Intel and Xerox, 1982). It is now one of the most widely used technologies for local area networks. At the beginning of the 1980s, a more or less identical version was defined to be an international standard designated IEEE 802.3. There are other IEEE 802 standards (IEEE, 1983–1986) for the LAN Token Ring (IEEE 802.5) and Token Bus (IEEE 802.4) technologies.

Connection characteristics

Ethernet is based on a coaxial cable as a bus, which is operated with a bit transmission rate of 10 million bits per second (a thousand times faster than a 9600 baud circuit). A cable segment may be up to 500 metres long and may carry up to 200 interface points (so-called *transceivers*). This version of the IEEE 802.3 standard is also known as *10base5*. There must be a distance of at least 2.5 metres between individual transceivers. Several Ethernet cables may be connected together through so-called *repeaters* or signal amplifiers, where no more than two repeaters may be inserted between two transceivers. Thus, the maximum length of all segments is restricted to a few kilometres. Moreover, there now exist repeaters with several ports and so-called *MAC layer bridges*, which make far larger networks possible (see Chapter 7). In addition, *fan-out units* or interface multipliers are available; these may be used for simultaneous connection of several hosts per transceiver.

Thin Ethernet (*Cheapernet*) is a variant of Ethernet that differs only in its electrical connection characteristics, and not in the data transmission protocol. This variant is known as *10base2*. The use of a thinner, more flexible cable simplifies installation and connection, in that the computer is connected directly to the cable via a transceiver integrated on the Ethernet controller card. Thus, the costs of the transceiver fall. Although the maximum cable segment length and the number of connectable stations are less than half that of Ethernet, this is no problem for small networks. Moreover, owing to the mechanical characteristics of the cable, Thin Ethernet may also be installed by non-professionals. Because Ethernet and Cheapernet are identical from the point of view of transmission speed and protocols, networks of both types may be appropriately connected via a repeater without problems.

Ethernet based on two-wire circuits (also known as *Twisted-Pair-Ethernet* or *10baseT*) is increasingly popular. Distances of up to 30 metres between the connected stations and a junction box may be bridged using the two-wire circuits. The stations are arranged in a star shape around each junction box.

At the same time, work is in progress to broaden the transmission bandwidth from 10 megabits to 100 megabits, to meet the increasing demands of distributed applications, for example, in the multimedia area. However, it will be some time before products based on interoperable standards are available.

Protocol

Ethernet uses the *Carrier Sense Multiple Access with Collision Detect* (CSMA/CD) protocol. In simple terms: before a station sends a packet, it checks to see if any other station is already active (carrier sense). If yes, it waits until the cable is free, otherwise it transmits immediately.

Should two or more stations begin by chance to transmit at the same time (collision), they recognize this situation, since they always compare the data sent with the data on the cable. If the data is corrupted, the transmission procedure is immediately interrupted and repeated after a brief waiting time. The waiting time is determined by a random number generator which, on retransmission, returns exponentially increasing delay values. This prevents two stations using the same waiting time for ever.

The addressing uses a 48-bit address, which is fixed in the hardware of every Ethernet controller. Since the IEEE distributes numbers to the manufacturers of Ethernet controllers, it is certain that every station worldwide has a unique address.

The structure of an Ethernet packet is shown in Figure 3.20. By way of illustration, the positions of the IP and TCP protocol headers in this packet are shown; thus, the individual protocol layers may be clearly identified.

The preamble to an Ethernet packet is a special bit pattern that serves to synchronize the receiving station. This is followed by the destination and source addresses. In the Ethernet standard, the address of the next highest protocol is entered (in our case, this is usually IP) in the packet-type field. Thus, various protocol layers above Ethernet may be simultaneously supported. In the IEEE 802.3 standard, the packet-type field is used as a length field; addressing of the higher level is carried out in the data section. (More of this later in the section about addressing the network layer.) After the data section of up to 1500 bits comes a 32-bit CRC checksum. Note that for technical reasons associated with transmission, a packet must be at least 64 bytes long. If less data is to be sent, the packet is artificially made up to this length by the Ethernet driver in the operating system.

Each station reads the packets on the bus cable and compares the destination address with its own. If the two are the same, the station is the destination and it receives the packet completely. Because of this property (all stations in the network read each packet), a message may be simultaneously sent to all stations (*broadcast*) or to a group of stations (*multicast*). Later we shall see how broadcasts are used in a protocol to be described.

Ethernet is often criticized because of the possibility of collisions, which however are infrequent in practice because of the high transmission rate and the carrier sense procedure. Tests have shown that the number of collisions shows an above-average increase when the theoretical transmission bandwidth is loaded at the 40% level and over with packets of various lengths. According to the predominant length of the packets in the network, the load may be significantly smaller or larger (up to 90% for packets of maximum length).

Packet start

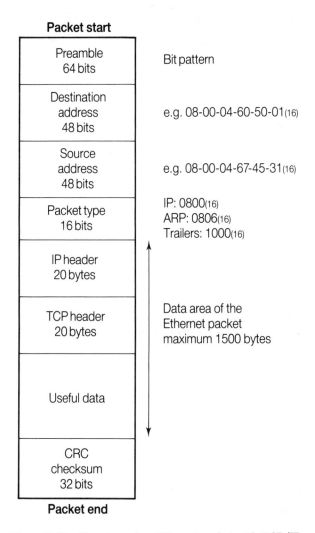

Preamble
64 bits — Bit pattern

Destination address 48 bits — e.g. 08-00-04-60-50-01(16)

Source address 48 bits — e.g. 08-00-04-67-45-31(16)

Packet type 16 bits — IP: 0800(16) ARP: 0806(16) Trailers: 1000(16)

IP header 20 bytes

TCP header 20 bytes — Data area of the Ethernet packet maximum 1500 bytes

Useful data

CRC checksum 32 bits

Packet end

Figure 3.20   Structure of an Ethernet packet with TCP/IP.

Addressing the network layer

In order to address the network layer, the Ethernet protocol header must contain an address entry. For IP, RFC 894 (Hornig, 1984) specifies entry of the value $800_{(16)}$ in the type field of the Ethernet packet.

The Ethernet 802 standard prescribes the use of the *Logical Link Control* (LLC) protocol on networks of the 802 family. The LLC protocol header contains the address of the next highest protocol. In fact, LLC has not penetrated the UNIX world and all current implementations use the mode specified in RFC 894. When, however, a host is required to use both

ISO protocols (with LLC) and TCP/IP simultaneously, it must be able to determine the type of a packet on hand. Luckily, packet-type numbers specified in the RFC are longer than the maximum length of an Ethernet packet; thus, we may assume that for values up to 1500 an LLC packet is on hand.

An extended LLC protocol, the *Subnetwork Access Protocol* (SNAP) for 802 networks was proposed in RFC 1042 (Postel and Reynolds, 1988). But for Ethernets and IEEE 802.3 networks, RFC 894 is the *de facto* standard as before.

Trailer encapsulation

Trailer encapsulation is a special way of sending packets in the link layer. Here, a special packet type is generated in which the IP, UDP and TCP protocol headers follow the data. In this way, the computer's receive buffer can be allocated in such a way that the data begins at a page or segment boundary of the main memory. The data length of a trailer packet is always a multiple of 512 bytes. Thus, it is possible to move the data by altering the memory management tables of the computer without copying into other address spaces. In conjunction with Ethernet, this mechanism is only advantageous for machines with small page sizes (for example, a VAX with page size 512 bytes), since the Ethernet packet itself can only be 1500 bytes long and since moreover too much bandwidth will be lost. A functional description of the protocol is given in RFC 893 (Leffler and Karels, 1984).

Ethernet trailer packets contain the values $1001_{(16)}$ or $1002_{(16)}$ in the Ethernet packet-type field, where the last position indicates the number of 512-byte blocks in the data part ($1002 = 2 * 512 = 1024$ bytes). The data is followed by the trailer of the same packet type ($800_{(16)}$), a 16-bit length field for the subsequent TCP/IP protocol headers and the TCP/IP protocol headers themselves.

In 4.2BSD, trailer encapsulation was active unless otherwise specified; since 4.3BSD, this form is on a per system basis agreed during the exchange of ARP (see later). In most UNIX systems, trailer encapsulation is no longer used today, although it is still supported on the receive side. When 4.2BSD systems are used in the network, care should be taken to ensure that either all other systems support trailer encapsulation or that they do not activate it in the first place (see *ifconfig*). Care is particularly advised in the case of non-UNIX systems, for example, Internet routers.

ARP and RARP

As outlined in the previous sections, Ethernet, like many other subnetworks, does not use Internet addresses but its own system. Worse still, Ethernet addresses with their 48 bits are longer than Internet addresses (32 bits) and so direct association is impossible. How then, when an IP packet is sent, is the Internet address converted into a subnetwork address? There are three basic possibilities:

(1) Static conversion using a table. This has the disadvantage that when alterations occur in the network a new table must be generated.

(2) Conversion of Internet addresses into subnetwork addresses using a formula. For example, a station with the Ethernet address 80-04-00-60-00-01 is allocated the Internet address 89.60.00.01, where part of the Ethernet address is used for the Internet address. However, it is possible that such a conversion may not be a one-to-one correspondence; for example, if the two Ethernet addresses coincide in the fields used for conversion then both hosts will have the same Internet address.

(3) Dynamic conversions, involving interrogation in the subnetwork. In this way, for example, alterations in the Ethernet address become transparent in the network.

The third possibility may only be meaningfully implemented on a LAN with broadcast. The *Address Resolution Protocol* (ARP) was designed for this purpose and is used for the interrogation. ARP was specified in RFC 826 (Plummer, 1982) and is now supported in all Ethernet-based products.

The hardware, protocol and operation fields in Figure 3.21 specify the type of the hardware address, the software address (IP here) and the message type (question or answer).

The functional description of ARP is as follows:

(1) IP presents a datagram at the Ethernet network interface of computer A, which searches for the corresponding Ethernet address in its own (temporary) table. If there is a valid entry, an Ethernet packet with this address is provided and sent.

(2) If there is no valid entry, an ARP broadcast packet with the Internet address of the target host is generated and sent.

(3) All computers in the network receive the ARP packet and compare the Internet address it contains with their own. The computer (B) with the same address sends an ARP response containing the desired Ethernet address back to computer A.

(4) Computer A enters the address from computer B in its table and sends the IP packet and the subsequent IP packets direct to computer B.

To make the association more dynamic, the entries in the temporary table are deleted after a certain time (1 to 20 minutes, depending on the

```
0           7           15                              31
┌───────────────────────────┬───────────────────────────┐
│         Hardware          │         Protocol          │
├─────────────┬─────────────┼───────────────────────────┤
│ Length of   │ Protocol    │        Operation          │
│ HW address  │ length      │                           │
├─────────────┴─────────────┴───────────────────────────┤
│          Source HW address (bytes 0–3)                │
├───────────────────────────┬───────────────────────────┤
│      Source HW address    │      Source IP address    │
│        (bytes 4–5)        │        (bytes 0–1)        │
├───────────────────────────┼───────────────────────────┤
│      Source IP address    │   Destination HW address  │
│        (bytes 2–3)        │        (bytes 0–1)        │
├───────────────────────────┴───────────────────────────┤
│         Destination HW address (bytes 2–5)            │
├───────────────────────────────────────────────────────┤
│         Destination IP address (bytes 0–3)            │
└───────────────────────────────────────────────────────┘
```

Figure 3.21   ARP protocol header.

implementation) and the interrogation is repeated. Since a search procedure only takes a few milliseconds, this process is practically transparent.

RARP stands for *Reverse* ARP and is used in the opposite case, to determine an Internet address, for example, by a diskless workstation during the load operation over the network. Such workstations require their own Internet addresses in order to communicate with a TFTP daemon. (The Ethernet address usually comes from the memory of the station's own Ethernet controller.) RARP is specified in RFC 903 (Finlayson *et al.*, 1984). Recently, this mechanism has been replaced by *BOOTP*, described in RFC 951 (Croft and Gilmore, 1985). The latter uses a much simpler mechanism for initiating the load operation of diskless workstations based on IP datagrams.

RARP uses the same packet format as ARP, but with different operation codes. RARP enquiries are also sent using network broadcast. One of the computers must have an active RARP server, which responds to enquiries using a table containing the Internet address corresponding to the Ethernet address. In order to operate an RARP server, direct access to the Ethernet layer from a user program is required; this is not implemented in all UNIX systems.

Serial line IP

4.3BSD included an implementation of the *Serial Line Internet Protocol* (SLIP). SLIP permits the connection of two computers over a serial line (for example, V.24). SLIP is a very simple protocol and was later specified in RFC 1055 (Romkey, 1988).

All SLIP packets begin with a byte with value $EB_{(16)}$, known in the protocol as ESC. The data is followed by a $C0_{(16)}$ (END). If these values occur in the data, they are sent as a 2-byte sequence ESC $EC_{(16)}$ or ESC $ED_{(16)}$ and reconverted into END or ESC by the recipient. No maximum packet length is prescribed, since by convention the expected upper bound is 1006 bytes.

SLIP does not contain addresses or other protocol fields and only serves to format the data into packets for transporting over a point-to-point connection. Any UNIX machine may be easily converted into a gateway (for example, to connect two Ethernets across building boundaries) using the SLIP driver delivered with most UNIX implementations and a serial line. However, for transmission rates of (usually) at most 19 200 bauds, there is a marked drop in performance in comparison with the Ethernet operation, to say nothing of the possible overloading of the UNIX processor due to the use of the serial line.

As a countermeasure, a protocol has been proposed in RFC 1144 (Jacobson, 1990), which decreases the packet size on SLIP links by compressing the TCP/IP protocol header. The algorithm is based on the fact that most of the information in the TCP/IP protocol header does not change during the lifetime of a connection (Internet addresses, port numbers, and so on). Using a private (SLIP) connection identifier, both sides only send the header fields that have actually changed since the last packet exchange. The benefits are overwhelming: the average TCP/IP protocol header is reduced from 40 to 3 bytes for most cases. Since the most used applications in the network are remote login and TELNET, which usually only send a character at a time, the ratio of user to protocol data in a packet is improved through compression by a factor of 10. Implementations of this, as yet non-standard, protocol are in use at various sites; however, they are not widely available from UNIX vendors.

Point-to-point protocol

Like SLIP, the *Point-to-Point Protocol* (PPP), specified in RFC 1331 (Simpson, 1992), is a protocol that may be used to link two systems over a serial line. Since PPP is slightly more recent than SLIP, precautions have already been taken within it to eliminate some of the weak points of SLIP. These essentially include:

- a facility to support different protocols in the network layer using a protocol field;

- the incorporation of a checksum following the data;

- the phasing out of ASCII control characters with the introduction of octets.

Like SLIP, PPP also uses a specific byte value $7E_{(16)}$ to identify packet boundaries. Unlike SLIP, but as in the X.25 protocol, a so-called flag byte is always sent when there is no data transmission: in other words, when the protocol is idling. The start of a packet is detected as soon as another byte value occurs after a flag. When a byte value corresponding to the flag occurs in the data part itself, an escape character $7D_{(16)}$ is inserted ahead of it and the sixth bit of the following character is complemented. The same procedure is used to eliminate ASCII control characters, such as XON/XOFF, which may lead to problems under certain circumstances.

Before a data exchange can take place under PPP, the connection between the two systems is configured and tested using the *Link Control Protocol* (LCP). LCP is also used when the connection is terminated. The LCP is a component of the PPP specification. In addition, another, so-called *Network Control Protocol* (NCP) is used to exchange special control information for the protocol used in the network layer. Each network layer protocol has its own NCP; the NCP defined for IP is called the *Internet Protocol Control Protocol* (IPCP).

X.25

In recent years, X.25 has become increasingly popular as a means of building *wide area* TCP/IP *networks* (WANs). Support for X.25 comes in two forms: either via a self-contained Internet router, which is connected as a station on the LAN, or via a network interface driver, turning the UNIX system into a gateway. The latter is less common, owing to the lack of UNIX reference implementations. In both cases, an X.25 connection is used as a direct link between two systems, or networks, in a very similar way to the SLIP protocol.

However, X.25 connections are not usually established statically, but created dynamically, depending on the Internet addresses of the packets arriving at the X.25-gateway subnetwork interface. If the X.25 connection is not used for some time, it may be severed temporarily with any TCP connections that are still active remaining unaffected.

A standard described in RFC 877 (Korb, 1983) specifies a way of transmitting IP datagrams over X.25. The most interesting feature of RFC 877 is that it specifies IP datagrams to be sent as complete packet sequences; that is, datagrams larger than a maximum size X.25 packet should not be fragmented by IP, but sent as multiple X.25 packets linked by the 'M' bit in the X.25 protocol header. Thus, the overhead of an additional IP protocol header per X.25 packet is saved; fragmentation and reassembly of the IP datagram is handled in the X.25 interface driver.

Other subnetworks

Since the volume of data exchange is steadily increasing, the bandwidth provided by an X.25 service is in many cases no longer sufficient. Thus, faster data transmission technologies are increasingly becoming established. These include, in particular:

- Integrated Services Digital Network (ISDN)
- Asynchronous Transfer Mode (ATM)
- frame relay.

The services listed above provide transmission speeds in the megabit area. As in the case of the linkage of networks via X.25, they are usually activated by a bridge or a router installed in the LAN, which executes the corresponding subnetwork protocols.

4

TCP/IP – layers 5 to 7

- TELNET

- File Transfer Protocol

- Simple Mail Transfer Protocol

- Trivial File Transfer Protocol

In the previous chapter, we were concerned with the protocols of the lower layers. However, as mentioned in the introductory chapter, the TCP/IP architecture also has a set of standardized application protocols (Figure 4.1). Even though these have recently been replaced in part by more modern services and applications, more in correspondence with the increased requirements in modern computing, it is still worth learning more about them. In what follows, we shall consider the protocols together with the corresponding UNIX commands.

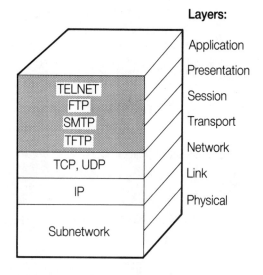

Figure 4.1   The higher protocol layers of the TCP/IP architecture.

TELNET

TELNET is specified in RFC 854 (Postel and Reynolds, 1983). It is intended to provide access, in the form of a terminal session (also called *remote login* or *virtual terminal*), to a computer connected to the network. In UNIX systems, the *telnet* command is used on the client side, while on the server side (the computer called over *telnet*) there is a so-called daemon or server known as *telnetd*. The TELNET service is attached to TCP port 23.

UNIX processors currently incorporate the *rlogin* command, which offers almost the same functionality as *telnet* but provides better support for the UNIX environment. In fact, the TELNET protocol contains elements that, in particular, support interworking with mainframe systems; thus, it is preferred for heterogeneous operation. (We shall return to *rlogin* in detail later.)

A *telnet* session

A computer name is usually supplied when *telnet* is called. A port number may also be entered: this allows for the manual execution of a dialogue with other services (for example, SMTP). If no computer name is given, *telnet* goes into command mode and issues a prompt. In the command mode, connections to computers may be created and cancelled, the operating parameters may be modified and much more. An escape character (usually ^], given by simultaneously pressing the keys ctrl and]) may be used at any time to change to this mode. In the case of an active connection, *telnet* returns to the network connection after each command.

On activation of *telnet*, a TCP connection to the target computer and to *telnetd* (whence to the server) is set up. *telnetd* then organizes the remainder of the procedure so that the login process to which one is usually accustomed on a local terminal proceeds over the newly created connection (over an 'artificial' terminal so to speak). The result is a window into the server computer, where there runs a shell in which programs may be activated as usual.

After this, in UNIX systems, every input or output character passes through three different processes (in both directions), as shown in Figure 4.2:

- the *telnet* command at the terminal;
- the *telnetd* server, which handles the TELNET protocol on the server side;
- the application program, which is started on the server computer over this connection;
- and all the way back to the terminal.

Certain UNIX programs, such as editors, operate only in conjunction with terminals and use modes that may only be selected in the terminal driver. Thus, applications and the *telnetd* process are connected via a so-called pseudo terminal driver. To the application program, the pseudo terminal looks like an interface to a normal terminal; *telnetd* sits at the point where the terminal hardware is connected, where it accepts outputs from the applications and forwards them to the *telnet* user program in the other computer. The pseudo terminal driver acts like a normal terminal

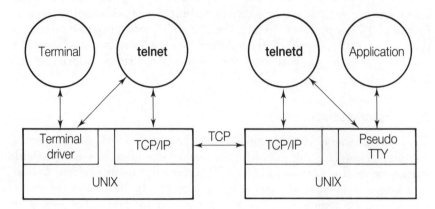

Figure 4.2   Schematic diagram of a TELNET session under UNIX.

driver: it processes control characters, generates echoes for all characters entered, and so on.

Mode of operation of the TELNET protocol

It is well known that the operation of computer systems and the capabilities of the terminals connected to them vary greatly from system to system. This area has been to some extent standardized for the user by the introduction of standard operating systems such as UNIX, MS-DOS and OS/2. A protocol that is required to operate between arbitrary systems in the very heterogeneous data-processing world must be either restricted as far as its permissible functions are concerned or very flexible in its ability to adapt to any behaviour encountered.

A middle road was selected in the TELNET protocol: this involves a small number of message-format specifications and anything else is negotiated between the two partners in the session.

Network virtual terminal

TELNET defines a so-called *Network Virtual Terminal* (NVT) to describe the capabilities of the data sources and destinations. The NVT consists of a virtual keyboard which generates only specific characters and a virtual printer which can only display specific characters. This determines the functional scope of the input and output sides. Every end point of a TELNET connection logically consists of an NVT keyboard and an NVT printer, as shown schematically in Figure 4.3. Precise details are given in the TELNET specification. The NVT is, as it were, a specification of the

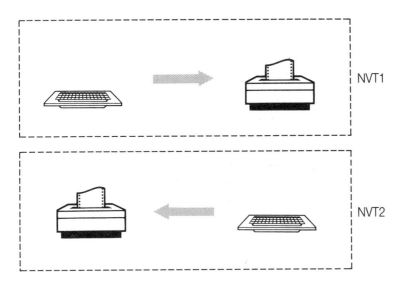

Figure 4.3 Schematic diagram of a network virtual terminal.

presentation layer and is thus of major importance. Outside TELNET, the NVT format is also used in the FTP and SMTP protocols.

TELNET options

Both parties to a TELNET connection provide services that may be switched on and off by TELNET protocol elements known as options. At the beginning of the TELNET session, client and server negotiate the modes to be set. However, options may also be negotiated at any time during the active session. In UNIX machines, the TELNET server and client set modes that correspond to the mode of operation of the UNIX terminal, including transfer of the terminal name and character-serial input with echo through the TELNET server. Other settings may be preferred on mainframes.

The transaction continues using four special protocol commands: *do, don't, will* and *won't*. Here, *do* and *will* are requests or offers to the communication partner to provide a certain service, and *don't* and *won't* are the opposite. Semantically, these protocol codes are defined in such a way that requests and offers for the same output act as answers to one another. Figure 4.4 shows the transaction of TELNET options between two UNIX systems using internal commands in the *telnet* program. Note how the change from the input mode to the command mode takes place and how the session is explicitly broken off.

```
$ telnet
telnet> toggle options
Will show option processing.
telnet> open train1
Trying...
Connected to train1.
Escape character is '^]'.
SENT do SUPPRESS GO AHEAD
SENT will TERMINAL TYPE (reply)
RCVD do TERMINAL TYPE (don't reply)
RCVD will SUPPRESS GO AHEAD (don't reply)
RCVD will ECHO (reply)
SENT do ECHO (reply)
RCVD do ECHO (reply)
SENT won't ECHO (reply)

System V UNIX (train1)

RCVD don't ECHO (don't reply)
login: test
Password:
UNIX System V/386 Release 3.2 i386
train1
Copyright (c) 1987 AT&T
All Rights Reserved
$ date
Sat Jun 10 19:17:34 GMT 1989
$ ^]
telnet> quit
Connection closed by foreign host.
$
```

Figure 4.4 A *telnet* dialogue with option handling and explicit interruption.

File Transfer Protocol

The *File Transfer Protocol* (FTP) is specified in RFC 959 (Postel and Reynolds, 1985). TCP port 21 is fixed as the command channel and TCP port 20 as the data channel. In UNIX systems, the protocol is the command of the same name *ftp* and the server is *ftpd*.

FTP differs from other file transfer programs in many respects. The most prominent differences include the use of separate channels for control information and data and the fact that FTP data transfers do not run in the background (work without a spooler).

As protocol elements, FTP uses ASCII text in the NVT format, terminated by a new-line symbol, consisting of a four-character command word with optional parameters. Return codes contain a three-figure digital code and an accompanying text which explains the success or failure of the action. Codes beginning with the numbers 1, 2 or 3 are positive return codes, while codes 4 or 5 stand for errors. The subsequent numbers give a more detailed description of the return code and the error. The fact that the protocol elements are coded in ASCII simplifies debugging and it is also possible to communicate interactively with the FTP server. The FTP protocol commands may be used to send, receive, delete and rename files, to create, delete and change directories, to send electronic mail, to append to files and much more.

For every data transfer, a TCP connection between client and server is opened, and closed again after transmission. In this way, FTP uses the reliability features of TCP and, since all necessary precautionary measures for error-free transmission are already in hand, it does not need to use any reliability features of its own.

Although many transmission modes (for example, data compression) are specified, only two modes are implemented on UNIX systems, namely, the text mode and the binary mode. In the text mode, text files are sent as ASCII lines separated by carriage return and new-line symbols; in this way, they can be transferred between two different types of system. In binary mode, a file is transmitted, without conversion, as a sequence of bytes, which is naturally a good deal faster. At the start, text mode is initially set. For transmissions between two similar systems (for example, UNIX systems), binary mode should also be used for text files, for reasons of speed.

ftp **command**

At the beginning of an FTP session, a connection to the server FTP must be set up. This is done by supplying the computer name with the *ftp* command, or using the *open* command in the FTP command mode, as for *telnet*. To execute a file transfer, it is necessary to obtain access rights to the file or permission to store it. This is done by logging on to the server computer, giving a login name and a password. After the login, one remains logically on the client computer, as before, and not on the server computer, as in TELNET. This should be noted when commands are executed.

Now one of the many FTP commands may be activated. In the example in Figure 4.5, the debug option has been switched on to show the exchanges that occur in the command channel. As can be seen, the execution of a session is very easy to follow. Arrows indicate a message from the client; lines with three figures at the beginning denote replies from the server. Regrettably, data transfer cannot be followed in this way. The

```
$ ftp -d
ftp> open train2
Connected to train2.
220 train2 FTP server (Version 4.4 Tue Dec 20 1988) ready.
Name (train2:kurs1):kurs1
331 Password required for kurs1.
Password: ...
230 User kurs1 logged in.
ftp> dir
--> PORT 192,9,150,244,4,57
200 PORT command successful.
--> LIST
150 Opening data connection for /bin/ls -1 (...
total 1
-rw ------- 1 kurs1   ixos    240 May 18 10:53 test
226 Transfer complete.
100 bytes received in 1 second (0.66 kbyte/s)
ftp> get test
--> PORT 192,9,150,244,4,59
200 PORT command successful.
--> RETR test
150 Opening data connection for test (192.9.150.244,1083)
226 Transfer complete.
local: test remote: test
250 bytes received in 0 second (0.24 kbyte/s)
ftp> quote HELP
--> HELP
214-These commands are recognized (*'s unimplemented)
USER    PORT    RETR    MSND*   ALLO    DELE
SITE*   XMKD    CDUP    PASS    PASV    STOR
MSOM*   REST*   CWD     STAT*   RMD     XCUP
ACCT*   TYPE    APPE    MSAM*   RNFR    XCWD
HELP    XRMD    STOU    REIN*   STRU    MLFL*
MRSQ*   RNTO    LIST    NOOP    PWD     SYST
QUIT    MODE    MAIL*   MRCP*   ABOR    NLST
MKD     XPWD
214 Direct comments to ftp-bugs@train2.
ftp> quit
--> QUIT
221 Goodbye.
```

Figure 4.5   Outputs of an FTP session.

quote command may be used to enter FTP protocol messages directly. The HELP message provides, for example, a list of the FTP protocol elements implemented in the server. PORT calls signal the address of a data channel on which the client is waiting to the server. If the PORT call is missing, TCP port 20 is used as standard.

The following *ftp* commands are used very frequently:

ftp command	*Explanation*
get	Fetch a file from the server.
put	Send a file to the server.
del	Delete a file in the server.
binary	Switch into binary transmission mode.
cd	Change the directory on the server.
lcd	Change the directory on the client.
pwd	Display the contents of a directory on the server.
dir	Display the directory on the server.
hash	Display a # character for each transmitted block.
quit	End the *ftp* command.

In addition, there are many other commands that are intended to facilitate work with *ftp*. Automation using a command file with the name *.netrc* in one's own Login directory is also possible. This may be used to construct a range of computer-specific command macros. As for *telnet*, you should run through some of the *ftp* commands from the manual yourself at the terminal, so you can better appreciate the capabilities of this program.

One disadvantage of *ftp* is that the program cannot transfer the access rights from the source file to the target file (this is not technically provided for in the protocol). Furthermore, file trees may not be transmitted.

Simple Mail Transfer Protocol

The *Simple Mail Transfer Protocol* (SMTP) is the Internet protocol for electronic mail specified in RFC 821 (Postel, 1982). TCP port 25 is defined for SMTP. Like TELNET and FTP, SMTP is distinguished by its simplicity; it incorporates many features of FTP.

As can be seen from the sample dialogue in Figure 4.6, a mail transfer can be accomplished with remarkably few protocol elements:

Command	Explanation
HELO	Introduction of the client to the server.
DATA	Message text in ASCII format (7 bits). The end of the message is indicated by a single full stop at the beginning of a line. If a line of the message begins with a full stop, the sender SMTP adds another full stop, which will be removed by the other party. If the destination SMTP replies with a positive acknowledgement, the message was successfully received.
QUIT	End of the SMTP dialogue.
MAIL	Declaration of the sender's address. Replies, error messages, and so on will be sent to this address.
RCPT	Declaration of the message destination. There may be several consecutive RCPT commands, so that data may be sent to several destinations but transmitted only once.

The three-figure codes of FTP are used for replies and acknowledgements. Address entry follows the conventions of the *Domain Name System* (DNS), which we shall discuss in Chapter 7 on internetworking.

```
220 balahe.ixos.de Sendmail 5.1 ready at Sat, 10 Jun ...
HELO mitsouko.ixos.de
250 balahe.ixos.de Hello mitsouko.ixos.de, pleased ...
MAIL From:<santi@mitsouko>
250 <santi@mitsouko>...   Sender ok
RCPT To:roland
250 roland...   Recipient ok
DATA
354 Enter mail, end with "." on a line by itself
Date: 10 Jun 89 11:22:33
From: <santi@mitsouko.ixos.de>
To: <roland@balahe.ixos.de>
Subject: All OK

Mitsouko is active again as of now.
.
250 Ok
QUIT
221 balahe.ixos.de closing connection
```

Figure 4.6   SMTP dialogue.

Other SMTP protocol elements are:

Command	Explanation
VRFY	Verification of a user name. The recipient attempts to return the full name of the user and the address of his mailbox in reply.
EXPN	Expansion of distribution lists. The recipient provides a list of the people with names and mailbox addresses.
SEND	Send a message to a user's terminal. In addition to SEND, there are also SOML (Send or Mail) and SAML (Send and Mail).
TURN	Change the send direction. The current recipient becomes the message sender.
RSET	Termination of the current mail transaction.
HELP	Request for help information.
NOOP	No operation.

sendmail

In UNIX systems, SMTP is implemented by the program
/usr/lib/sendmail. This is a very complex program, which can
communicate with mail services other than SMTP and which to some extent
also operates as a gateway between different mail systems.

It is possible for *sendmail* to function not only as an SMTP server,
but also as an SMTP client. However, the user never uses *sendmail*
directly, but usually through a so-called *front end*, such as *mailx* or
elm, which controls and simplifies the entry of the message; *sendmail* is
only activated to forward the message. If forwarding is not immediately
possible, the message is entered into an output queue in the directory
/usr/spool/mqueue. Regular attempts are then made to forward the
message from there to the destination. The job queue may be inspected
by the program *mailq*, which is a link to *sendmail* (*sendmail* command:
link mailq).

On the server side, *sendmail* is activated on system start together
with other servers on the computer; it then waits for incoming TCP
connection requests. This server process also takes charge of the repeated
forwarding from the queue.

A configuration file (*/usr/lib/sendmail.cf*) is used to control
sendmail, which makes the program very adaptable. In addition to the
definition of the local mail-forwarding program and many other things,
this file also contains the commands for converting the address for the
connected mail system. A great many system managers have already been
reduced to tears through attempts to understand the syntax and content

of conversion rules and many other options. Usually, *sendmail* is supplied with an operable configuration file, which need not be modified other than for local adjustments.

It is also worth mentioning the alias file, which is built into *sendmail* and which the network administrator may use to create distribution lists and for forwarding requests. (Another way involves the DNS management in which mail addresses may also be entered.) The alias file in */usr/lib/aliases* is edited by the network administrator and is then converted into an indexed database using the *newaliases* command. Like *mailq*, *newaliases* is a link to *sendmail*. Alias names may also be used to send messages to programs, for example, to set up an automatic answering service.

Mail management

The more important the availability of reliable electronic mail is, the more critical the management of the mail system becomes. One particular point is that all internal mail users within an organization should be reachable from the outside and should be able to access the worldwide mail network.

It is usually worthwhile installing a mail-distribution computer, to which all mail is initially sent and which then forwards the message to the private mailbox of the recipient. In this way, mail addresses of users only need to be held and managed on the mail-distribution computer, which can greatly ease the administration of the mail service, since the addresses of users (for example, the names of their workstations) often change. Mail may be forwarded in two ways:

- An alias may be used to permit forwarding to the destination address of the recipient.
- Users may also initiate the forwarding of mail themselves by creating a file with the name *.forward* in their Login directory. The message is then immediately forwarded to the forwarding address contained in this file, without detours over a local service. The disadvantage of this procedure is that every user must have a user ID on the mail computer.

As far as the sending of mail is concerned, there should also be a central system via which all outgoing mail is sent. Many UNIX systems already have facilities for configuring this function as standard, so that the installation by the system manager is inexpensive.

However, such procedures are not always amenable to sufficiently simple management, particularly in environments with a strong client–server orientation. For such environments it is best to use a so-called post office, from which the users collect their incoming mail and to which they send their outgoing mail, independently of the system on which they are currently working, using front ends that speak the *Post Office Protocol* (POP). This will gain in importance in the future with increasingly frequent *nomadic computing*, the use of laptops, notebooks and other portable devices and regular changes in the location of staff; in particular, electronic mail is the only efficient way of communicating with another person asynchronously (in other words, not on the telephone or face to face).

Trivial File Transfer Protocol

The *Trivial File Transfer Protocol* (TFTP) is a file transfer protocol with minimal requirements. It is specified in RFC 783 (Sollins, 1981) and uses UDP port 69.

Like FTP, TFTP also supports a text and a binary transmission mode. The main difference from FTP is the use of a connectionless transport protocol, UDP in our case. This has several consequences as far as the structure of the protocol is concerned. Firstly, TFTP must itself be responsible for transmission reliability via algorithms such as timeouts and packet retransmission. Moreover, the process does not involve logging on to the server computer; the TFTP server replaces this lack of authorization by restrictive access constraints, so that, for example, on UNIX processors, files may only be read and written if their access rights make them available to be read and written by all users. The protocol specification does not prescribe how a system should protect itself against illegal access over TFTP, so this is therefore implementation-specific.

The TFTP protocol codes are:

- Read Request (RRQ)
- Write Request (WRQ)
- Send Data (DATA)
- Acknowledgement (ACK)
- Error (ERROR).

Communication between the TFTP server and the client begins with RRQ or WRQ packets. In this way, transaction IDs, which are later used to identify the data packets, are exchanged. They also contain the file names and an entry regarding the transmission mode to be used. DATA packets are used to transmit the actual data and the server receives an ACK or an ERROR packet in reply. The transmission is deemed to be closed when a DATA packet of length less than 512 bytes is received.

It is not difficult to see that TFTP can have no advantages as

far as regular file transfer between systems is concerned. While TFTP
is used for such purposes in exceptional cases, this protocol is currently
mainly used in loading server programs and fonts in X window terminals
and in bootstrapping diskless workstations. In the latter case, TFTP is
used to transfer the system program into the main memory (see RFC 906
(Finlayson, 1984)). This is because of the low operational requirements of
TFTP: in addition to the protocol itself, only the IP base functions, the
very simple UDP protocol and a driver to access the network are required.
Such a protocol may be implemented very cheaply and the result stored in
a few kilobytes of memory, for example, on an EPROM.

tftp

As usual, UNIX systems contain a *tftp* command corresponding to the
TFTP protocol of the same name. The corresponding server is called
tftpd. The options available and the operation of *tftp* are very similar to
the *ftp* command, but less comprehensive (for example, the authorization
process is missing). The user should note the access constraints referred
to earlier. Figure 4.7 shows a sample *tftp* dialogue on a UNIX system.

```
$ tftp
tftp> connect train2

tftp> binary

tftp> trace
Packet tracing on.
tftp> verbose
Verbose mode on.
tftp> get /usr1/kurs1/test /tmp/test
getting from train2:/usr1/kurs1/test to /tmp/test [octet]
sent RRQ <file=/usr1/kurs1/test, mode=octet>
received DATA <block=1, 512 bytes>
sent ACK <block=1>
received DATA <block=4, 373 bytes>
Received 885 bytes in 0.1 second [50907 bits/s]
tftp> status
Connected to train2.
Mode:  octet Verbose: on Tracing: on
Rexmt-interval: 5 seconds, Max-timeout: 25 seconds
tftp> quit
$
```

Figure 4.7   Outputs of a TFTP session.

Here, the *connect* command does not establish a connection but determines the partner address for subsequent actions. The *verbose* and *trace* commands make the exchange of the protocol elements visible.

5

Berkeley r-utilities

- *$HOME/.rhosts* and */etc/hosts.equiv*

- *rlogin*

- *rsh*

- *rcp*

- *ruptime* and *rwho*

- *rexec*

The integration of TCP/IP into UNIX by the University of California in Berkeley was a decisive contribution to the success of the TCP/IP architecture. The developers in Berkeley did not restrict themselves to the implementation of existing protocols and services such as FTP and TELNET, but also developed their own, sometimes very UNIX-specific, commands. The commands are the consequent conversion of existing UNIX commands into a networked environment; thus, in an 'open' UNIX environment, the Berkeley r-utilities are used almost exclusively today. They are termed r-utilities because they begin with the letter r, as in *remote*. In addition to the r-utilities, a full range of commands (not discussed in detail here) has been developed over the years. This chapter is concerned with the attributes of the r-utilities.

$HOME/.rhosts and /etc/hosts.equiv

In addition to their particular suitability for UNIX systems, some of the Berkeley utilities have another special attribute: the equating of login names over computer boundaries. Correctly configured, this eliminates the tedious typing in of login names and passwords on accessing other computers in the network; access now follows without further checks. The relevant commands are *rlogin*, *rsh* and *rcp*. Moreover, all programs are TCP-based.

The mechanism for equating network-wide login names is very simple and therefore insufficient for systems with security requirements. The greatest weakness is, as in many other instances in UNIX systems, the status of the *superuser*. If a potential penetrator knows the superuser password for just one computer in the network, he may, having the necessary knowledge, penetrate all the other computers. In practice, the mechanism used by the r-utilities has provided adequate protection since, while there are people who know a superuser password, none of them has the necessary knowledge or criminal energy to take advantage of this.

The mode of operation is as follows: the server computer contains tables that specify the pairs of client and server login names that may work together. The client login name is transmitted immediately after connection set-up in the form of an ASCII character string. Server programs protect themselves from misuse in that they only trust the client's login name entry when the TCP connection on the client side comes from a region of privileged TCP ports (ports 1 to 1023). These ports may only be accessed by the superuser. Thus, all commands that use this authorization scheme have the Setuser-ID bit set and belong to the login name *root*. The function of the privileged ports, which exist in both TCP and UDP, is purely UNIX-specific; thus, these ports may be freely accessed in every other operating system. Moreover, this concept avoids passwords being transmitted in clear (when they might be intercepted) within the network.

```
$ hostname
aramis
$ id
uid=2015(santi) gid=100
$ cat $HOME/.rhosts
aramis santi
loopback santi
mitsouko santi
joop root
ixos santi
ixos roland
$
```

Figure 5.1   Example of a .rhosts file.

Access rights are controlled on the server computer by a configuration file, which may be system-wide or user-specific. An individual user may use the file .rhosts in his Login directory to allow other users on other computers to use his login name. On the other hand, the network administrator may declare all login names of another computer with host name entered in the file /etc/hosts.equiv to be equivalent; in this case, nominally identical login names have the same basic access. On most systems, for understandable reasons, the login name root is excluded from this; it can only be made accessible by specific permission in the .rhosts file of the superuser.

Files are searched for authorizing entries, firstly system-wide then user-specifically; the .rhosts file is only searched if no suitable entry is found in /etc/hosts.equiv. The .rhosts file must belong to the given login name or to root and must not be available for universal write access; this prevents the use of a 'Trojan horse'.

An entry in the .rhosts file consists of a computer name and a login name. The .rhosts file shown in Figure 5.1 permits the login name santi of computers aramis, loopback, mitsouko and ixos, the login name roland of computer ixos and the login name root of computer joop to access the login name santi on computer aramis. The inclusion of the original local login name in this list may be surprising, but in practice local access to one's own login name is commonly required for test purposes (for example, to check the functional integrity of the local TCP/IP system). The same effect would be obtained by entering the name of the original computer in /etc/hosts.equiv for all local login names.

rlogin

The name *rlogin* stands for *remote login*; thus, this command allows one to login on a different computer. The corresponding server is *rlogind*, which waits for connection requests on TCP port 513. As in *telnet*, so too here, a login procedure is initiated in the server computer and a pseudo terminal is set up. There are very few functional differences from *telnet* on UNIX systems.

The *rlogin* protocol is very simple. At the beginning of the session, three character strings ('(1)...(3)'), separated by zeros, are sent:

(1) This contains the original login name in the client computer, namely, the ID under which the *rlogin* was initiated.

(2) This contains the login name in the server computer that the user wishes to sign on to. As a standard, the same name is entered here as in the first character string; any other name may be entered using the option − *l*. If corresponding entries exist on the server computer, an automatic login takes place; otherwise a password and/or a login name must be explicitly given.

(3) This contains the login name and the transmission rate of the terminal at which the user is working on the client computer (for example, *vt100/9600*). The terminal ID is transferred in the server to the TERM variable, so that applications started there send the appropriate terminal control characters. The connection speed is stored as information within the internal structure of the pseudo terminal so that waiting times for terminal control characters may be correctly calculated.

The command*rlogin* does not use any other protocol; all characters entered at the keyboard are transparently sent to the server and all characters issued there are displayed on the user screen of the client computer.

As a rule, *rlogin* is terminated by termination of the local shell, for example, by entering ^D. If this control character has no effect (possibly because of a 'hanging program'), an explicit termination may be produced by entering ~. at the beginning of the line. The escape character ~ may be arbitrarily redefined using the − *e* option. In some systems, by entering ~!, it is possible to branch temporarily into a local shell or (if there is more text after the exclamation mark) to execute a local command.

It is possible to associate the *rlogin* program file with the name of a server computer. Thus, it is possible to initiate a session simply by entering the name of a computer.

rsh

The *remote shell rsh* and the corresponding server *rshd* (TCP port 514) allow the user to execute commands on a different computer. In System V, there is a 'restricted shell' of the same name as this command, but it has nothing to do with the command; in this case, the shell is sometimes available under the name *remsh* or *rand*.

Since *rsh* does not interpret command calls itself, it is not a shell in the true sense. The command line entered as a parameter is sent to the server, at which time *rsh* connects the UNIX standard input and output channels *stdin, stdout* and *stderr* of the newly initiated command with the process running locally, by means of two TCP connections. This means that many UNIX commands may be used without alteration. The few examples in Figure 5.2 clearly show how powerful the UNIX pipe concept can be when associated with the *rsh* command.

There are also some restrictions:

- The exit code of the command in the server computer is not returned. Thus, in shell procedures, it is not possible to check whether or not the command was successfully executed.

- Terminal-oriented programs, such as editors, either do not run under *rsh* or run only with restrictions, since they expect a terminal as input and output channel.

- Terminal names are not given; consequently programs such as *pg*, which expect this information, fail.

- The UNIX signals interrupt (SIGINT), quit (SIGQUIT) and terminate (SIGTERM), which are sent locally to the *rsh* process, should be forwarded to the sender and then sent to the process group of the command. We have however established more than once that this clearly does not work on various systems.

The command given as a parameter is interpreted in the server processor through a shell (for example, *sh* $-c$); thus, shell meta-characters, such as output rerouting by '>', may also be used. On the client side, these must be enclosed by quotes to protect them from interpretation by the local shell. The Login directory is used as the current directory on the server. The shell used in the server computer is that given in */etc/passwd* with the option $-c$. If individual shells, programs or shell procedures are entered they must be capable of understanding the $-c$ option. Shell configuration files, such as *.profile* or *.login*, are not executed; consequently, user-specific defaults for command directories and the like have no effect.

A prerequisite for operation of the *rsh* call is the presence of entries in *.rhosts* or */etc/hosts.equiv*; an interactive login is not possible. If there is no suitable entry, the message **Permission denied**

... Normal command ...
```
$ rsh aramis date
Wed Nov 22 23:50:16 GMT 1989
```

... Transfer of data from server ...
```
$ rsh mitsouko cat /etc/passwd | grep santi
santi:x:2015:100:Michael Santifaller:/usr/santi:
```

... Initiation of commands with local data ...
```
$ rsh joop −l reinhard lp <printfile
```

... Data backup on server computer ...
```
$ tar cvfb − 20 fred.c | rsh ixos dd of=/dev/rmt0 bs=20b
a fred 657 tape blocks
$ rsh ixos dd if=/dev/rmt0 bs=20b | tar tvfb − 20
tar:  blocksize = 20
r—r—r—2015/100 336120 Nov 22 22:42 1989 fred
```

... Pipelining of commands via several computers ...
```
$ tbl −D text | rsh aramis troff −mm | lp
```

... Copying by suppression of Shell meta-character expansion ...
```
$ rsh aramis 'cat>fred'<santi
```

Figure 5.2   Possible applications of *rsh*.

appears on the screen. Like the *rlogin* command, *rsh* also uses the original login name in the remote computer, but a different name may be entered using the option − *l*. It is also possible to shorten the call by association with a host name: *rsh* calls *rlogin* when no command line is given.

The programmer can use the services of the *rshd* process with the library routine *rcmd()* and build it into his own applications. *rcmd()* generates the connection to the server and executes the protocols needed for authentication and for transfer of the command line.

rcp

The Berkeley utilities file transfer command *rcp* operates like an extension of the *cp* command in the network. All applications of *cp* that may be useful in a network (for example, copying of local files from remote computers and vice versa, copying between three computers and local copying) are implemented by *rcp*. Recursive copying of whole data

---

... Normal command ...

```
$ rcp aramis:/etc/passwd fred
$ rcp fred aramis:.
$ rcp aramis:fred sam
```

... Transfer between third-party computers ...

```
$ rcp mitsouko:file1 aramis:file1
```

... Use of another user ID ...

```
$ rcp sam santi@joop:test
```

Figure 5.3   Possible applications of the *rcp* command.

trees is also possible with the $-r$ option (this is a function that *ftp* does not provide, but which is very frequently required in practice). Moreover, the access rights of the source files are transferred to the target files. The $-p$ option may also be used to permit the modification time of the source file to be transferred to the target file.

The command *rcp* extends the file names by adding a host name separated by a colon, as in *aramis:fred* (see Figure 5.3). Path names are interpreted according to the Login directory of the login name used in the server. Of course, absolute path names such as *aramis:/etc/passwd* may also be used. If no path name is given after the colon, the entry refers to the Login directory. For the login name in the server, the same login name is again used as standard. If this is not desired, the host name must be given with an extension: for example, *santi@aramis:test* (old systems such as 4.2BSD also use *aramis.santi:test*). It is possible to enter regular expressions in file names. Note however that these must be protected from expansion by the local shell.

The *rcp* program may operate as client or (with the internal option $-t$) as server; thus, two *rcp* programs work together at the same time. The *rcp* server process is in this case initiated by *rsh* in the server computer. This means that, as for *rsh*, the entries in *.rhosts* must be present. The command *rcp* does not function if the shell configuration file (for example, *.cshrc*) generates an output.

ruptime **and** *rwho*

The *ruptime* and *rwho* commands are services provided using the *rwhod* daemon (UDP port 513), which runs on every processor.

```
$ rwho
beate      shalimar:ttyp1 Jun 19 11:49
bogi       joop:tty03     Jun 19 07:07
cornelia chloe:ttyp0      Jun 19 09:18 :05
daniel     fidji:tty00    Jun 19 09:48
elli       drakkar:tty03  Jun 19 10:32
hsz        joop:tty09     Jun 14 15:48 :03
jan        chloe:tty00    Jun 19 06:13
snoopy     joop:tty08     Jun 19 07:23
$ ruptime
chanel   down 2+15:48
chloe    up       4:49, 2 users, load 0.06, 0.05, 0.00
dior     down     0:41
drakkar up     6+02:30, 1 user,  load 0.10, 0.01, 0.00
fidji    up     4+03:22, 2 users, load 0.12, 0.05, 0.00
halston up       3:31, 1 user,  load 0.18, 0.13, 0.09
ixos     up    17+22:23, 0 users, load 0.00, 0.00, 0.00
joop     up     9+16:07, 5 users, load 0.42, 0.25, 0.08
$
```

Figure 5.4   Outputs from *rwho* and *ruptime*.

The *ruptime* command displays a list of the computers in the network, their load, the number of users signed on and the elapsed time since the last system start (Figure 5.4). The 4.2/4.3BSD program *uptime* was a prototype.

The *rwho* command, as the name indicates, displays a list of all users signed on to the network, as in the local *who* command (Figure 5.4). This is possible using information from the *rwhod* daemon, which, on each processor, regularly sends a UDP broadcast packet containing entries about the system and its users in the network. In 4.2BSD, this happens every minute; in 4.3BSD, every three minutes. All other *rwhod*s in the network receive this packet and read it into the directory */usr/spool/rwho*. Thus, *rwhod* both generates and uses the messages.

The two commands *rwho* and *ruptime* only read the information from the files in */usr/spool/rwho* and process it. Both use the same conventions regarding the interpretation of the modification time:

- If a processor has not sent any messages for 11 minutes, it is deemed to be inactive and the users signed on there are no longer indicated.
- Users who have not entered anything at the terminal for an hour are likewise removed from the list, unless the −*a* option is given.

The method of persistent sending used by *rwhod* has a significant disadvantage: in very large networks it leads to an unnecessary loading of the network. In networks with diskless workstations, it has an even worse effect: in certain circumstances, on receipt of the packet, the program pages of all *rwhod* daemons must be fetched by the server computer and, moreover, the received packets must be stored on the server processor. Thus, there is considerable activity in the network each time a packet is sent, and this activity may hinder other processes. On the other hand, the information is in general only used sporadically.

Sun Microsystems has developed another solution in which the information is only fetched when it is actually required. Sun systems therefore contain server programs called *ruserd* and *rstatd*, which fetch the required information about RPC requests when needed by the commands *rusers* and *rstatus*.

rexec

The *rexecd* daemon provides another way of initiating commands on other computers. It uses TCP port 512.

The protocol used by *rexecd* is similar to that of *rshd*, with the major difference that an encrypted password is sent with the request and thus there is normal authentication, as for a login. The *rexec* service is as a rule only obtainable via a program interface in the C library in the shape of the routine *rexec()*. Some systems also have a corresponding *rexec* command.

The *rexec* interface has not succeeded in practice since users clearly prefer the more comfortable automation of *rsh*. However, it is supported in all implementations.

6

TCP/IP administration

- TCP/IP implementations

- Loopback driver

- Configuration files in */etc*

- *ifconfig*

- *arp*

- *ping*

- *trpt*

- *inetd*

Often, a user waits in vain for connection to another computer or a specific server. For most problems, on UNIX processors, the standard environment of the accompanying TCP/IP subsystem contains a range of diagnostic tools and utility programs that cover most administrative tasks. This chapter explains the structure and the content of the TCP/IP configuration files on UNIX systems: the system and network administrator must know and understand these in order to install and extend the network.

TCP/IP implementations

For UNIX systems there are at least two different methods of implementing TCP/IP: firstly, the original implementation of the BSD systems and, secondly, implementations within the STREAMS mechanism. These essentially differ only in the embedding of the protocols and network-interface driver in the operating system core; in other words, in the system-internal interfaces and functions that are used to support this embedding.

STREAMS was first issued with System V Release 3, as a general environment for integrating communication protocols and terminal connections into the UNIX operating system core (thus, not only for TCP/IP, but also for other protocols). Most STREAMS-based TCP/IP implementations, including that delivered with System V Release 4, are versions of the BSD code that have been adapted and ported to the new run-time environment. The STREAMS environment is generally viewed as the future standard.

The BSD UNIX also contains an infrastructure for protocol implementations. Although this is not as flexible and powerful as STREAMS, it is excellently tuned to the needs of TCP/IP and the BSD TCP/IP and is therefore very efficient. For this reason, some manufacturers have ported the BSD TCP/IP implementation according to System V almost without changes, although they do not necessarily use a BSD-based core as a basis for their UNIX implementations. Usually, these systems also have a STREAMS environment in which other protocols may be implemented.

Users will not be able to detect these differences and system administrators rarely penetrate these depths; however, there are a number of points where a knowledge of these differences is useful.

Loopback driver

The loopback driver is one of the most important aids for the network administrator as far as the testing of the TCP/IP subsystem is concerned.

The UNIX operating system core contains special software components for use by the peripherals, called device drivers. Within the scope of the TCP/IP subsystem, in addition to the drivers for the network connection peripherals (for example, the Ethernet controller), every UNIX system also contains a *loopback driver*. This serves a virtual (one that does not actually exist) output device whose function is to insert received data, immediately and without alteration, into an input queue to a protocol stack. In this way, local connections may be opened and the local TCP/IP system tested, without using an Ethernet controller and therefore without being affected by any hardware component.

So that data can be sent via the loopback driver, this driver must also be given an Internet network address, since it is known that packets will be sent by IP to networks. Thus, every UNIX system is a system with at least two network connections, where the virtual loopback network is however not visible from the outside. By convention, the network number of the loopback network is 127; any host ID may be chosen in it. The address of the loopback connection is entered in */etc/hosts* under the name *loopback* or *localhost* or other possible aliases.

If services cannot be accessed on one computer, the readiness of the TCP/IP system running there and of its servers may be tested using the loopback network. Thus, it is possible to determine where the problem lies. If a local connection is possible, the problem may lie in the network connection, the controller hardware or the controller driver. If attempted local connection is not successful, there is probably a fault in the server in question or else the problem lies in the TCP/IP subsystem of the operating system. Note that internal connections are usually set up over the Internet addresses of the real network interfaces: from a logical point of view the only difference between the two variants is that the connection is made from the viewpoint of the TCP/IP subsystem over a different Internet address.

Configuration files in /etc

Most configuration files of the TCP/IP system on UNIX computers are found in the directory */etc*. These files contain lines of ASCII text and may be modified by any editor. The structure varies from file to file, although in all files, in each case, a line serves as a data record; comments begin with the character #.

/etc/hosts

The purpose of the file */etc/hosts* is to provide a symbolic name for an Internet address, since, of course, users cannot be required to remember a cryptic, several-figure Internet address. An entry in */etc/hosts* consists of

```
# Local network host addresses
127.1              local localhost
192.9.150.202      train1
192.9.150.201      train2
0xC0.0x09.0x96.0x01 aramis   # hexadecimal
0300.011.0226.02    mitsouko # octal
```

Figure 6.1   Extract from */etc/hosts*.

an Internet address in decimal, hexadecimal or octal format and an official name, as shown in Figure 6.1. In addition, one or more aliases may be given after the official name. The network administrator enters new addresses, names and aliases here when more processors are connected to the network.

When the Yellow Pages or the Domain Name Service (see next chapter) is used, the data held in this and other files is replaced or supplemented by information in the directory services. Note the interrelation of these three sources of information in possible problems associated with the addressing of computers in a network.

/etc/networks

This file contains network names and their numbers. In some systems, many ARPA-Internet networks are listed here. The information stored is not important to most normal users and is used, as in the case of the following configuration files (see Figure 6.2), to display program output as meaningful names rather than numbers. Thus, the network administrator may enter his own network addresses and numbers here. An entry consists of network names, network numbers and alias names.

```
# network name database
loopback-net 127        software-loopback-net
ixos-net     192.9.150
```

Figure 6.2   Extract from */etc/networks*.

/etc/protocols

In this file, the protocol numbers of the transport protocols are entered as they appear in the transport protocol field of the IP protocol header (see

```
# Internet (IP) protocols
ip     0 IP    # Internet protocol, pseudo protocol number
icmp   1 ICMP # Internet control message protocol
ggp    3 GGP  # gateway-gateway protocol
tcp    6 TCP  # transmission control protocol
pup   12 PUP  # PARC universal packet protocol
udp   17 UDP  # user datagram protocol
```

Figure 6.3 Extract from /etc/protocols.

Figure 6.3). This file is not altered by the administrator. The structure is as follows: protocol name, protocol number and alias name.

/etc/services

This file contains the port numbers and the designations of existing network services (see Figure 6.4); it is read by the programs at start-up. A line consists of service name, port number and protocol type separated by /, together with optional alias names.

```
# Network services, Internet style
ftp    21/tcp
telnet 23/tcp
smtp   25/tcp    mail
tftp   69/udp
# UNIX-specific services
exec   512/tcp
login  513/tcp
shell  514/tcp   rcmd # no passwords used
who    513/udp   whod
```

Figure 6.4 Extract from /etc/services.

hostname

The simple command *hostname* tells the user the name of his own computer. This can be very useful in shell procedures. System V has a similar command called *uname* which, among other things (with the option $-n$), returns the node name of the computer.

The computer name is provided in the start-up files executed on system start-up. Entry of the computer name is very important since it is passed to many programs (which cannot function properly without it).

The information provided by *hostname* is insufficient for processors with access to several networks (multi-homing), since in this case an individual name should exist for each network. The name the administrator should enter is in this case open to question (he will usually choose the name most heavily used).

netstat

The program *netstat* provides the user with comprehensive information about the state of the local TCP/IP system; thus, it is the network administrator's most important aid as far as the diagnosis of TCP/IP problems is concerned. In 4.2/4.3BSD systems, in addition to local statements about the TCP/IP system, it also provides information about the local interprocess communication (UNIX domain), the resources of the Xerox Network System (XNS) and other active protocol stacks (manufacturer-dependent information).

The program *netstat* provides information about the most important TCP/IP related resources in the system:

- communication end points
- network interface statistics
- data buffers
- routing tables and statistics
- protocol statistics.

Communication end points

If no options are specified, *netstat* provides information about all active communication end points. If the option $-a$ is given, it also provides information about passive servers.

Figure 6.5 shows two active TCP connections (ESTABLISHED) set up by *rlogins*. The two TCP end points in the TIME_WAIT state are remnants of a completed *rsh* call and will disappear after 30 seconds (quiet time). All other end points have been opened for the server and are currently passive (LISTEN). UDP end points do not have a state. Each line shows the local and foreign addresses of the partner. Whenever possible, the Internet address and the port number are replaced by the computer name and the name of the service. A star denotes that the end point is not yet associated with an address or that several addresses are possible. The columns Recv-Q and Send-Q show the number of bytes for this end point in the data buffer.

```
$ netstat −a

Active Internet connections (including servers)
Proto Recv-Q Send-Q Local Address Foreign Address (state)
tcp        0        0 aramis.login   mitsouko.1023   ESTABL.
tcp        0        0 aramis.1023    balahe.login    ESTABL.
tcp        0        0 aramis.shell   balahe.1035     TIME_WAIT
tcp        0        0 aramis.1022    balahe.1036     TIME_WAIT
tcp        0        0 *.time         *.*             LISTEN
tcp        0        0 *.daytime      *.*             LISTEN
tcp        0        0 *.portmap      *.*             LISTEN
tcp        0        0 *.chargen      *.*             LISTEN
tcp        0        0 *.discard      *.*             LISTEN
tcp        0        0 *.echo         *.*             LISTEN
tcp        0        0 *.domain       *.*             LISTEN
tcp        0        0 *.finger       *.*             LISTEN
tcp        0        0 *.exec         *.*             LISTEN
tcp        0        0 *.login        *.*             LISTEN
tcp        0        0 *.shell        *.*             LISTEN
tcp        0        0 *.telnet       *.*             LISTEN
tcp        0        0 *.ftp          *.*             LISTEN
udp        0        0 *.who          *.*
udp        0        0 *.nfs          *.*
udp        0        0 *.echo         *.*
udp        0        0 *.ntalk        *.*
udp        0        0 *.portmap      *.*
udp        0        0 *.domain       *.*
udp        0        0 *.tftp         *.*

$
```

Figure 6.5   Output from *netstat* −a.

Network interface statistics

A call to *netstat* with the option −i produces a list of the statistics
of the network interface, for example, of the LAN controller driver. As
Figure 6.6 shows, this list includes the number of input and output packets,
the associated errors and the number of collisions on the Ethernet. Of
course, for non-Ethernet controllers, the entry for the number of collisions
is either empty or has another meaning (in the SLIP driver, this entry signals
that memory to accept further data was exhausted). Other entries include
the name of the interface (for example, 'lo0'), the maximum number of

```
$ netstat -i
Name Mtu   Network   Address    Ipkts Ierrs Opkts Oerrs Collis
ec0  1500 ixos-net aramis      94    0     107   0     0
lo0  2048 loopback localhost 35     0     45    0     0
$ netstat -I ec0 10
    input  (ec0  )      output          input  (Total)    output
  packets errs packets errs colls packets errs packets errs co
  0       0    113     0    0     0       0    113     0    0
  2       0    4       0    0     5       0    8       0    0
  7       0    10      0    0     10      0    12      0    0
  2       0    4       0    0     5       0    8       0    0
  2       0    4       0    0     5       0    8       0    0
  2       0    4       0    0     5       0    8       0    0
  7       0    10      0    0     10      0    12      0    0
$
```

Figure 6.6 Output from *netstat* with options *−i* and *−I*.

characters that a packet may contain (Mtu) (for example, 1500 for Ethernet) and the network and host addresses.

Entry of option *−I*, together with a time interval (in seconds), enables permanent monitoring of a given network interface. In this case, the sum of the statistics of all the computer interfaces and those of the monitored interface is shown for the previous time interval. This provides a clearer view of the distribution of I/O activity within the network connections.

Data buffers

The availability of data buffers is extremely important as far as the performance of the TCP/IP system is concerned; thus, particular value is attached to evaluation of the buffer statistics in the case of problems. BSD-based and STREAMS-based environments contain two completely different data-buffer management mechanisms.

BSD-based TCP/IP implementations divide the data-buffer area into so-called mbufs, while the STREAMS buffer pool consists of 'data blocks' and 'message blocks'. Of course the two methods have different internal structures and are therefore arranged differently and lead to different statistics.

```
$ /etc/crash
> strstat
                alloc  inuse   total  max  fail
streams:          128     52     140   58   0
queues:           512    268     760  304   0
mblocks:         1990    134  147104  178   0
dblocks:         1592    134  145764  177   0
dblock class:
    0 (   4)      256      0   59668    4   0
    1 (  16)      256     23    3629   31   0
    2 (  64)      256      7   64586   30   0
    3 ( 128)      512    103   15081  134   0
    4 ( 256)      128      1    1186    5   0
    5 ( 512)      128      0     570    3   0
    6 (1024)       32      0     638    3   0
    7 (2048)       16      0     403    2   0
    8 (4096)        8      0       3    1   0
^D
$
```

Figure 6.7   Data-buffer statistics under STREAMS.

Figure 6.7 shows the output of the STREAMS statistics. Statistics are given for data blocks of size from 4 to 4096 bytes and for the streamhead, queue, message-descriptor and data-descriptor tables. Usually, the command *crash* and the *strstat* function contained in it must be used to output these statistics. However, some systems provide for a query using the *netstat* command with the parameter −*m*. The individual columns contain the following information:

- The first column contains the names of the individual resources.
- 'streams' manages relationships between processes and the TCP/IP STREAMS protocol stack.
- 'queues' manages relationships between the individual protocol modules comprising the TCP/IP implementation in the core.
- 'mblocks' describes part of a message.
- 'dblocks' contains the data for a message.
- 'dblock class' describes the size of the individual data block classes.
- 'alloc' stands for the total number of units of each resource present in the system.

- 'inuse' contains the number of units that are actually in use at the given time.

- 'total' describes the number of requests executed for each resource, for all those used.

- 'max' is the current greatest occupancy for the resource and represents the greatest number of blocks simultaneously occupied at any one time to date.

- A non-zero entry in the 'fail' column indicates the number of failed attempts to request this type of resource.

A non-zero entry in the last column means that this resource is too tightly assigned and has led to delays in, if not a refusal of, a system request (for example, for connection set-up). In this case, the number of occupied units should be increased, since otherwise the system is not operating optimally. Under System V Release 3, for example, a new system core with modified parameters should be generated.

In the 4.2/4.3BSD system, the output has a very different structure, as shown in Figure 6.8. The data buffer pool now contains only two sizes of buffer: so-called small mbufs with a usable data section of 114 bytes and mbuf clusters (mapped pages) of size 1024 bytes. A small mbuf is also required for each occupied cluster. Small mbufs are used to store socket structures (communication end points), routing table contents, protocol headers and small amounts of data. A type field specifies the purpose; Figure 6.8 shows a list of the various usage types. In this case too there are counters for occupied and free mbufs and for unsuccessful requests. Both the number of allocated buffers and the number of buffers in use are shown (for example, 156 of 416 mbufs are in use in Figure 6.8).

```
$ netstat −m
156/416 mbufs in use:
        4 mbufs allocated to data
        9 mbufs allocated to packet headers
        61 mbufs allocated to socket structures
        80 mbufs allocated to protocol control blocks
        2 mbufs allocated to routing table entries
2/36 mapped pages in use
88 kbytes allocated to network (22% in use)
0 requests for memory denied
$
```

Figure 6.8   Output from *netstat* −*m* under 4.2BSD.

Routing tables and statistics

As soon as a network is connected to other networks, the routing tables must be modified and made available for inspection. The routing table may be listed using *netstat* with the option −*r*. Option −*s* also generates the routing statistics.

The list of table entries in Figure 6.9 includes the target address (the address of the network or the host to be reached through the gateway), the address of the gateway and a flag to show whether the route is active (U) and whether it leads to a host (H) or to a gateway (G). The reference counter ('Refcnt') specifies how many active connections may use a route. 'Use' contains the number of packets sent over this route. The statistics include unusable ICMP redirections and dynamically or newly (by ICMP) created, unobtainable and wild card routes. For wild card routes, packets are tentatively sent over the so-called *default* route (see *route* program).

```
$ netstat −r
Routing tables
Destination  Gateway     Flags  Refcnt  Use  Interface
localhost    localhost   UH     2       18   lo0
ixos-net     aramis      U      3       63   ec0
default      joop        UG     0       0    ec0
ixtrain-net  ixos        U      2       56   ec0
$ netstat −rs
routing:
        0 bad routing redirects
        0 dynamically created routes
        0 new gateways due to redirects
        0 destinations found unreachable
        0 uses of a wild card route
```

Figure 6.9   Output from *netstat* −*r* and −*rs*.

Protocol statistics

Finally, *netstat* may also be used with the option −*s* to provide the user with protocol statistics for IP, ICMP, TCP and UDP.

The TCP/IP protocol modules are implemented at many places and support counters for various situations, mostly error cases. The network administrator can use these statistics to determine if defective packets were received (whether the defective packet was produced by communication with a computer or by external effects such as an error in the communication medium). In newer implementations, the comprehensive statistics of

```
$ netstat -s
ip:
      102 total packets received
      0 bad header checksums
      0 with size smaller than minimum
      0 with data size < data length
      0 with header length < data size
      0 with data length < header length
      0 fragments received
      0 fragments dropped (dup or out of space)
      0 fragments dropped after timeout
      0 packets forwarded
      0 packets not forwardable
      0 redirects sent
icmp:
      6 calls to icmp_error
      0 errors not generated 'cuz old message was icmp
      Output histogram
              echo: 7
              destination unreachable: 6
      0 messages with bad code fields
      0 messages < minimum length
      0 bad checksums
      0 messages with bad length
      Input histogram
              echo reply: 7
              destination unreachable: 6
      0 message responses generated
tcp:
      0 incomplete headers
      0 bad checksums
      0 bad header offset fields
udp:
      0 incomplete headers
      0 bad data length fields
      0 bad checksums
$
```

Figure 6.10   Output from *netstat -s*.

Figure 6.10 are extended by many entries, including, for example, the total number of TCP connections opened and closed, the number of data bytes sent, and so on (see Figure 6.11). The figure also shows an example of the use

```
$ netstat -s -p tcp
tcp:
63208 packets sent
40732 data packets (3116300 bytes)
4 data packets (44 bytes) retransmitted
12229 ack-only packets (10200 delayed)
3 URG only packets
5 window probe packets
10670 window update packets
783 control packets
79194 packets received
37212 acks (for 3116896 bytes)
2881 duplicate acks
0 acks for unsent data
49252 packets (26840940 bytes) received in-sequence
1206 completely duplicate packets (17796 bytes)
0 packets with some dup. data (0 bytes duped)
208 out-of-order packets (2254 bytes)
0 packets (0 bytes) of data after window
0 window probes
192 window update packets
9 packets received after close
0 discarded for bad checksums
0 discarded for bad header offset fields
0 discarded because packet too short
277 connection requests
178 connection accepts
424 connections established (including accepts)
442 connections closed (including 0 drops)
31 embryonic connections dropped
3170 segments updated rtt (of 37451 attempts)
96 retransmit timeouts
0 connections dropped by rexmit timeout
0 persist timeouts
9196 keepalive timeouts
176 keepalive probes sent
31 connections dropped by keep alive
$
```

Figure 6.11 Output from *inetstat -s - tcp* with extended TCP/IP instrumentation.

of the −*p* parameter, which may be used to restrict the output to a specific protocol.

The text output with the individual statistics is largely self-explanatory; the knowledge about TCP accumulated from the previous chapters should be sufficient to enable readers to interpret the individual fields.

ifconfig

The *ifconfig* command is used to configure, activate or deactivate network interfaces such as the Ethernet controller drivers. This command may only be used by the network administrator and in the start-up files at system start-up. In its simplest form (see Figure 6.12), *ifconfig* provides information about the current state of a network interface. In our example, the interface ec0 is active (UP), and debug mode (DEBUG) and ARP protocol (ARP) are switched on; *ec0* can also transmit broadcasts (BROADCAST). These entries are followed by entries for the Internet address, the broadcast address and the network mask. The network mask defines the bits of the Internet address that should be included in address comparison in routing. Normally, this is the network ID of the Internet address; for subnetwork routing the mask should be extended by the subnetwork ID.

```
$ /etc/ifconfig ec0
ec0:   flags=807<UP,BROADCAST,DEBUG,ARP>
    inet 192.9.150.13 netmask ffffff00 broadcast
192.9.150.255
$
```

Figure 6.12   Output from *ifconfig*.

The *ifconfig* command recognizes the following options and parameters:

- An address or a computer name that is entered into the interface.
- The protocol type must also be entered in 4.3BSD systems, which in addition to TCP/IP also support XNS or ISO as network protocols. If no protocol type is given, system names and addresses are interpreted by *ifconfig* as TCP/IP related.
- Interface activation.

- Interface deactivation.

- Activate or deactivate ARP usage for this interface.

- Assigns a routing-cost entry to the interface (for example, number of nodes passed through). For preference, a route with the lowest costs is chosen.

- Activation or deactivation of driver debug mode (if present).

- Definition of the subnetwork mask for TCP/IP.

- Partner addresses for end-to-end connections.

- Definition of the broadcast address. When a program gives this target address, the interface sends a broadcast packet if possible. As a standard (from 4.3BSD), the broadcast address is the host ID with all bits set to 1; in 4.2BSD zeros were used. This option offers the facility to use existing programs, although both address variants may not be used at the same time.

- Trailer encapsulation activation or deactivation for this interface.

arp

The network administrator uses *arp* to manage the entries in the system ARP table. Possible actions are to list, delete, enter or load from a file (see Figure 6.13).

```
# arp
Usage:  arp hostname
arp -a
arp -d hostname
arp -s hostname ether_addr [temp] [pub]
arp -f filename
arp -t
arp -t interval killcom killinc
# arp -s santix 08:00:14:12:34:45
# arp -a
135 santix (89.1.2.3) at 8:0:12:12:34:45 permanent (0)
136 alpha (89.1.2.4) at 8:0:14:54:45:87
# arp -d santix
# arp -a
136 alpha (89.1.2.4) at 8:0:14:54:45:87
#
```

Figure 6.13   Output from work with *arp*.

Listing is per individual computer name or for the whole table, and involves the display of the Internet and Ethernet addresses and of any other known attributes of the entry.

It may, for example, be necessary to delete entries using the parameter $-d$ when a computer's Ethernet card is changed and the ARP table and the physical addresses no longer agree. In principle, every system entry determined by network enquiry is assigned a time limit, so a new Ethernet address would be automatically recognized, at the latest, on expiry of this time interval. Information about the time limit may be obtained using the parameter $-t$.

Values must be explicitly entered in the table, using the parameter $-s$, if it is desired to communicate with computers that do not support ARP. Such entries may incorporate other attributes, although these are normally permanent, but like all entries they may be given a time limit. Thus, it is possible to make one's own processor the ARP server, thereby enabling it to reply to ARP enquiries on behalf of other (non-ARP) computers. Entries may also be read from a file (parameter $-f$), for example, when the system is booted. The Ethernet address is entered byte-wise in hexadecimal form with the individual bytes separated by colons.

ping

Error messages such as `Connection timed out` may have a number of causes. In most cases, it is best to check first that the computer in question is active. The command *ruptime* may be used for this. Note that *ruptime* only declares a computer inactive after five minutes and that an active entry only shows that the computer in question can transmit packets. From 4.3BSD, the network administrator has another way of checking, using the command *ping*. This command operates at a very deep level, in that it sends out ICMP echo request calls. As long as the IP protocol module in the interrupted computer is still active, a reply is sent ('ICMP echo response') showing that the computer is reachable and active. The next step is for the network administrator to check whether the desired server is active.

The *ping* command sends a 64-byte packet to the given computer every second and measures the time until the reply is received. The command is terminated by entry of an abort signal from the keyboard (^C or DEL), whereupon statistics about received and lost packets and the mean measured response time are displayed. The time measurements are interesting in that they indicate whether an over-long elapsed time between the two computers or the overloading of the target computer is likely to be the underlying cause of the problem. Normally, the response times are of the order of $\leq$ 10 to

```
$ ping aramis 512 10
PING aramis:   512 data bytes
520 bytes from 192.9.150.13:   icmp_seq=0.   time=20.   ms
520 bytes from 192.9.150.13:   icmp_seq=1.   time=10.   ms
520 bytes from 192.9.150.13:   icmp_seq=2.   time=10.   ms
520 bytes from 192.9.150.13:   icmp_seq=3.   time=10.   ms
520 bytes from 192.9.150.13:   icmp_seq=4.   time=10.   ms
520 bytes from 192.9.150.13:   icmp_seq=5.   time=10.   ms
520 bytes from 192.9.150.13:   icmp_seq=6.   time=10.   ms
520 bytes from 192.9.150.13:   icmp_seq=7.   time=10.   ms
520 bytes from 192.9.150.13:   icmp_seq=8.   time=10.   ms
520 bytes from 192.9.150.13:   icmp_seq=9.   time=10.   ms

——aramis PING Statistics——
10 packets transmitted, 10 packets received, 0% packet loss
round-trip (ms) min/avg/max = 10/11/20
$
```

Figure 6.14   Output from *ping*.

20 milliseconds. Lost packets mean that either the target computer or the intermediate nodes have had to discard packets, whether because of insufficient buffer space, internal jams or transmission error.

The *ping* command also offers a further test possibility of sending a certain number of fixed-length packets, as shown in Figure 6.14. This enables us to determine the behaviour for large packets. Through the transmission of packets of length greater than 1500 bytes, it provides an excellent test of the behaviour of a computer on sending and receiving IP fragments. The option −*v* permits the display of other received ICMP packets.

In SunOS and in some SunOS-based systems, *ping* only produces a brief message ('XYZ is alive'). To use the facilities described here, the option −*s* must be used.

trpt

In searching for obstinate errors, the TCP specialist may use the TCP trace built into the UNIX core. TCP trace is activated by turning on the option SO_DEBUG at the communication end point (socket) using the system call *setsockopt()*. Most of the servers described here activate TCP trace when

```
# netstat -A
Active Internet connections
PCB       Proto Recv-Q Send-Q Local Addr.  Foreign Addr.  (state)
d1067000 tcp   0      0      aramis.1024  mitsouko.1023  TIME_WAIT

# trpt -p d1067000
d1067000:
569 SYN_SENT: output [a398dc01..a398dc05)@0(win=1000)<SYN>
    → SYN_SENT
570 SYN_SENT: input a399d601@a398dc02)<SYN,ACK> → ESTABLISHED
570 ESTABLISHED: output a398dc02@a399d602(win=fe0)<ACK>
    → ESTABLISHED
604 ESTABLISHED: input a399d602@a398dc02(win=1000)<ACK>
    → ESTABLISHED
878 FIN_WAIT_1:  output a398dc02@a399d602(win=1000)<ACK,FIN>
    → FIN_WAIT_1
879 FIN_WAIT_1:  input a399d602@a398dc03(win=fff)<ACK>
    → FIN_WAIT_2
897 FIN_WAIT_2:  input a399d602@a398dc03(win=1000)<ACK,FIN>
    → TIME_WAIT
897 TIME_WAIT: output a398dc03@a399d603(win=1000)<ACK>
    → TIME_WAIT
#
```

Figure 6.15 Output from *netstat* −A and *trpt*.

the option −*d* is given on start-up. Subsequently, all activities relating to this communication end point are written to a ring buffer. If the variable *tcpconsdebug* in the TCP module of the UNIX operating system core is set to be different from the default value 0, output is generated on the system console. Generally, turning on console output is not recommended, since console output from the operating system is very inefficient and there is a danger of interrupting the operator working there.

The contents of the ring buffer may be edited and displayed using the program *trpt*. Normally, all data records in the ring buffer are analysed, but the option −*p* may be used to select and separately monitor a given connection using the address of its protocol control block. The protocol control block contains all the details of an active communication end point. The address of the protocol control block of an active connection is obtained using the *netstat* command with the option −*A*. Other options determine the details of the output and whether the program should continuously search the ring buffer for new entries. Figure 6.15 shows an application of *netstat* and *trpt* to a connection that has already been terminated. The exchange of the flag and the consequent change of state of the TCP protocol machine may be clearly traced.

SYN_SENT, ESTABLISHED, FIN_WAIT_1, FIN_WAIT_2 and TIME_WAIT denote states of the TCP protocol state machine. Before the SYN flag is sent (in other words, before the establishment of a connection), the state of the TCP end point is CLOSED. It then changes to SYN_SENT, when the SYN flag is received, where the sender waits for the SYN to be acknowledged. After this acknowledgement is received the state of the connection changes to ESTABLISHED while at the same time the sender sends an acknowledgement of receipt of the acknowledgement back to the receiver, where the same procedure is followed. Once the ESTABLISHED state is reached on both sides data can be transferred between the two end points. When one side wishes to release the connection, it sends a FIN flag and changes its state to FIN_WAIT_1 until an acknowledgement of this flag is received, when it changes to FIN_WAIT_2, waiting for a FIN to arrive from the other end. If this FIN arrives, the state changes to TIME_WAIT. After the quiet time has elapsed both sides return to the CLOSED state and the connection between the two TCP end points is released.

inetd

On the first UNIX systems with TCP/IP software, all server programs were activated at system start-up so that they could announce themselves at their ports and take on jobs. After a connection was made between one of these servers and a client, a child process that inherited this connection was spawned and only remained active for the duration of the connection. For its part, the central server process closed the connection immediately and waited for further new requests. This arrangement led to the start-up of between five and fifteen processes (according to the configuration) that were possibly seldom or never required.

To help matters, the program *inetd* was provided in 4.3BSD. This central 'super-server' opens the ports instead of the server program and waits for incoming connections; thus, in the inactive state only one process runs. A client-specific server process is only started when the corresponding TCP connection to the client has been established. The existing connection to the client is delivered to the server process in file descriptor 0. The program *inetd* is capable of starting both TCP- and UDP-based servers.

The program is configured via the file */etc/inetd.cf*. Non-standard servers may also be used in this way.

```
#
# Internet server configuration database
#
ftp      stream tcp nowait root /etc/ftpd     ftpd
telnet   stream tcp nowait root /etc/telnetd telnetd
shell    stream tcp nowait root /etc/rshd     rshd
login    stream tcp nowait root /etc/rlogind rlogind
exec     stream tcp nowait root /etc/rexecd  rexecd
tftp     dgram  udp wait   bin  /etc/tftpd    tftpd
ntalk    dgram  udp wait   root /etc/ntalkd  ntalkd
echo     stream tcp nowait root internal
discard  stream tcp nowait root internal
chargen  stream tcp nowait root internal
daytime  stream tcp nowait root internal
time     stream tcp nowait root internal
```

Figure 6.16   Extract from a */etc/inetd.cf* file.

The format of an */etc/inetd.cf* entry is as follows (see Figure 6.16):

Service name

The designation of a network service, such as *telnet*, as given in */etc/services*.

Socket type

The type of communication mechanism (*stream*, *dgram* or *raw*).

Protocol

tcp or *udp* as given in */etc/protocols*.

wait/nowait

This is only valid for datagram servers and indicates whether *inetd* can immediately accept further connections at the same port or whether it should wait until the server has finished.

User name

This is the login ID under which the server should be started.

Server program name

This is the path name of the server program. Some services are implemented internally by *inetd*.

Parameters of the server program

These are the parameters (including the program name, parameter 0) to be delivered to the server on start-up.

Some Internet test and information services, such as *echo, discard, chargen, daytime* and *time*, are internally processed by *inetd*. These are trivial test servers that echo, consume or generate characters or return the current system time.

The configuration file is reread, possibly to make a modification effective, when the server receives a SIGHUP signal. Otherwise configuration occurs and the file is read when the system is started.

For some years, SunOS has incorporated a different form of *inetd*. In this case, at least up to SunOS 4.0, this server is controlled by the file */etc/servers*, as shown in Figure 6.17. Latterly, SunOS also has a 4.3BSD compatible *inetd* and a file */etc/inetd.cf*. In addition, the SunOS server can start up RPC servers. This involves registering the RPC service with the port mapper; thus, */etc/servers* and the file */etc/inetd.cf* (syntactically extended in SunOS) also contain entries for the RPC program and version numbers.

```
login tcp /etc/in.rlogind
tftp  udp /etc/in.tftpd
time  tcp /usr/etc/in.timed
rpc   udp /usr/etc/rpc.rstatd   100001 1-2
rpc   udp /usr/etc/rpc.rwalld   100008 1
rpc   udp /usr/etc/rpc.mountd   100005 1
rpc   udp /usr/etc/rpc.rusersd  100002 1-2
rpc   udp /usr/etc/rpc.sprayd   100012 1
rpc   tcp /usr/etc/rpc.rexd     100017 1
```

Figure 6.17 Extract from */etc/servers*.

7

Internetworking

- Gateways, bridges and routers

- Routing

- Domain Name Service

- Network management

Among the most important functions of a network architecture are the ability to switch packets between different sections of the network and the possibility of addressing network objects using symbolic names. Over recent years, the subject of network management has also increased in importance with the widespread introduction of networks and the increase in network sizes. The TCP/IP architecture was conceived for large and very large networks; it is currently the only manufacturer-independent architecture that can be said to have been proven in this context for some years. If you are planning to install a network that is larger than a single Ethernet segment, you should devote your attention in this chapter to the relevant concepts and the possibilities offered by the Internet architecture and the implementation on your UNIX computer.

Gateways, bridges and routers

In discussions about networks, the term 'gateway' is often used in one context or another. Since so-called gateway functions are implemented in very different ways, we shall look at the individual criteria for distinguishing them. Firstly, the dictionary definition (Schneider, 1983): [A gateway is] a communication processor between different computer networks whose job is to transmit messages from one network to another network. One important aspect is protocol conversion. A gateway is usually realized using a special-purpose computer. Protocol conversion (protocol translation) usually takes place at the line and transport protocol levels.

Transitions between the modes of operation of a switching computer are in practice often smooth; thus, we shall restrict ourselves to basics.

Routers

A router is usually defined to be a node in the network that forwards packets in a lower layer without a protocol change occurring in that layer. Routers operate at the network level, which in our case means the IP level. There may well be a protocol change in the underlying layers, for example, a transition from Ethernet to SLIP and RS232. Either a UNIX computer with several network connections or a stand-alone specialized processor, as offered by some manufacturers, may be used as a router. Internet routers are capable of taking routing decisions based on information in the IP protocol header and in their routing tables. As Figure 7.1 shows, only OSI layers 1 to 3 need be implemented in a router.

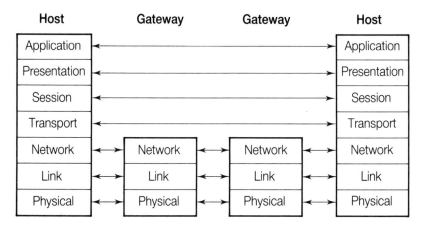

Figure 7.1 Communication between the layers of the OSI model.

Bridges

Bridges are nodes that link together (almost 'extend') two segments of a network over large distances. Usually, two bridges are linked by a serial line, for example, a leased line or X.25. A separate protocol is used on this line to transport packets from one segment to the other.

Bridges may operate in the network as Internet routers (B-routers). For LANs, usually only so-called *MAC layer bridges* (from Media Access Control) are used to receive data from the link layer of a LAN segment (for example, Ethernet) and to forward it to another LAN segment. MAC layer bridges do not carry out routing, since this activity takes place below the network layer in OSI level 3. An 'intelligent' or 'learning' MAC bridge does however 'listen in' to dynamically construct internal tables containing entries for stations connected to the segment. Thus, the bridge itself knows which packets must be transmitted between the segments. If a station sends a packet to an address in the other segment, the bridge automatically forwards the packet without being prompted or noticed by the sender station. MAC bridges are very popular since they are efficient and easy to install and to configure. In addition, they have the advantage of being independent of the protocol architectures used in a LAN.

Gateways

Gateways or relays are stations that link together two different protocols or protocol hierarchies and thus execute a conversion of the protocol. Examples of commercial gateways are the special-purpose computers through which

Macintoshes on the Apple LocalTalk LAN communicate with UNIX processors and NFS as file server. Here, relay functions are directly executed at several points: on adapting to the subnetwork medium (Apple LocalTalk → Ethernet) and on conversion of the network and transport layer protocols and of the file access protocol (Apple Filing Protocol → NFS).

In the TCP/IP literature, the term gateway is generally used for a router in the sense of the above definition. We shall adopt this definition for the purposes of discussion in the following sections.

Routing

Basic principles

Routing means that a packet must initially be sent through one or more nodes in order to reach another computer. This means that we must enter on one computer the address of the computer that provides for the transfer into the remote network, or that at least forwards the packet towards another computer. The latter may possibly pass the packet to the destination or itself forward it further. Networks with this capability are called *packet-switched networks*. There are also message- and line-switched networks. In the former, completely self-contained message units (for example, files in the *UNIX-to-UNIX copy* (UUCP) network) are transmitted; in the second case, fixed connections (as for example in a telephone circuit) are switched. Packet-switched networks have the advantage over line-switched networks that they share the physically existing network among all the connected computers and thus use the network more efficiently. The round-trip time for packet-switched networks is shorter than that for message-switched networks and thus makes on-line operation possible. However, packet-switched networks are a great deal more complicated to plan, install and operate, since various problems (for example, line failure or shifts in load behaviour) must be compensated for.

There are various ways of constructing routing tables in gateways:

(1) Fixed routing tables which are generated during configuration of the network and which may only be altered by restarting the node. This method is very inflexible in respect of changes in the network configuration.

(2) Loading of the table during operation through a central routing control point. This is much more flexible than method 1, but also very vulnerable: if failures occur in the network, it may in certain circumstances be impossible to load a table needed to remedy matters, since the node is unreachable.

(3) Dynamic adaptation of the table by evaluating messages on the fly and/or by interchange of information with the neighbour gateway. This method is the one most frequently used in Internet. It permits a self-contained and rapid adaptation of the routing table to changes in external circumstances.

A prerequisite for performance of the gateway function is that a computer must be physically connectable to at least two networks. As a rule, this is the case in TCP/IP implementations embedded in UNIX operating systems. Intelligent controllers that run TCP/IP, so-called 'front ends', may usually only be connected to a single network.

Gateway protocols

Gateways must exchange information about the other networks to which they have access. *Gateway protocols* are used for this purpose.

It has not been shown to be advantageous for all networks in the Internet (there could be several thousand at one time) to use the same routing algorithm. It is far better to allow networks under certain circumstances to use algorithms adapted to their own requirements. Moreover, malfunctioning of a gateway should not endanger the remainder of the network, even if this gateway sends faulty routing information.

Since networks should be available for through traffic, as before, a procedure for free information exchange (under certain conditions) must be implemented. This relates solely to the communication between networks; other prerequisites apply to internal network information exchange.

For semantic reasons, we now introduce a new term: the *autonomous system*. An autonomous system may be defined to be any subnetwork of the Internet whose structure is transparent from the outside. As far as relationships between gateways are concerned, according to the definition of an autonomous system, distinction is made between so-called *interior neighbours* (gateways resident within the same autonomous system) and *exterior neighbours* (gateways of different autonomous systems). This relationship is shown diagrammatically in Figure 7.2. Networks 1 and 2 are both autonomous systems with two exterior neighbours and the computers A and B as interior neighbours.

Message exchange between the exterior gateways is through the *Exterior Gateway Protocol* (EGP) as specified in RFC 827 (Rosen, 1982), RFC 888 (Sämonson and Rosen, 1984) and RFC 904 (Mills, 1984), or, more recently, through the *Border Gateway Protocol* (BGP), described in RFC 1267 (Lougheed and Rekhter, 1989). The concept of the autonomous system and the neighbour computer is also described in these documents.

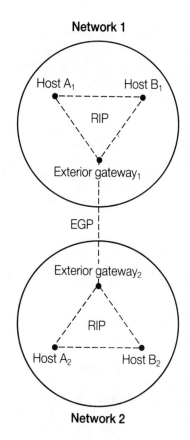

Figure 7.2   The Internet routing concept.

Non-gateway computers must be aware of the routes available to them. The most popular protocol for message exchange within an autonomous system is the *Routing Information Protocol* (RIP) developed by the University of California in Berkeley and specified in RFC 1058 (Hedrick, 1988). It was first implemented in the program **routed** in 4.2BSD. There is also the HELLO protocol, specified in RFC 891 (Mills, 1983), which incorporates other functions (for example, synchronization of the clocks of the computers in the network) in addition to the exchange of routing information and, more recently, the *Open Shortest Path First* (OSPF) protocol, specified in RFC 1247 (Moy, 1992). While EGP is as a rule only used in the Internet, where autonomous systems (connections between large networks) exist, RIP is also important in private networks with internal gateways, in which it is much used. HELLO is only available on a few processors and is thus not very common. OSPF is still relatively new, but is viewed as the future standard.

All the above protocols are based on the regular exchange of information (usually every 30 seconds); EGP establishes logical connections with neighbour gateways, while RIP broadcasts its messages into the network.

Route, routed **and** gated

In every TCP/IP system (even those that cannot be connected to more than one physical network), it is possible to specify routes into other networks. This is done by an entry in an internal system routing table, either manually, using the command *route*, or automatically by the daemon routed (which is available on almost all systems) or via gated (which is only found on a few systems, but which will be increasingly used in the future).

Both routed and gated are able to exchange RIP protocol messages with other daemons. In this way, they inform interior neighbours about the routes available on their own system and find out about existing routes in other networks, which routes they then enter in their own routing table. However, the two daemons are only used in networks containing gateways. There, for the purposes of automatic route entry, they should be active on all computers. In addition to RIP, gated can also process the EGP and HELLO protocols, taking into account the mutual effects the three protocols may have on one another. A separate implementation of EGP is available in the *public domain* and is described in RFC 911 (Kirton, 1984).

The *route* command can only manipulate one route per call. The routed and gated daemons may be used to specify static routes, which are automatically entered into the routing table on system start-up. The gated daemon also allows the network administrator to decide which gateways are to be trusted, since the reliability of the entries in the exchanged protocol messages influences the robustness of the whole route configuration. The routed daemon reads static route entries from the file */etc/gateways*, while gated is configured from the file */etc/gated.cf*.

For message exchange over a route to be operational, the route must be entered in both directions. If this is not done then, while the target processor will be able to receive messages, it will not be able to send its reply back, so that, for example, set-up is not possible over TCP. A new route should be tested using the command *ping* in both directions.

It is very practical to enter a *default* route in the routing table. This route has Internet address 0.0.0.0 and indicates a gateway. All packets with unknown Internet target addresses are first sent to this gateway, in the hope that the latter knows the remainder of the route and in certain circumstances returns an ICMP redirect with the Internet address of the required gateway. If the gateway is unable to forward the packet, it returns an ICMP message of type 'Destination Unreachable'.

Domain Name Service

Background

When we execute TCP/IP programs, we usually address the desired computer with a symbolic name. The network-wide mapping of symbolic computer names to Internet addresses was made centrally for the Internet in the file HOSTS.TXT on the NIC computer. This file had to be regularly read using FTP by all computers connected to the Internet. The local copies of this file for the connected computers were found in */etc/hosts*.

Over recent years, Internet has grown from a few hundred to several thousand computers. In view of this, it is increasingly difficult to keep the information in HOSTS.TXT constantly up to date, since there are ongoing alterations. In addition, because of its size, file transfer required considerable time and overloaded the network. The solution to this problem could only be a service that shifted the management of the data away from the centre to the originator of alterations and thus to organizations that operate parts of the network. This idea gave rise to the Domain Name Service (DNS), the Internet *directory service*. The term 'directory service' is usually applied to the case in which applications and users can retrieve information stored under a name. In our case, the information may include Internet addresses, port numbers and mailboxes, as in a telephone directory. Another directory service supported on UNIX computers is the Yellow Pages service, now termed *Network Information Service* (NIS), which is incorporated in NFS.

The concepts and protocols of the Internet DNS are described in RFC 1034 (Mockapetris, 1987a) and RFC 1035 (Mockapetris, 1987b), with supplements in RFC 1101 (Mockapetris, 1989) and RFC 1183 (Everhart *et al.*, 1990). In 4.3BSD, an implementation of this specification on UNIX systems was made available. The program *named* is a DNS-compatible *name server*. Its query section, called the *resolver*, is implemented in the form of library routines, which are linked into a program.

The procedure for participating in the worldwide DNS with one's own network is described in RFC 1032 (Stahl, 1987).

Structure of the name space

As the name DNS indicates, the name space of the network is divided into domains. The domains are arranged in a tree structure; there is a root and above that are so-called *top-level domains*, which are again subdivided into subdomains. Figure 7.3 shows part of the DNS. A domain is referred to by specifying a path from the branch in the direction of the root, for example, CS.PURDUE.EDU. At the ends of the branches are addressable objects such as host computers and mailboxes. The names of these objects are always unique within a domain.

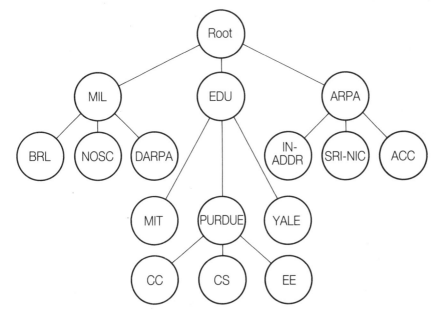

Figure 7.3 Extract from the domain name space.

The top-level domains are predefined by the NIC; they are user domains in the USA. Currently, these include:

- MIL for the US military;
- EDU for universities and other educational organizations;
- GOV for government organizations;
- COM for commercial industrial organizations;
- ORG for non-commercial organizations;
- ARPA for Internet-specific organizations.

In addition to these top-level domains for organizations within the USA, there is a top-level domain for each connected country, for example, DE for Germany and UK for Great Britain. In some countries, the national top-level domain includes a subdomain structure similar to that of the top-level domain in the USA; for example, in the UK, there exist subdomains CO for commercial organizations and AC for academic institutions.

DNS name servers

DNS name servers manage so-called zones. A zone begins at a node in the DNS tree and contains all underlying branches. A name server may now delegate authority over a subzone to another name server and thus control the sources of information in a subdomain. DNS consists of a large number of nested zones, in which name servers operate. These name servers each recognize their neighbour servers in the zones immediately above and below. For reasons of reliability, each zone has at least two active name servers (*primary* and *secondary*), which both provide the same information.

Information about addressable objects is stored in *Resource Records* (RRs), which are managed by name servers. User programs generate RR queries via the resolver. RRs consist of the following fields:

- owner of the information
- type
- class (for example, IN for Internet, ISO for ISO)
- period of validity
- data.

The syntax used for RRs in the name server databases is fully specified (Mockapetris, 1987b). The data is coded in ASCII and may therefore be exchanged between name servers without conversion. The name server databases include the following available RR types:

- *Start of Authority (SOA)*: Definition of a zone.
- *Address (A)*: Internet address of a host.
- *Name Server (NS)*: Name of a name server for a domain.
- *Host Information (HINFO)*: Entries relating to the operating system, hardware, and so on.
- *Canonical Name (CNAME)*: Alias for a computer.
- *Well-Known Services (WKS)*: List of services provided (TELNET, FTP, SMTP, and so on).
- *Mail Exchanger (MX)*: A mail manager for a domain.
- *Gateway Pointer (PTR)*: Gateway addresses.

Queries and replies to queries consist of four variable-length fields:

- A query field used to specify the information required.
- An answer field containing the required information.
- If the name server is unable to supply the information, the AUTHORITY field contains the names of authorized name servers that do have the information.
- An additional field for further (optional) information for the initiator of the query, for example, the address of the name server given in the AUTHORITY field.

Resolver

The resolver takes over name server queries on behalf of the application program and thus also on behalf of the user. The resolver is required (as far as possible) to store the information obtained locally (caching), so that this information may be used in similar queries without the need for further communication with the name server. The storage period depends on the period of validity specified in the RR, which determines the length of time the resolver should temporarily hold the information in the absence of a renewed request for it.

A resolver should also be able to settle so-called *iterative queries* and thus to forward queries that cannot be successfully answered by a name server, using the information in its AUTHORITY field, by contacting other name servers. It can however request the name server to execute this so-called iterative query, in which case the name server is responsible for the subsequent forwarding (this implies an increased load on the name server).

The UNIX resolver available in 4.3BSD is a very limited implementation, which cannot execute either local caching or iterative queries. However, both these functions are implemented in the BIND server (see later) and, moreover, the resolver is configured in such a way that queries outside of the domain pass to the name server. The resolver is designed to be a transparent replacement for existing routines to search the files in */etc* (such as */etc/hosts*); thus, as a rule, a program must only be linked to a new subroutine library and need not be altered.

For queries, the resolver may use either UDP or TCP, where UDP, as the standard protocol, has its own error protection (repetition of query). Iterative queries may under certain circumstances take a long time, so care should be taken to ensure that the repetitions are not sent too soon. If this is not possible, TCP should be used. The resolver API enables individual application programmers to specify the exact parameters of their queries.

If the NFS NIS and DNS are used at the same time, there may be overlaps in the information supplied by the two services (for example, in the system addresses). Some systems contain entries in the resolver's configuration file that point the resolver to maps of NIS.

Resolver configuration

If one of the hostname to IP address conversion routines is called in a program, the resolver library checks the file */etc/resolv* to find out which name server should be consulted to resolve the system name. A typical resolver configuration file is shown in Figure 7.4.

The **domain** statement defines the name of the DNS domain this host is in, and the following IP addresses (there may be more than two) are locations of name servers that can be queried, in the given order. The system on which this */etc/resolv.conf* was used was also a running name server,

```
domain      santix.de
nameserver  127.0.0.1
nameserver  192.9.200.100
```

Figure 7.4 Sample */etc/resolv.conf* file.

```
# The 'Network Configuration' File.
#
# Each entry is of the form:
# ⟨network_id⟩ ⟨semantics⟩ ⟨flags⟩ ⟨protofamily⟩ ⟨protoname⟩
# ⟨device⟩ ⟨nametoaddr_libs⟩
#
udp tpi_clts v inet udp /dev/udp switch.so,tcpip.so,libresolv.so
tcp tpi_cots_ord v inet tcp /dev/tcp switch.so,tcpip.so,libresolv.so
rawip tpi_raw - inet - /dev/rawip switch.so,tcpip.so,libresolv.so
```

Figure 7.5 Sample */etc/netconfig* file.

which is why the first IP address is the loopback address. The second address is that of a secondary name server in the same domain (the entire set-up for this example configuration will be shown in the section entitled 'BIND configuration').

On some newer versions of the UNIX system there is a file named */etc/netconfig* in which the shared libraries containing name-to-address mapping routines must be defined. An example is shown in Figure 7.5.

If the resolver is to be enabled, the entries for *tcp*, *udp* and *rawip* in the file must contain a reference to the library *libresolv.so*.

Solaris 2.x systems also have a */etc/nsswitch.conf* file that defines which of the various name services available on Solaris should be used.

BIND

The *Berkeley Internet Name Domain* (BIND) server incorporated in 4.3BSD is a complete implementation of the DNS for UNIX systems. It is available under the program name *named* and is configured from a number of files. It executes caching and iterative queries and may be configured in three different modes: as a primary server, a secondary server or a caching-only server. In the last case, the server does not manage a database of its own, but, as mentioned earlier, only takes over functions that the resolver itself is unable to execute. Even caching-only servers need not be started on every processor: the resolver may be configured in such a way that it is possible to contact up to three different non-local name servers.

BIND configuration

The first file that the BIND daemon reads when it is launched is the boot file, usually located in */etc/named.boot*; an example of this file is shown in Figure 7.6.

The semicolons in this file, as in all named files, are used to introduce comments. The `directory` statement defines the directory (*/var/named*) in which all named files referenced later are located. The `cache` statement defines the file that contains resource records with which the cache of the name server is primed, in other words, which do not need to be looked up remotely. We shall show an example of this later. The following `primary` statements define the files in which resource records for different aspects of the local domain are specified: first the mappings for the local domain (*santix.de*) in the file *santix.hosts*, then the so-called reverse mapping for the local domain (*200.9.192.in-addr.arpa*) from the top of the DNS root in the file *santix.rev*, and lastly the reverse mapping for the loopback domain (*0.0.127.in-addr.arpa*), which should be present in the file *named.local* on all systems that run a local name server.

Let us first have a look at the *santix.hosts* file, which contains the systems in our example domain (Figure 7.7).

```
;
; Boot File
;
directory /var/named
cache          .                     named.ca
primary    santix.de                 santix.hosts
primary    200.9.192.in-addr.arpa    santix.rev
primary    0.0.127.in-addr.arpa      named.local
```

Figure 7.6   Sample */etc/named.boot* file.

```
;
; santix.hosts (primary)
;
@ IN SOA mozart.santix.de.  santi.mozart.santix.de.  (
        8; serial number
        10800; secondary server refresh (3 hours)
        3600; secondary server retry (1 hour)
        604800; secondary server expiration (1 week)
        86400); minimum time-to-live (1 day)
;
; (name) (ttl) (class) (recordtype) (data)
;
; name server
;
santix.de.   IN NS    mozart.santix.de.
santix.de.   IN NS    santix.santix.de.
santix.de.   IN NS    ns.Germany.EU.net.
santix.de.   IN NS    ns.EUnet.ch.
;
santix.de.   IN MX 10 santix.santix.de.
*.santix.de.  IN MX 10 santix.santix.de.
;
; systems
;
santix    IN A     192.9.200.100
          IN HINFO Sparc3/10 SunOS4
bach      IN CNAME santix.santix.de.
;michael
mozart    IN A     192.9.200.101
          IN HINFO Sparc2 SunOS5
;christa
strauss   IN A     192.9.200.102
          IN HINFO 386PC PC/TCP
;localhost
localhost IN A     127.0.0.01
```

Figure 7.7 Sample host mapping file.

The file starts with a Start-of-Authority record which defines the start of a zone in the DNS hierarchy. The @ symbol is shorthand for the domain for which this file contains the resource records (*santix.de*), as defined in the *named.boot* file. The DNS names contain the name of the primary name-server system and the mailing address of a person (*santi*) on a host (*mozart.santix.de*) to which mail should be sent in case of problems with the name service for this domain. The following numbers contain a serial number that indicates the version of this file (to be used by other name servers in determining whether the file has been changed, which means that the administrator has to increase the number after each modification, otherwise the changes will not be propagated to any secondary servers) and time values in seconds for various timer functions: how often a secondary server should refresh its copy of the master database, how often it should try to get the information in case there is a problem accessing the primary name server, how long information should be kept if it is not possible to obtain a fresh copy, and the minimum lifetime of each record; the last value applies to all records in this file and specifies a lifetime of one day, in other words, another name server keeps the information in its cache for at least a day. Please also notice the parentheses, starting at the end of the SOA line and ending after the last time value, that allow entries to span multiple lines.

The next section in our file usually contains resource records for name servers (NS) that serve the local domain; in our case there are two servers in the local domain (one primary on *mozart.santix.de* and one secondary on *santix.santix.de*) and two servers outside the local domain (*ns.Germany.EUnet* and *ns.EUnet.ch*), for reasons of reliability. Please note that all domain names in the named configuration files must have a '.' (dot) at the end. The third section contains mail exchange resource records (MX) to indicate where mail for this domain should be sent. The first line defines the system *santix.santix.de* to be the recipient for all mail addressed to the domain *santix.de*, while the second entry defines the same system to receive also mail addressed to any system within the domain. If set up in this way, a designated system can function as a mail server for all systems in the domain, which is more convenient from a reliability and management point of view. The number (10) behind the MX token defines the priority of this record, in case there is more than one mailhost defined.

The last section in this file defines the names to address mappings (A) for systems in this domain, plus some useful information (HINFO) about the system, and in one case, an alias or canonical name (CNAME) for a system. The HINFO record has the system type and the operating system version as parameters. You have probably noticed the IN token in every definition line; it denotes the entry to be an entry in the Internet domain.

The next file, *santix.rev*, contains the reverse mappings, in other words, from address to name, for the domain (Figure 7.8).

As you can see, it also starts with an SOA statement, containing the same parameters as the *santix.hosts* file, to instruct any secondary name servers, followed by names of server systems. The last part of the file defines pointer (PTR) records that provide a way to map both the hostids of IP addresses from this domain into host names. Since our example domain has been assigned a Class C address, the hostid is only one byte long. As can

```
;
; santix.rev
;
@ IN SOA mozart.santix.de.  santi.mozart.santix.de.  (
      6; serial number
      10800; secondary server refresh (3 hours)
      3600; secondary server retry (1 hour)
      604800; secondary server expiration (1 week)
      86400); minimum time-to-live (1 day)
;
    IN NS  mozart.santix.de
    IN NS  santix.santix.de.
    IN NS  ns.Germany.EU.net.
    IN NS  ns.EUnet.ch.
;
100 IN PTR santix.santix.de.
101 IN PTR mozart.santix.de.
102 IN PTR strauss.santix.de.
```

Figure 7.8   Sample reverse mapping file.

be seen, they match the hostids defined in the *santix.hosts* file.

Since each server system must also serve its own loopback domain, there needs to be a *named.local* file (Figure 7.9).

```
;
; named.local
;
@ IN SOA mozart.santix.de.  santi.mozart.santix.de.  (
      2; serial number
      10800; secondary server refresh (3 hours)
      3600; secondary server retry (1 hour)
      604800; secondary server expiration (1 week)
      86400); minimum time-to-live (1 day)
;
  IN NS  mozart.santix.de
1 IN PTR localhost.santix.de.
```

Figure 7.9   Sample loopback mapping file.

```
;
; named.ca
;

;; ANSWERS:
.                      518400     IN NS NS.INTERNIC.NET.
.                      518400     IN NS AOS.ARL.ARMY.MIL.
.                      518400     IN NS KAVA.NISC.SRI.COM.
.                      518400     IN NS C.NYSER.NET.
.                      518400     IN NS C.TERP.UMD.EDU.
.                      518400     IN NS NS.NASA.GOV.
.                      518400     IN NS NIC.NORDU.NET.
;                      518400     IN NS NS.NIC.DDN.MIL.
GERMANY.EU.NET.        99999999   IN A 192.76.144.66
NS.GERMANY.EU.NET.     99999999   IN A 192.76.144.0
NS.EUNET.CH.           99999999   IN A 146.228.10.15
NS.INTERNIC.NET.       518400     IN A 198.41.04
AOS.ARL.ARMY.MIL.      518400     IN A 128.63.4.82
AOS.ARL.ARMY.MIL.      518400     IN A 192.5.25.82
KAVA.NISC.SRI.COM.     518400     IN A 192.33.33.24
C.NYSER.NET.           518400     IN A 192.33.4.12
TERP.UMD.EDU.          518400     IN A 128.8.10.90
NS.NASA.GOV.           518400     IN A 128.102.16.10
NS.NASA.GOV.           518400     IN A 192.52.195.10
NIC.NORDU.NET.         518400     IN A 192.36.148.17
NS.NIC.DDN.MIL.        518400     IN A 192.112.36.4
```

Figure 7.10   Sample cache file.

Not surprisingly, it contains an SOA record, a PTR record for the
local system and an NS reference to the local name server.

The last file shown here is the cache file; it contains the IP addresses
of systems that are fairly well known and do not change their names and
addresses very often, such as name servers that serve the top-level domains
of the DNS system and other often-used domains (Figure 7.10).

Of course, the name server does not only fill its cache with *named.ca*
entries; it also holds information obtained when interrogating other name
servers on behalf of a user request, as described earlier. A dump of the
current cache contents can be made by sending an INT signal to the bind
daemon. The process ID of the bind daemon can be found in the file
/etc/named.pid, where it is deposited when the daemon starts up. A
debug trace of the *named*'s activity can be enabled by sending a USR1

signal; the output goes into the file */tmp/named_dump.db*. Sending more USR1 signals increments the debug level. The trace is disabled by sending a USR2 signal, and sending a HUP signal forces the daemon to reread the *named.boot* file and reinitialize itself from the configuration files described above.

The configuration files for a secondary name server in the same domain are set up similar to the primary server, with the relevant fields changed accordingly. Although a secondary server copies the information of the primary server at regular intervals (as defined in the SOA statement), it should have its own configuration files in case the primary server is not accessible for some prolonged amount of time. Also, if a domain is to be connected to the global Internet, it is usually done through some local Internet access service provider organization. Please contact the DNS administrator of your Internet access provider for the IP addresses specific to your DNS environment and any local policies that should be adhered to by its clients.

There is a utility called *nslookup*, which can be used by the system administrator to look up entries in any name server; it is therefore an ideal tool to test if the local *named* is configured properly and operational.

Network management

As the size of networks increases, network management (the administration of hosts and gateways in the network) is an increasing challenge. The task of network management is to monitor the elements of the network in order to identify malfunctions (for example, due to capacity bottlenecks), faults or structural changes at an early stage and to take countermeasures. In some network architectures, this also includes the control of access to the network and the allocation of information for metered accounting.

Although there is a whole range of programs for local management of the TCP/IP subsystem, and although network management protocols to manage the Internet Message Processor (IMP) in the original BBN ARPANET have already been introduced in practice, promising activities as far as general network-wide management protocols in the Internet are concerned have only been undertaken in recent years.

Network management is an area in which evolution is still rife. The basis for the Internet activities in this area is the Simple Network Management Protocol (SNMP), which was described in RFC 1157 (Case *et al.*, 1990). Like the OSI management architecture, it is based on the manager/agent paradigm. SNMP is used by a manager (for example, an application program), which accesses data in the management information base (MIB) implemented in the agent. To access this data the manager uses the operations GET and SET to read and write variables in the MIB and the operation GETNEXT, which returns the next variable. Messages about events in the agent are sent to the manager via so-called SNMP traps. All SNMP packets are encoded in a format standardized by the OSI under the name *Abstract Syntax Notation One/Basis Encoding Rules* (ASN.1/BER) (ISO standards 8824 and 8825). However, in the current implementations only a subset of the possible formats according to this standard is used.

MIB variables are also specified in RFCs; the current standard MIB II is specified in RFC 1213 (Rose and McCloghrie, 1991). MIB variables contain entries about system names, TCP connections, routing tables, network interfaces, and so on.

In addition to the standard MIB, manufacturers may also define private, so-called enterprise MIBs, to manage their own non-standardized devices or resources. These private definitions also follow the format specified in RFC 1155 (McCloghrie and Rose, 1990a) and thus may be read in or interpreted by management stations from other manufacturers; this guarantees the ongoing interoperability of different management components. There are also a number of MIBs for various subnetworks and network components. In addition, we note that SNMP management is increasingly extending to the management of systems, since it can operate over an existing network-management structure.

In the design of SNMP, great attention was paid to simplicity; thus, this protocol can be implemented and operated relatively inexpensively, for example, in routers and network controllers and also in PCs. This simplicity was to be the main reason for the appearance of an astonishing number of SNMP products within the briefest of periods; in the meantime, SNMP agents with an implementation of the standard MIB are now delivered as standard on some UNIX systems.

This is to be compared with the standard comprehensive approach of the OSI world, which is described in the two standards *Common Management Information Service* (CMIS) (ISO/IEC 9595) and *Common Management Information Protocol* (CMIP) (ISO/IEC 9596-1, 1991). MIBs conforming to OSI comprise objects consisting of attributes, methods and event messages, which are arranged in a tree-like structure and specified in a definition language derived from ASN.1. Where the functionality of the OSI management is required in a TCP/IP environment, CMIP with its associated OSI application, presentation and session layers may be used over a TCP/IP link. The key to this is provided by an additional adaptation layer above TCP, which offers OSI applications the functions of an OSI transport protocol; this is described in RFC 1006 (Rose and Class, 1987). (This version of CMIP over TCP is therefore known as CMIP 1006.)

In addition to SNMP and CMIP 1006, increasing numbers of individual management interfaces for the various objects in the network, which are tailored to the management requirements of their servers, will become established. The first implementations are likely to be based on RPC, though here too, the trend towards greater object-orientation should catch on. Examples of this include the activities of the OSF in the Distributed Management Environment (DME) programme. SNMP is the management standard for network components; CMIP 1006 is used in TCP/IP networks, essentially for reasons of compatibility with the OSI management.

8

Introduction to ONC/NFS

- Origins of the ONC/NFS technology

- Steps to network integration

- Alternatives to NFS

This chapter begins the second part of the book, on the *Network File System* (NFS). First, we shall consider the ONC/NFS technology generally; there then follows a brief discussion of the scope and applications. Finally, we look at two of the most important network file systems.

Origins of the ONC/NFS technology

NFS was developed and brought to the market by Sun Microsystems Inc. Sun is primarily a manufacturer of UNIX workstations, but it has also been one of the strongest forces in the UNIX movement over recent years.

Sun Microsystems has taken on board the philosophy of distributed and open systems. Thus, from the beginning, NFS was designed so that it permitted the connection of computers from different manufacturers with very different operating systems running on them. Naturally, this philosophy was not followed without some selfishness. Sun only produces workstations, which are primarily used in networks with systems from other manufacturers. Nevertheless, the fact that NFS could be used in heterogeneous network environments was probably its greatest advantage over other products, such as AT&T's *Remote File System* (RFS: see 'Alternatives to NFS' at the end of this chapter).

Set against previous customs, in which manufacturers produced new developments solely for their own hardware platforms, in the hope of binding clients to a particular computer system, Sun has trodden a completely new road. The specifications of the NFS protocol have been published and a reference implementation for UNIX is available to all interested parties at a favourable price (in comparison with its cost). Most manufacturers of UNIX systems have ported this reference system, or a variant of it, to their computers and pay licence fees to Sun. Thus, at least in the UNIX world, NFS has become the *de facto* standard for distributed file access and is today available for practically every UNIX system. NFS is a component of the System V Release 4 of December 1989 and is thus incorporated in the *System V Interface Definition* (SVID). The NFS protocol is also a component of the specifications in the X/Open Portability Guide.

A few manufacturers and software houses have used the published specifications to implement the NFS protocol themselves and to integrate it into their products. These products may be operated without a licence and may be made public. More recent versions of the BSD UNIX also contain a reimplementation of NFS, as does the Open Software Foundation's OSF/1 operating system.

Modes of application and operation

NFS is usually supplied as an extension of the operating system offered by the manufacturer and, under certain circumstances, must be acquired

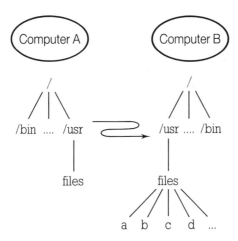

Figure 8.1   Mounting of a remote file system with NFS.

as an add-on. Most technical workstations are exceptions to this and include NFS and TCP/IP protocols and commands as part of the basic configuration. This trend will increase with the integration of NFS into System V and other leading UNIX derivatives and with the imminent networking of all workstations and personal computers. NFS products are available for operating systems other than UNIX, for example, for MS-DOS, VMS, MVS, and so on. Almost all TCP/IP products for PCs also contain an NFS client implementation.

NFS allows programs read and write access to files on NFS server computers. This access is transparent to the programs, which need no alteration, special preparation or additional parameters before operating over NFS. The files on the NFS server are made accessible in that the NFS client computer mounts individual file systems (or sections) from file systems of the NFS server into its own file system, as shown in Figure 8.1. The allocation of these access capabilities is not usually made in response to a request from the program desiring the access but must be granted to the local system before the access is made.

One aspect of this transparency is the speed of the data access over the network, which must be so high that there is no noticeable difference from a local disk access. The original goal in developing NFS was to achieve 80% of the data throughput rate for a local hard disk. Thus, it is possible that access over NFS to a dedicated NFS server with a very fast hard disk may, under certain circumstances, attain a better throughput than that possible locally on a computer with a cheap but slow hard disk. High-grade optimized workstations, in particular those that may be operated without a local hard disk, may commonly have read or write speeds in excess of several hundred kilobytes per second over NFS.

NFS implementations on UNIX systems with local hard disks can usually operate symmetrically; thus, a processor may be a client and a server at the same time. Two computers may thus share their files, provided this is permitted by the network administrator for the given configuration. Depending on the NFS implementation and on the nature of the operating system, most non-UNIX systems only allow a specific mode of operation. Integration of the NFS client into an operating system is much more complicated than the implementation of a server.

Thus, manufacturers of mainframes and minicomputers mostly offer server implementations that make good use of the hard-disk storage space that is generally plentiful on these systems. For PCs, client implementations are almost always the rule, since the allocation and management of disk space for a large number of PCs is most cheaply achieved using a central server. Since MS-DOS (which is predominant on PCs) only permits *single-tasking*, it is impossible to use client and server programs simultaneously.

NFS is sometimes termed a *distributed file system*. A more correct terminology would be 'network file system', which in any case is the meaning of the initials NFS. NFS does not distribute file systems in the network, but converts local accesses into requests to one or more servers.

This concept is not new; it has already been successfully used in many other systems. Many such solutions have been developed for UNIX systems over the past ten years. Network file systems have also been implemented for other operating systems, in particular for PCs and the MS-DOS operating system.

Genesis

NFS was announced in 1984. The first implementation on a Sun workstation was introduced in the following year. This product had version number 2.0 and contained a client and server implementation of NFS (embedded in the *Virtual File System* (VFS)), together with the directory service then called *Yellow Pages* (YP).

In 1986, the companies The Instruction Set Ltd and Lachman Associates Inc. ported the reference implementation of NFS Version 2.0 to System V Release 2 for a DEC VAX. This porting was needed since the Sun reference implementation was based on 4.2BSD, from which SunOS also descended. The porting to System V showed that it was possible to make NFS available on practically all UNIX computers. In the same year, Sun issued a new version of NFS, Version 3.0, which was distinguished from its predecessors mainly through improvements to the YP protocol. In addition, Sun also released the first implementation of NFS for PCs under MS-DOS (PC-NFS) in the same year.

Version 3.2 was introduced in 1987. As a major extension, this offered the possibility of network-wide file locking, a function that had been requested by many users since the start. It also incorporated the *Remote Execution Service* (REX), a network service enabling one to initiate processes on other machines; these processes then accessed local files via NFS. In addition, NFS support for diskless workstations was improved to allow them to be supported using special files and named pipes. In the same year, Lachman Associates Inc. ported NFS to System V Release 3 under the *File System Switch* (FSS).

Version 4.0 of NFS, released in 1989, contains encryption facilities, which may be used to guarantee that file access cannot be spoofed. At this point the Yellow Pages service was renamed the *Network Information Service* (NIS). In 1992, NFS was licensed to more than 300 manufacturers. With 3.1 million installed units in 1992, NFS was one of the most successful UNIX technologies ever. At that time there was a total of 100 different implementations of NFS.

Open network computing

When NFS is used, a number of services with very different functions are also exploited. For example, providing access to files involves the execution of administrative tasks in the network. An individual protocol is usually defined for each of these services. The NFS protocol of the same name is only used to access files.

SunSoft, a company to which Sun Microsystems has hived off its operating-system software activities since 1991, markets NFS and its associated protocols under the name *Open Network Computing* (ONC). The latest version of ONC, ONC+, was introduced in 1992. Its architecture is shown in Figure 8.2, in which the boxes shaded in grey represent the components of ONC+. We shall consider each of these technologies in more detail later.

Not all NFS products offer the same functional scope as ONC and ONC+. Usually, one may initially assume that all implementations of the NFS protocol interoperate with each other. At first, the other functions in the NFS implementations from different manufacturers based on the NFS reference implementation were quite similar; however, later, certain services such as NIS or the Lock Manager were omitted from some manufacturers' products, partially outdated versions of protocols were supplied and there were serious differences in the administration.

The *Common Open Systems Environment* (COSE), an initiative founded by UNIX manufacturers, including IBM, Hewlett-Packard, Novell, SunSoft, Santa Cruz Operation and USL, in 1993 set itself the objective of

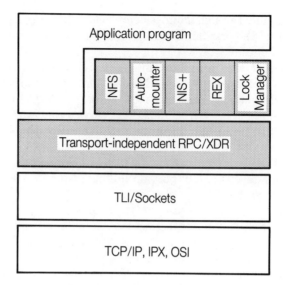

Figure 8.2 ONC+ architecture.

specifying a universal software platform for open systems. Because ONC+ is a component of this specification, this therefore leads to a stronger unification of the NFS environments. The compatibility of individual implementations is checked by comparing the protocols used in the NFS product and their version numbers; only implementations with the same protocol version are compatible.

Steps to network integration

Principles

Since the breakthrough of the so-called *time-sharing* principle in commercial operating systems, networking in electronic data processing has greatly increased. Central processing is increasingly being replaced by desktop PCs or workstations. In what follows, we shall discuss the possible steps towards integration in a network.

Step 1: Time sharing

The most widespread method of data access, which is heavily predominant in the area of large-scale, serial computers, involves a central processor in which all the data is stored and which handles all applications. In this case, the resources are not distributed over a network. UNIX systems are constructed according to this principle. The disadvantages of this are the capacity limits of the central processor, since once this is fully loaded an extension may be expensive or technically impossible. The suitability of the central computer may be another problem. There may be important reasons against migrating new applications to a computer that is already in operation, for example, security requirements, availability of special applications, graphical capabilities, and so on.

Step 2: File transfer

This step refers to the transfer of all the data to another computer, for example, using FTP. The processing takes place locally, on the same computer on which the processing application runs. It is basically unimportant whether the file transfer is carried out over a network or using a storage medium such as a floppy disk. Both cases involve the problem that the file may be altered on each computer and thus at times the copies will differ from the most recent state. These differences must be eliminated by a periodic and possibly complicated procedure.

Step 3: File access in the network

In this case, NFS (for example) is used to access individual blocks of a central file, where the data structures are interpreted in the processing computer. The same is true for the writing of data – files are in principle modified centrally. There is another difference from file transfer, namely, that only the file section required at that moment is transmitted. However, as a prerequisite, all applications that access the file must expect an identical file structure.

Step 4: Data queries in the network

This involves structured access to individual data records using a query language such as the *Structured Query Language* (SQL). In this case, the data is preselected in the server according to criteria specified in the query; thus, only the relevant data within a file is transmitted. The level of abstraction is higher than that in step 3; instead of files, the server manages and stores logical entities, possibly in an optimal manner.

Each of these steps towards integration has cost implications. These must be in keeping with the requirements.

Fields of application of NFS

Like all mechanisms, file access in the network has its advantages and disadvantages, which consequently determine the preferred applications and scope.

NFS permits optional access to file blocks in the form in which they are stored on the hard disk, without interpretation of the internal structure; thus, it operates 100% according to the UNIX philosophy, which leaves these tasks to the application programs. Since index sequential files are implemented differently in each operating system, the developers of NFS have not attempted to incorporate a high-level access mechanism for this either. For these reasons, the operation of UNIX databases over NFS, while possible, is not sensible, since all the index information must be transmitted over the network in order to find the required data. An additional factor is the throughput rate for the necessary locking of individual data records in the case of multiple access, which is decreased when a network is used. It is better in this case to install a database with distributed access on a central database server; this amounts to step 4 integration as currently offered by database manufacturers.

The preferred application areas for NFS are development, design and office automation, where common data in the form of source-code files, object libraries, letters, and so on is accessed. In combination with a database server, the most appropriate access mechanism is used for each type of data.

Alternatives to NFS

Naturally, as a mechanism, NFS has competitors. In particular, integration of MS-DOS systems with file servers will certainly not be achieved by equipping all PCs with PC-NFS. In this section, we look at technologies that are similarly used in local area networks on UNIX systems.

RFS

The Remote File System (RFS) was released by AT&T together with the System V Release 3 in 1986. This system has never been as successful as NFS, one reason being that NFS reached the market two years earlier. Another reason may have been the inept licensing politics for System V Release 3 with which AT&T pushed the thoroughly desirable standardization of UNIX rather too blatantly for the taste of their competitors. In System V Release 4, the coexistence of RFC and NFS was made possible, for reasons of backwards compatibility. We assume that the RFS technology will not be developed further.

Without going further into the protocols used by RFS and its implementation, we shall briefly look at the differences between RFS and NFS. The functionality of RFS from the user's viewpoint is almost identical to that of NFS. Both products offer transparent networking and are not visible to the user and his applications. In RFS also, file systems are locally mounted on the server computer. Unlike NFS, RFS also permits access to special files. Support for diskless systems is not provided for in RFS. Although this is in principle possible, RFS incorporates no arrangements to provide an implementation for diskless systems. The management of the two systems is different, although a unification of the administrative commands was undertaken for System V Release 4. Unlike NFS, RFS is solely designed for use on UNIX systems. Integration with MS-DOS, VMS or other operating systems is practically impossible. However, the UNIX systems used in RFS networks may be based on various processor architectures. As far as the preservation of the local UNIX file system semantics is concerned, RFS is better than NFS. The RFS protocol does not use file access primitives but issues UNIX system calls to dynamically generated processes in the server computer. This also enables access to special files.

OSF/DCE DFS

The *Open Software Foundation*'s (OSF) *Distributed Computing Environment* (DCE) includes the *Distributed File System* (DFS), which has its roots in the Andrew File System developed at Carnegie Mellon University and incorporates many improvements on the latter design.

The DCE is the OSF's answer to SunSoft's ONC; like ONC, it contains a number of services that permit and are intended to facilitate the development and operation of distributed applications, some of which we list below:

- Remote Procedure Call
- Directory Service
- Security Service.

These DCE services are used in the implementation of DFS, and were also used to help create a reference implementation for the use of the DCE technologies. In the first version of DCE, the DFS implementation was still very unreliable and consequently was not supplied with the rest of DCE by most manufacturers. In the meantime, these teething problems have been solved, and increasing use of DFS is to be reckoned with.

The advantages of DFS over NFS include:

- a complete mapping of the local file system semantics by a full state protocol;

- improved data throughput by file group replication and extensive caching in the DFS client;

- increased security by integration with the DCE Security Service;

- worldwide file access using the DCE Directory Service.

OSF's implementation of DFS also contains an improved local file system, which incorporates a journal mechanism, similar to those in databases, that permits faster restarting of a file server. In addition, it is delivered with tools to support diskless clients. Implementations of DFS clients and servers have been announced for UNIX systems and for OS/2 and various mainframe systems.

LAN Manager/X

Anyone interested in the networking of PCs will surely be familiar with the terms PC-NET, MS-NET, NETBIOS and LAN Manager. These terms stand for a technology created by the two protagonists of the MS-DOS world, IBM and Microsoft.

PC-NET and MS-NET enable a PC to access a dedicated server computer, in that they make the server's file system appear to the client as a virtual additional disk drive. Both contain a *redirector*, a software module that converts accesses to this disk drive into messages to the server, which has been integrated into MS-DOS since 1985. The protocol used for this is called the *Server Message Block* (SMB); its messages are sent via calls to another interface, the NETBIOS. NETBIOS defines an interface that must serve implementations of transport protocols in order to work with PC-NET. Many manufacturers also supply NETBIOS-compatible network software, including software for TCP/IP.

Over recent years, the SMB protocol has evolved considerably, and we now speak of Core SMB and the Extended SMB protocol, where the latter is upwards compatible. The Extended SMB protocol contains extensions for the networking of UNIX and/or OS/2 computers. A UNIX-to-UNIX file system based on the SMB protocol was once offered in the mid 1980s in the form of the XENIX-NET product. Because of the dominance of NFS in homogeneous UNIX-to-UNIX networking, this product had little success and disappeared from the market. However, it was capable of serving MS-DOS client PCs with a UNIX server. Subsequently, there were other implementations of the LAN Manager for UNIX. However, it was clear that UNIX-based implementations of the LAN Manager, and other PC networks, are at a disadvantage compared with dedicated PC file servers, because of the lack of integration into the operating system; thus, they should only be used in mixed environments. The LAN Manager client implementation for UNIX should also be reserved for these environments.

For Microsoft, the LAN Manager (and thus also SMB) is the strategic network product. In the fight for dominance in the PC-network market against the overpowering opponent Novell with its NetWare product, Microsoft now has an important trump card in its hand with its Windows NT operating system.

Novell NetWare

With the majority of the PC-network installations, Novell's NetWare product is the *de facto* standard in the PC area. NetWare consists of an independent operating system for PCs, which is optimized for file-server operation, and a proprietary protocol stack including a file access protocol. Novell's own transport protocol, Internet Packet Exchange (IPX), is very similar to TCP/IP, since the two protocol worlds have common ancestors in research.

NetWare may be used to provide applications on the file server that run in so-called *Netware Loadable Modules* (NLM). The interfaces supplied for programming NLM programs are proprietary and thus of little attraction for clients with a strategic orientation towards open systems with standardized interfaces, such as, for example, POSIX. This is one reason why Novell wishes to complement NetWare with JnixWare for application-server tasks.

NetWare is the most common network environment, with a market share of more than half the PC systems installed worldwide. Thus, numerically, IPX is the most common transport protocol, since there are umpteen million PCs with IPX capabilities.

Although NetWare is primarily relevant in the PC area, there are a number of points of contact with UNIX and NFS.

- Some manufacturers provide NetWare servers for UNIX systems, which are used in heterogeneous environments.

- Novell's NetWare NFS is an NFS server implementation on file server software, so that it is possible to integrate UNIX workstations into NetWare environments. An FTP server and an implementation of the BSD UNIX printer spooler protocol *Line Printer Daemon* (LPD) are also built in.

- After taking over the *UNIX System Laboratories* (USL), which produced System V and other System-V-based products, Novell now has a foot in the UNIX camp. In addition to support for NFS, UnixWare, Novell's first UNIX-based product, also contains the IPX protocol and is Novell's answer to Windows NT.

- The COSE consortium is forcing NetWare and IPX, together with NFS, as industry standards.

9

ONC protocols

- Classification of ONC protocols

- Remote Procedure Call

- External Data Representation

- Port mapper/RPC bind

- Network File System protocol

- MOUNT protocol

In this chapter, we look at the most important protocols of the NFS technology and consider their characteristics. The corresponding commands and their functional descriptions will be discussed in the next chapter.

This split has been made in order to confine the description of the overall operation of NFS as far as is possible to a single chapter and to separate this clearly from more theoretical considerations of the protocols. Thus, there will be many references to the attributes described in this chapter.

Classification of ONC protocols

ONC is based on a protocol layering that largely corresponds to the layering defined in the OSI model (see Figure 9.1). The protocols shown in Figure 9.1 are those most often used in ONC products. Being modelled on OSI, ONC is theoretically protocol-independent; in other words, every layer of the protocol hierarchy may be exchanged for a functionally identical variant, transparently to the remaining system. In practice, however, this exchangeability is difficult to achieve and is usually only possible in certain groupings of layers:

- the subnetwork levels (layers 1 and 2)
- the transport levels (layers 3 and 4)
- the so-called 'higher' levels (layers 5, 6 and 7).

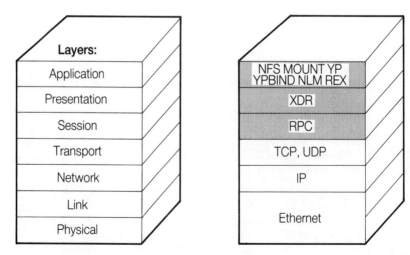

Figure 9.1 Comparison of OSI and NFS protocol layers.

Table 9.1 ONC protocol standards.

Layer	Protocols	Standard
Physical/Link	CSMA/CD	Ethernet IEEE 802.3
Network	IP	RFC 791
Transport	TCP	RFC 793
	UDP	RFC 768
Session	RPC	RFC 1050
Presentation	XDR	RFC 1014
Application	NFS MOUNT	RFC 1094
	NIS REX NLM	Industry standards

As we have seen in the previous chapters, TCP and UDP, together with IP, form a closely related unit; thus exchanging one of the protocols would make little sense. We have also already discussed the fact that Ethernet may be exchanged for another protocol such as, for example, X.25 or Token Ring. In this chapter, we shall also see that the implementation (but not necessarily the design) of RPC-based protocols gives rise to a certain dependence on the RPC technology used and thus it appears impossible to separate the two components. In the best cases an exchange may be conceivable in the presentation layer, although this does not usually take place.

Table 9.1 lists the standards that are normally relevant to the protocols used in ONC. ONC was initially based on the TCP/IP protocols since these are common on UNIX systems. In more recent implementations a *Transport Independent Remote Procedure Call* (TIRPC) library is used to avoid the dependence on TCP/IP protocols; thus, it is now possible to use ONC applications, such as NFS, over an OSI or IPX protocol stack. Because of the high data-throughput requirements of NFS, a LAN such as Ethernet with a correspondingly large bandwidth is a prerequisite for sensible and transparent operation.

Remote Procedure Call

Remote Procedure Call (RPC) is a session-layer protocol, although this description is not completely true, since there is, admittedly, some mixing with the application protocols implemented using RPC. The RPC principle was originally developed by researchers working for Xerox.

To implement NFS, Sun's engineers developed their own RPC technology which is usually referred to as SunRPC or ONC/RPC in professional circles. ONC/RPC is used not only in the implementation of NFS, but also in many other networked applications. ONC/RPC is specified in RFC 1050 and in the documentation supplied with NFS systems and products. SunSoft plans to hand over the control of the specification of ONC/RPC to the IETF, which would lead to the creation of an open standard.

An RPC forms the basis for message exchange in all ONC applications. ONC/RPC may be used to design and implement network services, which, as the name indicates, are used in a similar way to subroutine calls or *procedures* in high-level programming languages. This mode of working eases the programmer's tasks in the design and implementation of distributed programs. The source code for ONC/RPC (and for the *External Data Representation* (XDR)) is in the public domain and is therefore available free of charge.

There are other RPC technologies apart from ONC/RPC, including the DCE RPC, which we have already mentioned. Although both RPC techniques follow the same conceptual approach, they have a different internal structure and are therefore not interoperable.

Mode of operation

The mode of operation of an RPC is similar to the local procedure call (Table 9.2). In the case of a local procedure call, the parameters are assigned

Table 9.2 Comparison of RPC with the local procedure call.

Remote procedure call	Local procedure call
Activation by the client program. The request parameters are packed into a data packet.	The calling module executes a procedure call; the code generated by the compiler writes transfer parameters to the stack.
Sending of the request and unpacking of the parameters in the server program.	Jump to the subprocedure.
Parameters are unpacked in the server and passed to the subprocedure in the server.	Parameters are loaded from the stack into local variables or registers of the subprocedure.
Execution of the request (the procedure) in the server.	Execution of the subprocedure code.
Packing and returning of the results to the client.	The results and the return value of the subprocedure are stored in a register.
Unpacking of the results by the client and continuation of the normal program execution.	The calling procedure accesses the data.

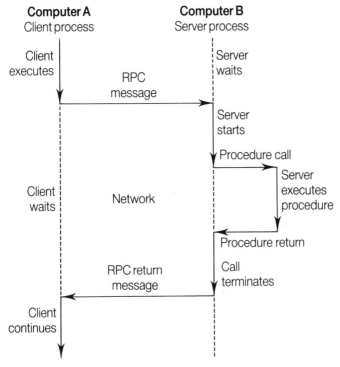

Figure 9.2 Execution of an RPC.

to the calling procedure at a specific point (for example, the stack). The program then branches into the subprocedure, which carries out its work and returns. The results of the subprocedure can now be received by the calling procedure in a register.

The calling module for the RPC now runs in the client program and the procedure called runs in the server. The execution of an RPC consists of the steps shown in Table 9.2 (see also Figure 9.2).

The packing and unpacking of the parameters and the results, the creation of a full RPC protocol header and the sending and receiving of the message are executed by code and library routines linked into the program, known as the RPC run-time system. A list of the library routines and an example of an application are given in the third part of the book in the section entitled 'RPC/XDR programming' (Chapter 13).

Tools for programming

The creation of RPC clients, in other words the programming of RPC requests, can be simplified using tools. For this, one may use a compiler for a language in which the RPC requests, their parameters and return values are defined; the compiler generates the code to call the RPC run-time routines, known as *stubs*. Stubs have calling interfaces like normal procedures, so that they can be linked into a program like any other module, and are transparent in the program code.

A separate language is used for the definition for the following reasons:

- A separate language makes the RPC system more independent of the programming language used to program the application program. The RPC compiler can, optionally, be provided with several code generators and can generate the stubs for different programming languages, such as C and Pascal, and their different calling syntaxes, from a single definition of an RPC request.

- The definition of the RPC request can also be used to generate code for parts of the RPC server that will later execute the procedure.

- The management and control of the RPC system requires additional static parameters for the RPC request that are not provided for in the syntax of normal programming languages.

A description of the definition language developed for ONC/RPC, the *Remote Procedure Call Language* (also known as the XDR language), and the associated compiler *rpcgen* can also be found in the third part of the book.

Unfortunately, RPCL and *rpcgen* are only very simple tools, which do not use the existing facilities to their fullest extent and do not generate a perfect mapping of a local procedure call, but only provide partial support by generating the XDR conversion routines (we shall discuss the purpose of these shortly) and fragments of client and server code.

Thus, other tools that provide better support for the ONC/RPC programmer have been developed by external software houses; these include, for example, Netwise's RPCTool.

This shortcoming was one of the reasons why OSF did not opt for ONC/RPC when choosing the RPC technology for its DCE. The *Interface Definition Language* (IDL) currently contained in OSF/DCE leaves little to be desired in this respect. IDL is also the basis for the RPC technology used by Microsoft for its Windows family of operating systems.

IDL may be used to define almost all (sensible) procedure parameters, from extremely complex data types to so-called 'call-by-reference' parameters in which only a reference (or pointer) to the parameter data is supplied to the procedure. This is a major problem when using RPC, since the calling procedure runs in another process and usually on another system and cannot access the data referenced. IDL now generates stub code that sends the referenced parameter together with the call to the server and

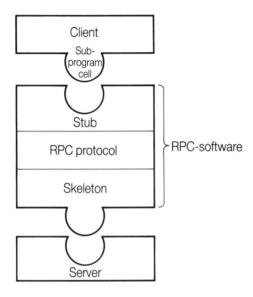

Figure 9.3   Function of the stub.

stores them again in the client program after the execution of the procedure, so that changes to the data are returned.

The tools contained in ONC only provide for so-called 'call-by-value' parameters in which only a copy of the actual value of the parameter is supplied to the procedure by the call. The mapping of the RPC procedures created in this way using the IDL stub is then complete, to the extent that theoretically a client program without source-code alterations can be linked either to the RPC stub or to the actual procedure that normally runs in the server (see Figure 9.3).

ONC/RPC protocol

The ONC/RPC protocol is, so to speak, the chassis for transporting requests to the server, where they flow into *procedures*. The programmer can define an arbitrary number of procedures between the client and the server, together with parameters and results. A functionally coherent group of procedures is called a *service* in RPC jargon or a *program* in the case of

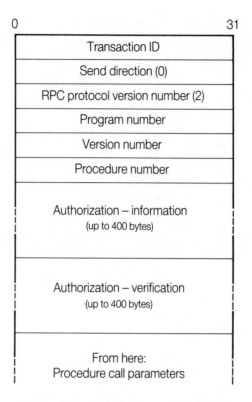

Figure 9.4 ONC/RPC protocol header.

ONC/RPC. Each service is assigned a so-called *program number*, which identifies this program. When, in NFS discussions, we talk of an *application protocol* (a concept from the non-RPC-oriented TCP/IP world), it is such an ONC/RPC program that we have in mind, since the definition of a service represents an application-layer protocol. Of course, the NFS protocol is itself also such a group of RPC procedures. OSF/DCE uses the term *interface* instead of program, based on a somewhat more abstract concept from the world of distributed, object-oriented models, in which objects export their interfaces.

As can be seen from the ONC/RPC protocol header of a request packet in Figure 9.4, an ONC/RPC packet contains the following items defining a request:

- a program number, to find the server that implements the program;
- a version number to check program versions in case there has been an evolution of the interface definition;
- a procedure number to identify the target procedure in the server.

These entries are used by the ONC/RPC execution environment, which is linked into the server, to branch into the correct subprocedure. All the fields of the RPC protocol header are coded in the XDR format.

Sun has defined the conventions outlined in Table 9.3 for the allocation of the program number.

Sun provides a registration service for RPC developers, where they can allocate unique program numbers to avoid collisions with other RPC programs. Developers send electronic mail to rpc@sun.com and ask for a new number.

The individual procedures of a program are usually numbered sequentially by the developer. The version number associated with the program allows several versions of a procedure to be supported within a server; if there is no procedure with the the same procedure and version number, the request is rejected. By convention, procedure 0 of each program is used for test purposes: it contains a null routine, which returns immediately supplying a void result. Thus, it is very easy to test RPC servers for signs of life.

The transaction ID at the beginning of the ONC/RPC protocol header identifies each individual RPC request. Since it is returned in the response, the client may use it to allocate incoming messages to that request. Servers recognize from the transaction ID whether a request is repeated by the client. No particular properties are specified for transaction IDs, they must simply be different from request to request. The transaction ID is followed in the protocol header by the field for entry of the send direction; it contains the value 0 in the RPC request and 1 in the response.

Table 9.3   Specification of the program-number area.

Beginning	End	Use
0	1FFFFFFF	Sun
20000000	3FFFFFFF	Free for developers
40000000	5FFFFFFF	Transient programs
60000000	7FFFFFFF	Reserved
80000000	9FFFFFFF	Reserved
A0000000	BFFFFFFF	Reserved
C0000000	DFFFFFFF	Reserved
E0000000	FFFFFFFF	Reserved

Security

The topic of security in distributed data processing is increasingly important, even for organizations that, unlike banks and the military, have no particular axe to grind in this respect. With the move away from central computers, for which security was relatively easy to achieve since they were always located in the computer centre and only accessible to a few people, and the transition to a decentralized architecture, there is a need to avoid security loopholes. At the same time, for better or for worse, companies today rely on their EDP being operational and their company data being correct. Security is something that cannot be belatedly imposed on a system; it must be taken into account from the beginning, even during the design of the technology and the applications that will run on it. For this reason, security services are an integral component of modern distributed systems. Before we discuss the security in ONC and NFS, we first include a brief review of the most important terms in this area.

Data protection terminology

The aim of all security measures in EDP is *data protection*. Many people initially associate the term security solely with the concept of keeping data secret and with encryption procedures. However, we shall see that these two aspects represent only a subarea of the security problem and that security questions are relevant whenever data is accessed, not only for read access (as when data is kept secret) but also for write access. The same applies to the use of data that the user himself cannot read but uses as a device that may be accessed in a certain way (one example of this is the execution of a program, which is itself a form of data). The procedures used for this are called *access control mechanisms*. For example, the UNIX file system controls the access to files using algorithms that are influenced by the so-called 'permission bits' associated with each file, which assign specific rights to certain users.

Access control is only sensible and effective if one can reliably determine who is performing the access. This is the task of *authenticating* the accessing entity (subject) to the entity being accessed (object). Of course, authentication also takes place in the opposite direction, since the subject would also like to ensure that it is accessing the right object. In the case of RPC-based applications, the client is a subject and the server or the individual entities (such as files) managed by the server are objects. Usually, a client is associated with a certain user or *sponsor* for which it acts.

Since distributed processing involves the transmission of data over lines that may not be secure, the *confidentiality* of the data is protected by *encryption* (encoding with a secret key) against unauthorized reading. The *integrity* of the data is ensured by encrypting a checksum over the data; the recipient can thus be certain that the spoofer did not also falsify the checksum. Because even the best security measures can be overcome by appropriate means or with sufficient time, unauthorized access should also be detected by an *audit* or logging of all security-related events and, if possible, traced back to the originator.

Cryptographic procedures

At this point, we should like to say a word about encryption. There are many procedures for cryptographic encryption of data, the two most important of which are the *Data Encryption Standard* (DES) and the RSA procedure (named after its authors, Rivest, Shamir and Adleman). DES was developed by IBM for the US Department of Defense. The DES procedure uses a single key to encrypt and decrypt the data. Because the sender and the recipient use the same secret key, this is also known as a *secret key* procedure. RSA, on the other hand, uses two keys, one of which is public and the other known only to its holder. In comparison with DES, RSA has the advantage that, unlike DES, it does not require the exchange and regular renewal of a common secret key between the partners, which is an expensive administrative task; instead, RSA's public key can be made automatically accessible to all potential partners. Moreover, it is generally assumed that the cryptographic strength of the code (the improbability of breaking the code) is greater for RSA than for DES. On the other hand, DES is very common and is easy and efficient to implement, while RSA is computationally very intensive.

ONC/RPC and security

ONC/RPC itself only contains interfaces for authorization and does not have a general model for access control. Other security functions are currently not supported. In the following paragraphs we shall consider the implementation of these concepts in ONC/RPC in detail.

Authentication As previously mentioned, an RPC message must sometimes also contain information that authenticates the client to the server, so that the server knows which user the client is representing when issuing the request. The server must also be able to check the validity of this authentication information. The areas provided for this follow directly after the procedure definitions or the return status entry in the ONC/RPC protocol header. This enables servers to restrict access to services (such as the reading of specific information) to authorized clients. The authentication information consists of two parts: the actual information about the identity of the sender (analogous to a name, date of birth, and so on) and a *verifier* (analogous to a password, signature, and so on). Recipients may use this second part to determine whether the identity is authentic, in other words, that it comes from the sender. ONC/RPC itself does not specify how the authentication should be carried out; it only makes an area of up to 400 bytes available for the relevant information. At the beginning of each area is a label that specifies the type and length of the authentication information. From this label, the recipient of the message can determine the structure of the information (and evaluate it accordingly).   The mechanism caters for any type of authentication information. Currently, the following types are predefined:

- AUTH_NONE: No authentication information; both parts of following area have length 0. AUTH_NONE is used when it is not required to check the authorization.

- AUTH_UNIX/AUTH_SYS: UNIX access rights based on user and group IDs to be entered by the client. This type is used in the NFS protocol. It was previously known as AUTH_UNIX, but has been renamed AUTH_SYS in a recent version of ONC/RPC; both terms refer to the same procedure. AUTH_UNIX/AUTH_SYS information is not accompanied by a verifier, and the area provided for it is occupied by AUTH_NONE.

- AUTH_SHORT: Short version of the authentication identification, generated and returned by the server. Usually, this is a reference to AUTH_UNIX/AUTH_SYS authentication information from a previous RPC request, which the client may use instead of the original authentication information in future calls to the server, in order to increase performance.

- AUTH_DES: Authentication information in the form of a character string as data with a DES-encrypted time stamp as verifier. This type of identification information is used by *secure NFS*.

As the alert reader will immediately note, a file access system such as NFS that uses AUTH_UNIX without a cryptographically encrypted verifier for access protection cannot be secure. A clever programmer would be able to generate counterfeit NFS requests and so gain unauthorized file access. Secure NFS closes this security loophole. This variant may be obtained with SunOS Version 4.0 and System V Release 4.

Access control   As previously mentioned, ONC does not contain a uniform scheme for the provision of access control functions; each ONC program has to develop its own scheme. This can undoubtedly be traced back to ONC/RPC's original role as the basis for the NFS protocol. Because, in the case of UNIX file systems, the access control model was defined by the permission bits, there was no need to invent anything new for this. Only read access to the other ONC services is available and they do not provide any confidential information; the administration for these takes place elsewhere so that there was no urgent need in this case either. This shortcoming was first clearly recognized with the propagation of ONC/RPC as a general procedure for distributed applications.

Dependence on the transport protocol

An RPC program can in principle be operated over both TCP and UDP. Some servers provide their services via both transport protocols and leave the choice to the client. However, as a result of the differences in the performance of the two protocols, the selection of the transport protocol gives rise to a number of differences in the behaviour of the RPC program, which should be taken into account when designing an application protocol.

Data volume

Very often, RPC is used with UDP, since the majority of RPC-based applications are transaction-oriented. When UDP is used, the maximum size of the data section of an RPC packet is restricted since, for practical reasons, UDP packets cannot be arbitrarily large. There is no theoretical upper limit for TCP; therefore, if large data volumes are to be sent, this protocol should be preferred.

Normally, it is assumed that data volumes of up to 8 kbytes may be sent over UDP. In most systems with integrated NFS, this upper limit is used up by UDP packets with a maximum of 8800 bytes (8 kbytes data plus RPC/XDR additions). When TCP is used, RPC messages are packed into blocks with a 4-byte length field; thus, theoretically, several thousand million bytes may be moved in a single RPC.

Idempotence

Because reliable transmission of a message in the transport layer is not guaranteed when UDP is used, the RPC layer must take charge of reliability here. This is provided using a timer in the client, which retransmits unanswered ONC/RPC messages after a given time interval has elapsed. The duration of the timer and the permissible number of retransmissions may be altered by the client program.

However, the issuing of a timer does not necessarily mean that the execution of a request has been prevented by an error. It is equally possible that the processing of the request in the server has been delayed or that the response packet has been lost. In the latter case, if the request in the server has already been executed, its retransmission after the timer has expired would start it up again. Of course, there are precautions that may be taken against what is known in the technical jargon as *at most once* behaviour; for example, increasing RPC transaction codes may be assigned and a state field for each client–server context may be introduced. However, in ONC/RPC, these expensive mechanisms have not been included in the RPC run-time library for performance reasons; they are very similar to reliability procedures used by TCP and thus should only be implemented by this layer.

Thus, the ONC/RPC application protocol design for UDP applications should ensure that a request with the same parameters always delivers the same result; thus, that it may be arbitrarily repeated. The best example of this is the NFS read request which always provides the exact file position and length; in this case, inadvertent repetition would only recover the same data again. This is another reason why NFS does not allow access to special files; many devices, for example terminals, only operate serially and do not usually allow for repetitions. This repeatability is called *idempotence* in RPC jargon. Some servers attempt to improve performance here using the transaction ID in the ONC/RPC protocol header; in order to avoid surplus repeated requests, they check whether a request has already been seen and is now being or has just been processed.

When TCP is used, no retransmissions may be initiated at the RPC level since TCP itself retransmits the message until it reaches the recipient. In other words, the server receives the message either once only or not at all (at most once). If message forwarding is unsuccessful, the RPC layer will be notified and may inform the application program. The same is also true for the RPC response message from the server.

Since data transmission with TCP is reliable, another mode of operation is available when required: batching. Batching involves the sending of RPC requests in rapid succession without waiting for the response to the previous call, for example, for the data-transmission phase of a file transfer implemented with RPC. This results in a considerably higher transfer rate between client and server, since the waiting times between request and response are omitted. To execute batching, client and server must have previously agreed that the server should not send response messages.

External Data Representation

In our tour of the individual protocol layers, we have now reached the presentation layer. If we define the term 'protocol' to mean a declaration of the form of communication between two peers, then the External Data Representation (XDR) also falls into this category. As specified in RFC 1014 (Sun Microsystems, 1987), XDR is concerned with the definition of a format for data encoding. XDR does not have a protocol header or other protocol elements like other protocols.

Background

The object of data communication is to exchange data between computers and operating systems of different origins and types. For a computer to understand data sent from another computer, the data must be presented in the same form or in a form agreed between the two computers, otherwise the recipient cannot convert the data into its own internal format. We have already come across this problem in our discussion of the TCP/IP protocol headers.

There are two modes of operation for the protocols of the presentation layer. In the *explicit format*, a description of the individual elements is transferred with the data, thus enabling the recipient to recover the structure of data records (as in ASN.1 *Basic Encoding Rules* (BER)). The *implicit format* involves an agreement between the two communication partners, prior to the data transfer, regarding the structure and presentation of the elements. Within the implicit format there are two different data-encoding formats, namely the so-called *canonical* format, in which the sender always converts the data into a common uniform format which is reconverted by the recipient, and the *server makes it right* format, in which the sender leaves the data in its own local presentation format and adds an identifier to the message that signals the sender's format to the recipient. XDR uses an implicit, canonical format.

Data encoding

Different computer systems differ greatly as far as the representation of data is concerned. These differences may be determined by both hardware and software. In addition to the representation of integers and floating-point numbers, there are different ways of encoding text and differences in the arrangement of the elements within complex data objects such as unions and structures.

Encoding of numbers

Binary integer processing is used in all modern processor architectures. However, in the case of integers, the processor may store words consisting of several bytes in different ways, either with the least order byte (*little-endian*) at the lowest memory address or vice versa (*big-endian*).

Figure 9.5 illustrates the arrangement using a 32-bit word. Theoretically, the same difference could arise for the bit sequence within a byte, but in practice all processors use the big-endian format to arrange the bits in a byte.

Similarly, in the past, there were great differences in the representations of floating-point numbers. Table 9.4 shows the format defined in the IEEE standard 754 (IEEE, 1985), which is today used in many standard processors and coprocessors.

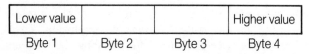

Motorola 680x0, IBM 370, SPARC

Higher value			Lower value
Byte 1	Byte 2	Byte 3	Byte 4

Intel 80x86, VAX, NS32000, MIPS, SPARC

Lower value			Higher value
Byte 1	Byte 2	Byte 3	Byte 4

Figure 9.5   Big- and little-endian formats.

Table 9.4   ANSI/IEEE 754-1985 floating-point number format.

Function	Size
Mantissa	23 bits
Exponent	8 bits
Sign	1 bit

Encoding of text

While the encoding of numerical values is usually determined by the processor hardware, the software is critical in the encoding of text and complex data objects. Without a mapping from codes to characters, text is simply a (meaningless) sequence of bytes. Standardized mapping tables linking numerical values and an alphabet include the ASCII and EBCDIC codes. Unfortunately, these have fundamentally different structures, for example, the letter 'A' is represented by $41_{(16)}$ in ASCII and by $C1_{(16)}$ in EBCDIC.

Complex data objects

Unions and structures are complex data objects constructed from the basic data types described above; they are defined by the programmer or the compiler. While program declarations are in principle interchangeable, the most frequent problem on binary exchange of these objects is the different alignment of the elements they contain.

An optimal access to data structures in the main memory usually assumes that the individual elements lie on the processor word boundaries (thus, their start address is even and/or divisible by four). Most processors

```
struct example {
    char c;  /* begins at position 0 */
    short s; /* begins at position 1, 2 or 4 */
    long l;  /* begins at position 3, 4 or 8 */
};
```

Figure 9.6   Example of a structure with various word boundaries.

require an additional cycle for operations over word boundaries, and some (for example, most RISC CPUs) cannot work at all with unaligned addresses.   Since elements within structures do not always have a length that is a multiple of the word size, most compilers cater for this with automatically inserted padding, so that, according to the system, consecutive elements begin at addresses divisible by two or four.   The structure shown in Figure 9.6 (given in C notation) may consist of 7, 8 or 12 bytes on different systems.   For all the areas shown, appropriate specifications must be determined by XDR.

Specifications

The data elements converted into XDR format are sequentially written to the data buffer (serialized) (this process is also referred to in jargon as marshalling) and then sent.   The conversion from XDR (decoding) into an internal, possibly different, format is the job of the receiving computer (canonical).

XDR uses a format of 8-bit bytes with a big-endian bit sequence. All integer data types (in C notation *char*, *short* and *long* together with the type *enum*) are converted to 4-byte integers in big-endian format.   In addition to the defined C data types, there is a 64-bit integer *hyper* and a Boolean type *bool*, which are treated analogously.   The IEEE format is used for floating-point numbers.

The canonical format procedure used in XDR, in which, under certain circumstances, every value must be converted by the sender and reconverted by the receiver, is not uncontroversial.   While there are no disadvantages for computers whose processors operate using the byte order specified by XDR, message traffic between computers with the little-endian format requires a double (totally unnecessary) conversion.   It would, for example, be possible to send a label with the message that would permit the recipient to recognize the byte order and convert it only when necessary (server makes it right).

Byte sequences are, as before, sent as a sequence of bytes, padded to be a multiple of 4.   For a variable-length sequence, a length field is used to enable the recipient to distinguish between data and padding. The same applies to arrays of structures or unions, which XDR processes as byte sequences. Text is encoded in the ASCII format. Structure elements are aligned to 4-byte boundaries (here the requirement for a total length divisible by 4 is naturally met).

Definition language

As previously mentioned, a special language, RPCL, similar to C, has been developed to describe XDR data formats. This may be used to describe the data objects exchanged in the application protocols and to define RPC services. There is also a compiler that generates C programs from XDR definitions (see RPC/XDR programming in Chapter 13). XDR need not always be installed together with RPC or networks. In principle, the systems involved may agree upon a common data format for a data exchange, even when this exchange involves files. Thus, the implementation of XDR also contains functions that support a use of XDR outside RPC.

Packet structure

Now that we have discussed all the protocol layers from the cable to the application, the RPC packet structure shown in Figure 9.7 should be

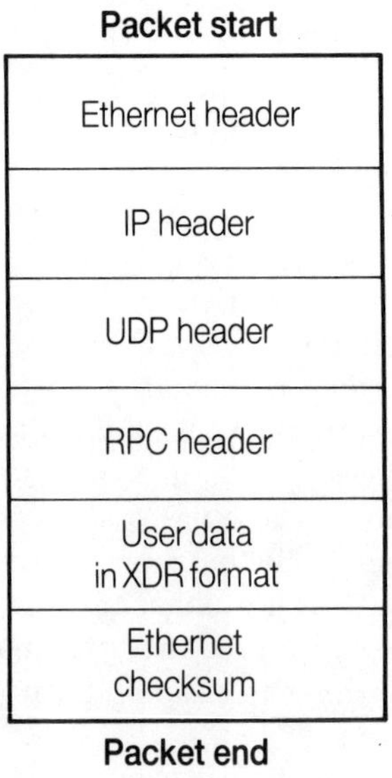

Packet start

Ethernet header
IP header
UDP header
RPC header
User data in XDR format
Ethernet checksum

Packet end

Figure 9.7   Structure of an Ethernet packet with RPC data.

practically self-explanatory. (Clearly, this packet is intended for an Ethernet network with UDP as the transport protocol.) The individual protocol headers (and thus also the protocol layers) are clearly identifiable in the Ethernet packet.

Port mapper/RPC bind

As outlined in the discussion of TCP/IP, a rendezvous between client and server processors is made by calling a server port number, which must be known to the client. If this principle of a defined port number were also to be used for RPC programs (with the increase in computer networking, there may be thousands of these in the future), there would soon be a problem with the allocation of free port numbers. Thus, the *port mapper*, which dynamically binds port numbers to RPC programs, was created for the RPC protocol.

For TIRPC the function of the port mapper was extended from the concept of port numbers to the conversion of arbitrary address formats. Thus, this new implementation is known as RPC bind.

Mode of operation of the port mapper

The port mapper server operates like a directory service. It controls a mapping table relating RPC programs and their version numbers to the local UDP or TCP port numbers for which a service (server) is available. The port mapper or RPC bind service itself occupies port 111 in both TCP and UDP, because it must be available under a well-known port number.

An RPC server is usually allocated a free port number by the system on program start-up. It then registers this number with the port mapper together with the parameters of the service it offers. When a client wishes to access an RPC service, it first sends an enquiry including the program, procedure and version numbers together with the type of transport protocol desired to the port mapper of the target computer (the computer on which the procedure is to be executed). It receives the port number of the service by return and can then send the request directly to the server. Since the client caches the port number, it is not necessary to repeat the port mapper enquiry for subsequent RPC requests. Since in the client the port numbers are not stored in a file but in main memory, a new enquiry cycle is needed whenever a client program is started.

In addition to its many advantages, this dynamic mapping also has the disadvantage that if the port mapper breaks down the RPC service cannot then be obtained.

Port mapper protocol

Client and server both communicate with the port mapper via RPC procedures. The parameters of this protocol are shown in Table 9.5.

The RPC procedures defined in the port mapper protocol may be taken from Figure 9.8. It is not appropriate to give the exact description of the procedure parameters and the results at this point. The symbolic names used should provide a clear description of the corresponding functions. Further information may be found in the NFS documentation and in RFC 1050 (Sun Microsystems, 1988a).

As Figure 9.8 shows, here too there is a procedure 0 which, by definition, does nothing, has no parameters and returns a void value. The procedures PMAPPROC_SET and PMAPPROC_UNSET are used by the server to register or (respectively) de-register a service. PMAPPROC_GETPORT and PMAPPROC_DUMP supply an individual port number or the complete port mapper table. A client may use the procedure PMAPPROC_CALLIT to broadcast an RPC message to all existing servers (in the network) of a given service.

Table 9.5   RPC protocol parameters for PORTMAP.

Name	Value
Program number	100000
Version number	2
Transport protocol	TCP, UDP

RPCBIND protocol

The RPCBIND protocol is a more recent version of the port mapper protocol that is supplied with System V Release 4 and systems based on that such as SINIX 5.4, UnixWare, Destiny and Solaris 2.x. The parameters of this protocol are shown in Table 9.6.

Consideration of the specification shown in Figure 9.9 shows that the new version no longer refers to the specifics of TCP/IP, such as port numbers and IP addresses, but uses universal fields for these purposes. Otherwise, the protocol contains essentially the same operations as the port mapper protocol, together with a number of new procedures.

Table 9.6   RPC protocol parameters for RPCBIND.

Name	Value
Program number	100000
Version number	3
Transport protocol	TCP, UDP

```
/*
 * Procedure 0, Does nothing:
 */
0. PMAPPROC_NULL ()
          returns ()

/*
 * Procedure 1, Sets an entry:
 */
1. PMAPPROC_SET (prog, vers, prot, port)
                        returns (success)

/*
 * Procedure 2, Deletes an entry:
 */
2. PMAPPROC_UNSET (prog, vers, dummy1, dummy2)
                        returns (success)

/*
 * Procedure 3, Searches for an entry:
 */
3. PMAPPROC_GETPORT (prog, vers, prot, dummy)
                        returns (port)

/*
 * Procedure 4, Transfers the whole table:
 */
4. PMAPPROC_DUMP ()
   returns (maplist)

/*
 * Procedure 5, Indirect broadcast:
 */
5. PMAPPROC_CALLIT (prog, vers, proc, args)
                        returns (port, results)
```

Figure 9.8 Port mapper protocol, version 2.

As can be seen from the figure, the GETPORT procedure is replaced by GETADDR in RPCBIND. It provides a so-called universal address (*uaddr*) in the field *r_addr* in the *rpcb* structure. Universal addresses may be converted into true transport address structures (*netbuf*) for delivery to the TLI interface (see Chapter 13), using library routines or the

```
/* STRUCTURE WHICH DESCRIBES THE CONVERSION TABLE */
struct rpcb {
  u_long r_prog; /* RPC program number */
  u_long r_vers; /* RPC version number */
  string r_netid<> /* Protos.  for which service provided */
  string r_addr<> /* Address of the server */
};

/* CHAINED LIST OF RPCB STRUCTURES */
struct rpcblist {
  rpcb rpcb_map; /* Information */
  struct rpcblist *rpcb_next /* Pointer to next element */
};

/* ARGUMENTS & RESULTS OF RPCBPROC_CALLIT PROCEDURE */
struct rpcb_rmtcallargs{
  u_long prog; /* Calling RPC program */
  u_long vers; /* Calling version number */
  u_long proc; /* Calling procedure */
  opaque args_ptr<> /* Call parameter */
};

struct rpcb_rmtcallres{
  string addr_ptr<>; /* Address of the executing server */
  opaque results_ptr<> /* Results */
};

/* RPCBIND PROGRAM DEFINITION */
program RPCBPROG{
  version RPCBVERS
    void RPCBPROC_NULL(void) = 0;
    bool RPCBPROG_SET(rpcb) =1;
    bool RPCBPROG_UNSET(rpcb) =2;
    string RPCBPROG_GETADDR(rpcb) =3;
    rpcblist RPCBPROG_DUMP(void) =4;
    rpcb_rmtcallres RPCBPROG_CALLIT(rpcb_rmtcallargs)= 5;
    unsigned int RPCBPROG_GETTIME(void) =6;
    struct netbuf RPCBPROG_UADDR2TADDR(string) =7;
    string RPCBPROG_TADDR2UADDR(struct netbuf) =8;
  } = 3;
}; = 100000;
```

Figure 9.9   RPC bind protocol in RPCL, version 3.

UADDR2TADDR procedure (or, conversely, using TADDR2UADDR). In addition, the GETTIME procedure returns the time on the local computer.

Recent RPC programs initially use the RPCBIND protocol to interrogate server systems. If this protocol is not supported by these, the query is repeated with the old port mapper protocol. RPCBIND servers, which are the only ones used in more recent system versions, support both the RPCBIND and the old port mapper protocol.

Server binding

One of the greatest disadvantages of the original ONC/RPC implementation is the fact that a client must know exactly on which computer and at which address a given server is available. The port mapper or RPC bind service initially only solves part of the problem. When the mapping of servers and computers changes, manual intervention is generally required on the client side.

It would be desirable to have a service that would search for a server on behalf of the client. This service is known as *binding* in RPC jargon. In OSF/DCE, this work is carried out by the cell directory service. YPBIND could provide a similar service for ONC systems, but regrettably its use is restricted to the NIS subsystem. NIS itself is not dynamic enough to take on directory service functions. NIS+ in ONC+ satisfies the conditions for efficient client–server binding. NIS is described in Chapter 11.

Network File System protocol

The NFS protocol (Sun Microsystems, 1989) consists of a number of RPC procedures similar to the port mapper protocol.

Table 9.7 shows the constants of the NFS service. The current version of the NFS protocol is number 2; version 1 was never issued.

The NFS protocol has remained unchanged since 1984. A revision of the NFS protocol was worked on briefly in the late 1980s; however, because of concerns that incompatibility with the current version would make the

Table 9.7   RPC protocol parameters for NFS.

Name	Value
Program number	100003
Version number	2
Transport protocol	UDP
Port number	2049

market uncertain, a new version was not released. Competing products are now beginning to overtake NFS as far as reliability and performance are concerned; for this reason, SunSoft and its partners announced a new version of NFS some time ago.

The specification of port number 2049 is surprising. However, as noted earlier, port numbers may be arbitrarily chosen, and the mapping between services and port numbers is made by the port mapper! The explanation is simple; this number is a relic from the past which has been retained, at least until the next version of NFS. This port number was accidentally set to 2049 as a result of negligence in the implementation and, once its removal had been neglected at the start, later correction was impossible for reasons of upward compatibility.

Specification of the NFS protocol

Although RPC services, like the NFS protocol, are best specified using RPCL, in our opinion, a formal definition with RPCL would be too general and of little help at this point. Instead, we shall introduce the NFS protocol using a somewhat simpler and clearer representation, which is also found in the NFS manuals (in which the specifications are usually given).

As in the representation of the port mapper protocol, a procedure with its parameters and return values is represented in the following form:

```
<Procedure number>.<Procedure name> (<Parameter>)
                                   returns (<Results>)
    <Declaration of the arguments>
    <Declaration of the results>
```

Before we consider the NFS procedures in detail, we must take a more detailed look at some of the data objects and structures that they use.

Discriminated unions

In RPCL, the term *discriminated union* stands for a labelled area that may contain various data objects. The label provides information about the type of the data object. The data area of a discriminated union also begins physically with a label followed by the data itself. It is interesting that explicit formats, avoided in the XDR protocol, are here reintroduced through the back door. The approach is also pragmatic, since only a single message channel is used to transmit results and error codes. More modern technologies use the concept of *exception* to signal the error state via an additional interface (necessarily internal, but using a different procedure), but this requires a greater abstraction of the interface than that currently provided for in ONC/RPC.

In RPCL, a discriminated union is represented as shown in the following example:

```
union switch (status) {
    ERROR:
        int errorcode;
    OK:
        string text<MAXDATA>;
    default:
        struct {}
} result;
```

The object **result** begins with a label **status**, which may take the values **ERROR** or **OK**. This is followed by either a field **errorcode** or a character string **text**. Every other value denotes an empty set.

The entry in pointed brackets **<MAXDATA>** indicates that **text** is a variable-length character string, where the value of **MAXDATA** is the maximum length. Fixed-length objects are denoted by square brackets, as in **[MAXDATA]**. These length entries are also used in other array definitions.

Discriminated unions are (as our example demonstrates) often used as results of procedures: an error code is returned in the case of an error; data is returned in the case of success. In programming local subprocedures in C, in such a case, one would return a pointer to the data, which would have value 0 in the case of error. When computer boundaries are crossed, this method cannot be used since, unlike local calls where cross-references to data may be given as parameters (call by reference), in the RPC context the data itself must always be exported (call by value). (This difference should always be noted when defining RPC procedures.)

NFS protocol constants

The following constants are defined for the NFS protocol:

```
/*
 * The maximum number of bytes in a READ or
 * WRITE request
 */
const MAXDATA = 8192; /* const defines a constant */

/*
 * The maximum number of bytes in a path name
 */
const MAXPATHLEN = 1024;

/*
 * The maximum number of bytes in a path name component
 */
const MAXNAMLEN = 255;
```

```
/*
 * Size of the file entry pointer 'cookie'
 * returned by READDIR
 */
const COOKIESIZE = 4;

/*
 * Size of a file handle
 */
const FHSIZE = 32;
```

NFS data types

The most important data object in the NFS protocol is the *file handle* (*fhandle*). This contains entries that uniquely identify a file on the NFS server. File handles are given as parameters in all NFS procedures and are references to the files with which the operation itself should be executed. They are thus very similar to the file descriptor in standard UNIX system calls. Since the NFS protocol must be valid for various systems, the file handle is defined to be a 32-byte (FHSIZE) format-free data field or so-called *opaque* object. Its contents are generated by the NFS server as a result of various RPC procedures and can only be understood by the server (in other words, the client receives the handle and sends it on every operation with the file; it cannot and should not manipulate it). The definition of this object is also unformatted:

```
typedef opaque fhandle[FHSIZE];
```

File handles are delivered to the client as a result of the procedures LOOKUP, CREATE and MKDIR.

Naturally, we know the information that the server usually stores in the file handle in UNIX systems (although different implementations of this also exist):

- the *major/minor device number* of the device driver of the file system containing the file;
- the *index node (inode) number* of the file addressed;
- a local inode generation number that fixes the instance of the inode.

These entries are sufficient to enable the NFS server to recognize a file uniquely. We shall go into the function of the generation number in more depth in our discussion of the weaknesses of the NFS protocol.

In some calls, path names and file names are given, which are defined as follows:

```
typedef string path<MAXPATHLEN>;
typedef string filename<MAXNAMLEN>;
```

The results of NFS procedures may take the following values:

```
typedef enum {
    NFS_OK = 0,
    NFSERR_PERM = 1,
    NFSERR_NOENT = 2,
    NFSERR_IO = 5,
    NFSERR_NXIO = 6,
    NFSERR_ACCES = 13,
    NFSERR_EXIST = 17,
    NFSERR_NODEV = 19,
    NFSERR_NOTDIR = 20,
    NFSERR_ISDIR = 21,
    NFSERR_FBIG = 27,
    NFSERR_NOSPC = 28,
    NFSERR_ROFS = 30,
    NFSERR_NAMETOOLONG = 63,
    NFSERR_NOTEMPTY = 66,
    NFSERR_DQUOT = 69,
    NFSERR_STALE = 70,
    NFSERR_WFLUSH = 99
} stat;
```

Most of these definitions are well known to UNIX programmers; they correspond to the error codes defined in */usr/include/sys/errno.h*. Only two values are new. NFS_OK stands for the successful execution of a procedure. NFSERR_STALE stands for invalid (stale) file handle. The error code NFSERR_WFLUSH is not currently used.

The file types known in NFS are defined by *ftype* ('file type'). Here, the similarities to UNIX situations are not purely coincidental:

```
typedef enum {
    NFNON = 0, /* no file */
    NFREG = 1, /* regular file */
    NFDIR = 2, /* directory */
    NFBLK = 3, /* block-oriented file */
    NFCHR = 4, /* character-oriented file */
```

```
            NFLNK = 5   /* symbolic link */
        } ftype;
```

No other data types are defined. System V FIFOs (which are also
known as named pipes) are not stand-alone file types in NFS Version 2,
since they do not exist on BSD systems (and thus neither do they exist on
the earlier SunOS versions). They may be emulated by a combination of
invalid entries in other fields and should be included in a later NFS protocol
version.

The structure *fattr* ('file attributes') defines the attributes of a file
as far as they are important to the NFS client. Elements of *fattr* include
time stamps, for which there is an individual type definition, *timeval*:

```
        typedef struct {
            unsigned seconds;   /* seconds */
            unsigned useconds;  /* microseconds */
        } timeval;

        typedef struct {
            ftype    type;       /* file type */
            unsigned mode;       /* access rights */
            unsigned nlink;      /* number of links */
            unsigned uid;        /* owner's user ID */
            unsigned gid;        /* owner's group ID */
            unsigned size;       /* size in bytes */
            unsigned blocksize;  /* size of a file block */
            unsigned rdev;       /* major and minor device */
            unsigned blocks;     /* size in blocks */
            unsigned fsid;       /* file system ID */
            unsigned fileid;     /* catalogue number */
            timeval  atime;      /* time of last access */
            timeval  mtime;      /* time of last modification */
            timeval  ctime;      /* time of installation */
        } fattr;
```

UNIX specialists will immediately recognize the similarity with the contents
of the structure declared in */usr/include/sys/stat.h*, which is here only
extended by a few entries.

The *sattr* ('set attributes') structure contains those attributes
which may be set by system calls:

```
        typedef struct {
            unsigned mode;  /* access rights */
            unsigned uid;   /* user ID */
```

```
    unsigned gid;    /* group ID */
    unsigned size;   /* size */
    timeval  atime; /* time of last access */
    timeval  mtime; /* time of last modification */
} sattr;
```

The discriminated union *attrstat* ('attributes and status') is supplied as a result in almost all NFS procedures. In the case of success, it contains the attributes of the altered file, otherwise it contains the error code defined by *stat*:

```
typedef union switch (stat status) {
    NFS_OK:
        fattr    attributes;
    default:  struct {}
} attrstat;
```

The structure *diropargs* ('directory operation arguments') and discriminated union *diropres* ('operation results') contain the arguments and results of operations with file directories:

```
typedef struct {
    fhandle  dir;
    filename name;
} diropargs;

typedef union switch (stat status) {
    NFS_OK
        struct {
            fhandle file;
            fattr    attributes;
        }
    default:
        struct {}
} diropres;
```

NFS protocol specification

In this section, the NFS procedures of the NFS protocol are presented and discussed in detail.

Null

```
0.  NFSPROC_NULL () returns ()
```

Like all other RPC services, the NFS protocol begins with the procedure 0, which does not contain any arguments and returns a void result.

Fetch file attributes

```
1.  NFSPROC_GETATTR (file) returns (reply)
        fhandle  file;
        attrstat reply;
```

This procedure returns the attributes of the file specified in the file handle, for example, as a result of the UNIX system calls *access, open, stat* and *fstat*. File attributes are held in the NFS client in a cache, so that this frequently used information is always ready. Entries in the cache are time stamped. If the difference between the time of the time stamp entry and the actual time is greater than three seconds for files or 30 seconds for directories the information is fetched again from the server. Thus, it is possible that alterations to file directories by a second client only appear after this time interval has elapsed.

Set file attributes

```
2.  NFSPROC_SETATTR (file, attributes) returns (reply)
        fhandle  file;
        sattr    attributes;
        attrstat reply;
```

This procedure is used to set file attributes, for example, via the UNIX system calls *chown, fchown, chmod, fchmod, truncate, ftruncate* and *utime*. The altered attributes are returned as a result.

Read file system root

```
3.  NFSPROC_ROOT () returns ()
```

This procedure is obsolete and is not used.

Look up file name

```
4.  NFSPROC_LOOKUP (which) returns (reply)
        diropargs which;
        diropres  reply;
```

LOOKUP supplies the client with a file handle corresponding to a file name in a specified directory (*which*), thus making the subsequent operations with the file or the directory possible. The client uses this procedure to find its way around in the file system of another computer or NFS server.

The client uses LOOKUP to conduct a step-by-step search through path names given to it in a program and, in certain circumstances, may even call a separate RPC procedure for every path name component. This procedure is best explained with an example.

Let us assume that a server file system is mounted locally in the directory */nfs*. In order to find a file handle for the file */nfs/a/b/c/file*, the client system first searches the file system root / for the directory *nfs* whose attributes it has stored locally. In so doing, it determines that *nfs* is the mounting point of an NFS file system and now uses LOOKUP to search for the file handle for the directory *a* on the server. Then it searches for *b* in *a*, and so on, until it finally finds the file handle for *file*.

Why does the client not simply send the last part of the path name (*a/b/c/file*) to the server, leaving the server to return the file handle for *file* and thus saving time and system resources? Let us see what would happen if we used this method with path names such as */nfs/a/b/../../tmp/file*. In this case, in the NFS server file tree, */nfs/a/b* is switched backwards twice by .. , and in fact the file */tmp/file* is located on the client computer. In other words, this method of path name evaluation would create insoluble problems for the server.

UNIX path names of this type are however completely legal. Of course, they are not generated by a user, but by shell procedures or programs. Thus, we have shown that the step-by-step search for a path name using the LOOKUP procedure is the best solution. The time spent searching for path names may be shortened if the client uses a directory cache. The file handles for directories that are frequently searched will be stored in this cache; thus, there is little or no loss of performance.

Read the contents of a symbolic link

```
5.   NFSPROC_READLINK (file) returns (reply)
        fhandle file;
        union switch (stat status) {
            NFS_OK:
                path    data;
            default:
                struct {}
        } reply;
```

BSD systems define symbolic links or files that contain the path name of another file instead of data and are thus pointers to other files. If the system recognizes a symbolic link file, the pointer is read by the system even under NFS. It is then evaluated and the specified file is addressed. Up to five embedded symbolic links may be used. In order that programs such as the command *ls* may also evaluate symbolic link files, there is a system call named *readlink*. The RPC procedure READLINK allows access to symbolic links over NFS.

Read a file

```
6.  NFSPROC_READ (file, offset, count, totalcount)
    returns (reply)
        fhandle file;
        unsigned offset;
        unsigned count;
        unsigned totalcount;
        union switch (stat status) {
            NFS_OK:
                fattr  attributes;
                string data<MAXDATA>;
            default:
                struct {}
        } reply;
```

With this procedure, which is activated following a *read* or *exec* system call, the NFS client reads from a file belonging to the server; the latter, for its part, returns data and file attributes. The *offset* parameter explicitly sets the file read counter in the server at each call. The parameter *totalcount* is unused.

Write to cache

```
7.  NFSPROC_WRITECACHE () returns ()
```

This procedure is not used in the current version of NFS.

Write to file

```
8.  NFSPROC_WRITE (file, beginoffset, offset,
    totalcount, data) returns (reply)
        fhandle file;
        unsigned beginoffset;
        unsigned offset;
        unsigned totalcount;
        string   data<MAXDATA>;
        attrstat reply;
```

This procedure, which is activated following a *write* system call, is used by the NFS client to write to a file belonging to the server. The parameters *totalcount* and *beginoffset* are unused. The length of the data to be written is given in the length field of the *data* area.

Create file

```
9.  NFSPROC_CREATE (where, attributes) returns (dir)
        diropargs where;
        sattr     attributes;
        diropres  dir;
```

CREATE, which is activated by the system calls *creat*, *mknod* and *open*, generates new files in the server. The result of this call is the file handle for the new file.

Delete file

```
10.  NFSPROC_REMOVE (which) returns (status)
        diropargs which;
        stat      status;
```

This procedure, which is activated by the system call *unlink*, deletes files on the server.

Rename file

```
11.  NFSPROC_RENAME (from, to) returns (status)
        diropargs from;
        diropargs to;
        stat      status;
```

RENAME supports the atomic renaming of a file or directory, for example, in the BSD system call *rename*.

Generate link

```
12.  NFSPROC_LINK (from, to) returns (status)
        fhandle   from;
        diropargs to;
        stat      status;
```

This is activated by the system call *link*. It generates a so-called hard link (another directory entry for a file) within a file system.

Generate symbolic link

```
13.  NFSPROC_SYMLINK (from, to, attributes)
       returns (status)
          diropargs  from;
          path       to;
          sattr      attributes;
          stat       status;
```

This procedure is activated by the system call *symlink* and generates a symbolic link.

Create directory

```
14.  NFSPROC_MKDIR (where, attributes) returns (reply)
          diropargs  where;
          sattr      attributes;
          diropres   reply;
```

This procedure is activated by the system call *mkdir* and generates an empty directory with the entries . and .. (where .. denotes the directory above in the file system tree).

Delete directory

```
15.  NFSPROC_RMDIR (which) returns (status)
          diropargs  which;
          stat       status;
```

This procedure is activated by the system call *rmdir* and deletes a directory. The system calls *rmdir* and *mkdir* were not available in the first versions of System V (System V.2 and earlier); thus, for upward compatibility with older systems they are emulated by some NFS clients.

Read directory

```
16.  NFSPROC_READDIR (dir, cookie, count)
       returns (entries)
          fhandle  dir;
          opaque   cookie[COOKIESIZE];
          unsigned count;
```

```
union switch (stat, status) {
    NFS_OK:
        typedef union switch (boolean valid) {
            TRUE:
                struct {
                    unsigned fileid;
                    filename name;
                    opaque   cookie[COOKIESIZE];
                    entry    nextentry;
                }
            FALSE:
                struct {}
        } entry;
        boolean eof;
        default:
    } entries;
```

The result of this procedure is a list of directory entries, each of which consists of a file name, the inode number and the so-called 'cookie'. A 'cookie' is a pointer to a position in the directory.

Before giving further details of the parameters and results of READDIR, we should ask why it is actually needed. Why is it not possible to read the contents of a directory just as we would a file? The explanation for this is simple and enlightening. Every operating system has its own physical file system structure and its own directory format; they are not even fully compatible between different UNIX derivatives. Only now are UNIX systems being supplied that support several hard-disk file systems at once (for example, System V with several different UNIX file systems, MS-DOS and CD-ROM file systems). Since NFS is also required to function in a heterogeneous environment, there is a specific format for the exchange of directory information. More recent versions of UNIX (from System V.3 or BSD versions with NFS) contain generic system calls to read from directories (*getdents* or *getdirentries*). However, the UNIX programmer never uses these calls directly, but always through functions, such as *readdir*, supplied in the *directory* library routines. Attempts to read a directory over NFS using READ are rejected by the server with an error. However, for upward compatibility with old programs, some UNIX systems convert standard directory read operations within the NFS client to READDIR calls; under certain circumstances, this may harm performance. Other server operating systems do not have directories similar to UNIX; in this case, if, for example, a file is not accessed sequentially, emulation must take place in the server.

The format of the results of the READDIR procedure shows many similarities to UNIX, for example, the field *fileid* contains the inode number used in UNIX. The use of 'cookie' certainly needs to be explained. Since it is possible that, because of its size, a directory may not be contained

in a single RPC message, it must be readable in sequential steps. The cookie
is used to mark the position reached. In UNIX, the cookie is a file position;
in other systems, it may be an index key. Because of these differences, the
client cannot and should not evaluate the contents of the cookie. This data
is, like a file handle, declared to be *opaque*.

The rather complicated results structure is the XDR version of a
chained list, where the switch *valid* shows whether another directory entry
follows (thus, it acts like a NULL pointer in C). The Boolean *eof* tells us
whether the end of the directory has been reached.

Read file system attributes

```
17.   NFSPROC_STATFS (file) returns (reply)
          fhandle file;
          union switch (stat status) {
              NFS_OK:
                  struct {
                      unsigned tsize;
                      unsigned bsize;
                      unsigned blocks;
                      unsigned bfree;
                      unsigned bavail;
                  } fsattr;
              default:
                  struct {}
          } reply;
```

This procedure returns information about the mounted file system, the
number of blocks present (*blocks*), whether they are available (*bavail*) or
free (*bfree*) and their sizes (*bsize*), together with the optimal transfer size
(*tsize*) for READ and WRITE requests, and so on. STATFS is executed,
for example, by calling the UNIX command *df*. Sadly, the number of free
inodes in the file system is not returned; thus, this value in the output of
df is always 0. STATFS is activated by the system call *ustat* in System V
or by *statfs* in BSD NFS systems.

Particular features of the NFS protocol

Server restart

The designers of NFS were interested in designing a very robust file access
service which, above all, would eradicate the painful problem of restarting
after a failure of the server or client computer. The solution was a *stateless*
protocol, in which the server did not have to store any information about
the current state or the progress of the dialogue with the client (for example,

whether or not a file was open or closed). Thus, the NFS protocol does not have the usual open and close operations. Unlike in standard UNIX I/O routines, the read and write positions are always supplied to the server on application.

Since the *fhandle* for a file must always be unambiguous, it is now possible, after a server failure and a subsequent restart, to continue a read operation transparently, as far as the client program is concerned. While the server is not available, the client system retransmits the read request with the same parameters to the server at regular intervals, until the server responds. This behaviour is particularly advantageous for diskless workstations, which cannot execute a meaningful function without the server.

The repeated issuing of requests when there is no answer is a component part of the RPC mechanism. The waiting time between the repeats (which increases exponentially according to the number of unsuccessful attempts) and the number of repeats before total cut-off may be parameterized using the command *mount*.

Idempotence

The semantics of RPC procedures have to be defined in such a way that repetition is not a problem. However, in the NFS protocol, in some procedures (REMOVE, CREATE, RMDIR, MKDIR, LINK, SYMLINK and SETATTR), this is not the case. Thus, for example, a file delete may not be arbitrarily repeated (since after the first call the file is no longer present, a second call would return an error message of the form 'File does not exist'). Since NFS cannot be 100% protected against either overloaded servers with high response times or lost response packets, here too we must also reckon with redundant RPCs. So that these calls do not cause problems, the NFS server implementation under UNIX uses a cache to log previously terminated calls of all non-repeatable procedures together with their transaction ID. The cache is used to recognize repeats of such requests from RPC transaction IDs already stored in the cache; a positive response is now returned in place of an error code. Attempts have been made to extend this cache to WRITE procedures (Juszczak, 1989), to decrease the server load due to redundant repeated write operations.

There is one other situation in which the stateless NFS protocol is not always an advantage, for example, in mapping the UNIX semantics over NFS. We shall discuss this problem and its solution in the next chapter, on the implementation of NFS.

MOUNT protocol

As we have seen, files are allocated and accessed in NFS servers by mounting a file tree on the server computer into the local file tree of the client computer. Then, the files of this tree may be accessed using the normal resources (system calls, programs). However, the NFS protocol is a protocol for file *access*, and thus it does not itself define procedures to activate the mounting process.

The file system mounting procedure should be viewed as a totally separate problem, which is solved using the MOUNT protocol specified in RFC 1094 (Sun Microsystems, 1989).

Background

The only information that an NFS client requires initially for access to a remote file system is the file handle of a directory, for example, a file system root. From this point on, the client may penetrate more deeply into the file system on its own, using the procedure NFSPROC_LOOKUP. The job of the MOUNT protocol is now to provide this file handle in the first place. The name of the file system will be given in the call.

In addition, the MOUNT protocol also contains other procedures, for example, to interrogate the so-called export list of the file systems available via NFS and MOUNT. Another task is to record the mounts between clients and servers, since knowledge of these considerably simplifies network management. Because these relationships are beyond the scope of NFS itself, this is taken care of by *mountd* (the server for the MOUNT protocol), which notes the computer and path names for every mounting procedure. Because of this division between mounting and file access, there is no feedback to the NFS server after the mounting procedure. All operations in the MOUNT protocol involve only the MOUNT server. The NFS client may access the server so long as it is in possession of a valid file handle (here it does not matter if the MOUNT server has altered its tables in the meantime).

Specification of the MOUNT protocol

The procedure DUMP (see Figure 9.10) provides a list of the file systems on the server that are currently mounted on the client computer. The procedure EXPORT provides a list of the exported file systems. UMNT and UMNTALL delete one or all (respectively) of the entries of a client in the corresponding server. We again note that there is no guarantee that the *mountd* information agrees with those NFS client–server relationships that are actually active (this is, in particular, the case if the client computer has crashed). For this reason, a general UMNTALL call to delete all existing entries on all MOUNT servers is usually broadcast when the client computer

```
0.  MNTPROC_NULL () returns ()

1.  MNTPROC_MNT (directory) returns (reply)
        dirpath  dirname;
        fhstatus reply;

2.  MNTPROC_DUMP () returns (mountlist)
        union switch (boolean more_entries) {
            TRUE:
              struct {
                  name      hostname;
                  dirpath   directory;
                  mountlist nextentry;
              }
          FALSE:
              struct {}
        } mountlist;

3.  MNTPROC_UMNT (directory) returns ()
        dirpath directory;

4.  MNTPROC_UMNTALL () returns ()

5.  MNTPROC_EXPORT () returns (exportlist)
        union switch (boolean more_entries) {
            TRUE:
              struct {
                  dirpath      filesys;
                  typedef union switch (boolean more_groups) {
                      TRUE:
                        struct {
                            name   grname;
                            groups nextgroup;
                        }
                      FALSE:
                        struct {}
                  } groups;
                  mountlist nextentry;
              }
          FALSE:
              struct {}
        } exportlist;
```

Figure 9.10   MOUNT protocol.

Table **9.8**   RPC protocol parameters for MOUNT.

Parameter	Value
Program number	100005
Version number	1
Transport protocol	UDP

starts up. You will find more about this in the discussion of the *mount* and *umount* commands in the next chapter. The result produced by the MNT procedure has the following structure:

```
typedef union switch (unsigned status) {
    0:
        fhandle directory;
    default:
        struct {}
} fhstatus;
```

Table 9.8 lists the parameters of the MOUNT protocol.

10

Implementation of NFS

- NFS software packages

- Implementation of NFS under UNIX

- Import of file systems

- Export of file systems

- Diagnosis of RPC and NFS problems

- Lock manager

- NFS-based services

- NFS specialities

After our consideration of the protocols used by NFS in the previous chapter, we now turn our attention to the implementation of NFS on UNIX computers. Initially, we shall consider the embedding of the NFS server and client in more detail. Then follows a tour through NFS-specific and NFS-based programs and commands.

NFS software packages

Reference versions

As we have already seen in earlier chapters, System V and BSD-based systems differ in respect of the functional environment implemented and the options of individual commands. Thus, it is now appropriate to name the version of NFS we have taken as our reference version; as an example of an implementation based on System V Release 3 (SVR3), we have used the NFS version for Interactive Systems 386/ix 2.0 (System V Release 3.2). This implementation originally came from the company Lachman Associates. Most of the NFS products available on the market for SVR3 are based on the Lachman implementation. Since the release of System V Release 4 (SVR4), which contains NFS and TCP/IP as integral components, system manufacturers no longer have to implement and integrate these systems separately. We use a version of System V Release 4.2 from the company Consensys, although we also had the possibility of working with SINIX 5.41 on SNI computers.

On the BSD side, we had access to many different systems, including the DFS under SINIX V 5.2 on various Siemens MX computers, NFS under Ultrix on the DECstation 3100, and 4.2BSD with 3.2NFSSRC extensions on Digital Equipment's VAX; 3.2NFSSRC is the reference implementation of NFS for Sun and as such is the basis for most implementations, on both System V and BSD systems. In addition, Solaris 1.1 (SunOS 4.1.3) is also used in our company.

Naturally, the system variants include other manufacturer-specific restrictions or extensions, which we shall not discuss in detail here since we are only concerned with the basic functions, which in all probability are available on all systems. Readers with a deeper interest are referred to the manufacturers' documentation, in which all specific differences should be recognizable.

At this point, SunOS 4.0 deserves a brief mention. This version of the system introduced many new services, commands and options, which to a large extent also appeared in SVR4. It will be some time before the new functionality, in whatever form, is taken up by other manufacturers. This book has, in part, attempted to describe these new functions; however, it has not provided a detailed treatment (at least at the current time) of those that are regarded to be too manufacturer-specific.

Directory conventions

In addition to differences in the options supported and in the functionality, there are also differences between the available systems as far as the location of commands is concerned. Regrettably, in SVR3 there are no particularly binding conventions as to where NFS commands are stored. As far as the following examples of screen dialogue are concerned, care has been taken to keep them as general as possible (and to mark deviations as such). If particular commands cannot be called directly on your system, the directories */etc* and */usr/etc* are probably the best starting points for a search. YP administrative commands are found in either */etc/yp* or */usr/etc/yp* or in */var/yp* in more recent SunOS versions.

The directory */usr/etc* is used by Sun as an additional place in which to store system programs and data that are not required at the time the system is started; many of the NFS servers and commands are also located there.

However, as networking increases, the usual conventions for system-specific directories on UNIX systems are increasingly obsolete. While one objective is that data and programs used by several systems in the network should only be stored once, there will always exist data that is only valid for a specific computer in the network (for example, a configuration file */etc/passwd*). Since not all computers in the network use the same processor, the distinction between the different architectures must be made.

As far as the user of the system is concerned, this new distribution of files does not represent a visible alteration, since PATH variables and symbolic links render practically all these changes transparent. However, the network administrator must re-adapt himself in no uncertain way.

Implementation of NFS under UNIX

Embedding of the NFS client

One advantage of the implementation of NFS under UNIX is the transparent interface. A program does not notice whether it is accessing a file locally or over NFS. To achieve this, the corresponding system calls must be executed at a level external to the program in the UNIX operating system kernel. In other operating systems, this mechanism is known as a *redirector*, since it redirects normal system calls.

Access to files in operating systems consists of at least two complementary functions; firstly, the management of the file access (access

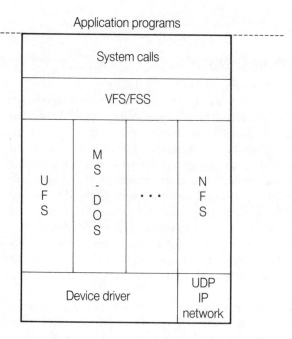

Figure 10.1   Embedding of NFS and other file systems in the UNIX kernel.

control) on opening and closing files and, secondly, the actual allocation of storage medium data. In classical UNIX operating system kernels, the modules for the file access were amalgamated with the access control itself and there was no separation at all between the management and the 'insides' of the file system. For NFS operation, for example, UNIX had to be extended by functions to generate RPC requests to an NFS server.

In order to integrate the NFS client in an architecturally clean way, the Sun developers have provided a new internal system interface, the *Virtual File System* (VFS). VFS makes it possible to operate several different file systems in a system at the same time. The system I/O calls are in a higher layer, which is independent of the file system. Access is managed in this layer before a lower (file-system dependent) layer is called.

Figure 10.1 shows the structure of the layers in the NFS UNIX kernel. Several file systems, such as UFS ('UNIX file system'), MS-DOS and NFS, may coexist below VFS.

VFS is used almost exclusively in BSD-based systems. In System V Version 3, AT&T implemented a similar concept, the File System Switch (FSS), for which an NFS variant is available. For future UNIX versions, the VFS interface has prevailed; it is of a higher level of abstraction and therefore more independent of the underlying file system. (In SVR4, FSS has already been replaced by VFS.)

Functionally, VFS is object-oriented; the operating system kernel contains file system objects (files), directories, and so on, represented in the form of *vnode* objects (vnode stands for virtual node). Every vnode is accompanied by references to the possible operations associated with this object. Thus, system calls such as *read* contain an additional step, namely, the evaluation of the vnode information and a jump to the corresponding file-system-specific routine. This routine carries out the steps needed to fetch the data, such as calling the disk controller or sending an RPC request, before finally handing the data over to the user program.

Asynchronous I/O in the NFS client

In order to improve the data throughput, the data blocks in UNIX are held in a buffer, also termed a *buffer cache*. This mechanism is also used for data written or read via NFS. Usually, the physical I/O operation occurs asynchronously from the system call of a user program; the UNIX I/O system reads the next block of a file in advance (the data block should be in the buffer already) when requested by the user program. Conversely, data blocks are initially written to the buffer and later transferred to the disk when space is required in the buffer or on the next regular 'flush' of the buffer. These procedures are known as *read ahead* and *delayed write*.

In order to execute an RPC, such as those issued by NFS requests, a process context is required. This is made available in the UNIX operating system via the *biod* daemon, which supports read ahead and delayed write. The *biod* daemon improves the data throughput on the connection between the NFS client and server, but is not absolutely necessary for operation. Without this daemon, there would be no asynchronous reads or writes over NFS. Usually, several *biod* processes (normally four) are active at the same time, thus enabling several operations to be executed in parallel. The program code executed by the *biod* process is stored in the operating system kernel and is activated by the system call *async_daemon ()*. Starting up too many *biod* daemons may in certain circumstances have undesirable consequences, namely, when through simultaneous delayed write of all the daemons the capacity of the UDP output buffer is exhausted. In this case, system performance is actually degraded.

Delayed write to a specific file is inhibited if a file is or has been locked by the lock manager: the blocks of this file are then sent immediately to the server and a so-called *write through* occurs.

Embedding of the NFS server

As a process, the NFS server is logically located above the VFS interface and issues calls to the underlying file systems. In principle, it could be implemented under UNIX as an arbitrary RPC server like a normal user process. However, in order to obtain the greatest possible throughput, the NFS server in UNIX must be installed within the operating system kernel. In particular, this avoids the copying of data blocks between system and user address space.

In fact, the server process *nfsd* is started like a normal UNIX program when the NFS system is brought up. Immediately after opening the UDP port and registering with the port mapper, it executes the system call *nfs_svc()*, from which it only exits in the case of (involuntary) abnormal termination. As for *biod*, the server code itself is found in the operating system kernel. Although the NFS server registers itself with the port mapper, it always uses UDP port number 2049. Nowadays, NFS clients do not request the port number, but send RPC requests automatically to port 2049. This peculiarity is supported for compatibility with earlier NFS versions, but it should be removed in the next version of the NFS protocol.

Like every other UNIX process, the NFS server must also remain inactive during a hard-disk read procedure and wait until the execution has been completed. During this time, other NFS requests for other clients may be processed. For this reason, several NFS servers (typically four) are simultaneously started up in order to serve a number of clients. The NFS servers take on requests from a common queue and process them sequentially.

Supported access types

The NFS server only supports access to normal files and directories; while special files and named pipes (FIFOs) may be opened, they are interpreted and processed as resources on the local computer.

Named pipes and special files have one thing in common: the access method used for data exchange with them is not implemented in the file system itself; instead, the catalogue entry associated with the name entry in the file system only contains pointers to other modules such as device drivers in the UNIX operating system. For special files the *major device number* is an index in the device driver table. Equally, the data exchange between two computers over a named pipe does not involve storing and reading the data block in the 'named pipe' file on the disk, but uses the operating system data buffer. The NFS client never uses a file handle for these file types for a read or write operation, but simply evaluates the information contained in the file attributes. Thus, the floppy disk drive connected to the client computer is accessed by, for example, opening the file */dev/floppy* on the server. Two processes on different NFS client computers that open the same named pipe on an NFS server cannot communicate with one another over the pipe.

These restrictions are understandable when we consider the additional complications that would be associated with the operation of devices within the NFS protocol and the NFS implementation. A good example of this would be the need to support the system call *ioctl*, which almost exclusively involves data structures known only to the application program and the device driver, which thus cannot be converted by XDR. For communication between two processes, it is sensible to use a TCP connection rather than a named pipe. This is much more efficient than exchanging messages over an NFS server, which would also have to make provisions for flow control, and so on.

For diskless workstations, the behaviour mode implemented in NFS is, however, sensible since the system must always be able to access its (own) peripherals.

Restrictions on the operation of NFS

While NFS was designed to permit operation equivalent to the local file system, there are problems in marginal areas with the reproduction of local semantics, which are difficult to resolve and must be accepted as quirks of NFS. Some of the problems may be avoided (or at least alleviated) by additional intelligence in the client. These are in all cases a result of the stateless nature of the NFS protocol and the fact that the NFS server cannot and should not determine which files the clients have opened.

The most famous example of this behaviour is the deletion of an open file. Applied in the local file system, this leads to the file physically remaining for as long as it is kept open by a process. These semantics cannot be expected in the stateless NFS server. A partial simulation of the local semantics is obtained in that the client renames the file to be deleted in the server; thus, the original file name disappears and the file itself is finally removed on closure. Renamed files have names in the format *.nfsxxxxxxxx*, where *xxxxxxxx* is a number chosen by the client. The files are not usually visible since they begin with a full stop. If the client crashes before the file is closed and before it can remove it, the file is preserved. Thus, on systems that are used as servers, a procedure should be regularly run (for example, on system start-up) to remove these remnant files. This emulation only functions when the opening and deleting processes are on the same client, otherwise the file in question is actually deleted.

This brings us to another problem: under certain circumstances a file may be deleted by another station between two accesses by a client. The server recognizes such situations and rejects further accesses with error code NFSERR_STALE; the user program receives the error code ESTALE. Invalid file handles may be recognized using an additional data field in the file handle and in the inode: in addition to the reference to a file system in the server and to the inode number of the required file therein, the system also stores the generation number of the inode. This generation number is increased by the system when the inode is released (the file is deleted) and on each access the server compares the generation number in the file handle with that in the inode.

Other restrictions are:

- The removal or absence of read or write authorization (with *chmod*) on an open file leads to an error in the case of access other than by the owner of the file (who over NFS always has read and write access to this file in the server). Since program files may also be accessed over NFS, the system reads instructions and data over NFS using *paging*. For this, the program file must be readable or else it must be executed by the owner himself, otherwise access is rejected by the NFS server. Note in addition that this refers to all files that are already open, where the access authorization is altered during the course of access. As in local file systems, the NFS client verifies the access rights before allowing a file to be opened or a program to be executed. The operation is rejected by the client if there is no authorization, although the server permits it in accordance with the above rules.

- Although the System V file append mode is supported by NFS, appending is not guaranteed when several processes on different clients write simultaneously to a file. This is due to the nature of the implementation, whereby the end of file stored in the file attributes is used as write position. The attributes stored in the client in a cache are usually only updated every three seconds; thus, in the case of multiple access to a file by several clients, they may not necessarily be up to date. In this case, it would be sensible for a programmer to lock the file for the duration of the append operation to prevent overwriting. In more recent versions of NFS, this time interval can be individually set.

- Write operations with length exceeding the maximum RPC output length set in the client are not atomic and cannot be mixed with other simultaneous write operations on the same file.

- As for files, directory attributes are also buffered in the client. Since they are only updated every 30 seconds, alterations to the directory may, in certain circumstances, only be visible to another client after this time interval. More recently, this time interval can also be set individually.

- Problems may arise with some UNIX programs in the case of unsynchronized clocks on the client and server computers, since the time on the server is used for file time stamps. (More about this in the section on the time daemon.)

Simultaneous access by several clients to one server and to the same file may result in data inconsistencies. This is also the case for local file operation; however, here the time windows for inconsistencies are smaller. The current version of NFS avoids additional integrity-related costs to the benefit of the performance in the normal mode of operation and leaves it to the application programs to guard themselves against data inconsistencies by appropriate means, such as file locking.

NFS and security aspects

Although this chapter and the previous one might give the contrary impression, a UNIX system with NFS is in practice no less secure than a UNIX system without NFS. Basically, we must realize that every time a system is connected to a network the possibility of unauthorized penetration of the system is increased many times over. In NFS implementations to date, sufficient precautions have been taken to make accidental compromise of data difficult. Probably only very few systems could withstand a determined attack, since there are increasingly many loopholes in the day-to-day operation. Version 4.0 of NFS improves security further in that access authorizations are exchanged between client and server in encoded form (AUTH_DES).

One major security loophole in UNIX is the almost unrestricted privilege of the superuser (user ID 0). All files, without restriction, may be accessed under the login name *root*. Such behaviour is undesirable in networked operation, on security grounds; thus, the user ID 0 in the server is changed to the user ID -2. Consequently, files stored in the server under the user *root* have user ID -2 as owner. In this way, user ID -2 is subjected to the same access restrictions as a normal user. In some systems, user ID -2 is entered in */etc/passwd* as *nobody*. Since in the System V data structures the user ID is stored as an unsigned value, -2 is $65\,534$ (which can sometimes be confusing).

Version 4.0 of SunOS allows a general conversion of user ID 0 to any other user ID.

This conversion is bypassed by the system call *exportfs*, which can be used to make file systems on most NFS server implementations accessible to the superuser. This is a necessity for diskless workstations, which must be able to execute their own system administration with their own files on a server. The call to *exportfs* associates a normal user ID for the superuser access with the file system; all accesses to user ID 0 are then mapped to the ID set apart for this file system. Thus, programs started under the name *root* may access the server, the ID used being individually selectable. The network administrator allocates an individual partition to each diskless workstation with a corresponding 'pseudo superuser ID'.

To prevent unauthorized access to data via RPC requests with falsified user IDs, the NFS server offers the possibility of permitting only RPC requests from privileged port numbers (less than 1024). In this case, higher port numbers are rejected with messages such as `NFS request from unprivileged port, source IP address = 192.9.150.240`. Regrettably, some NFS client implementations use unprivileged port numbers as standard, so that when monitoring is switched on, even mounting by the client is deemed to be unauthorized access. Monitoring may be turned on or off by the network administrator, by setting the variable *nfs_portmon* in the operating system kernel to 1 or 0 (for example, using a debugger). A similar mechanism exists in the mount daemon, in which case however external access by the debugger is usually impossible since it is supplied without a symbol table. Furthermore, the mount daemon may be permitted to compare the Internet address and the name of the client with the local information in */etc/hosts* and to reject requests when there is a discrepancy. All three monitors are normally switched off, although there are systems with other settings.

The performance of NFS

Since the user under NFS sees no difference between mounted file systems and a local hard disk, he expects the same performance in both cases, which is sometimes impossible. The first limitation is given by the server's hard disk, since, of course, NFS cannot transport the data faster than it can be supplied by this peripheral device. The access speed is also affected by factors such as the performance of the TCP/IP implementation and the Ethernet controller used, which must have sufficient buffer capacity to accept read and write requests of maximum length (8800 bytes).

One should always realize that when NFS is used, system and hard disk are linked not by a highly integrated hard-disk controller specifically designed for this purpose, but by a coaxial cable, two Ethernet controllers and thousands of computer instructions. Satisfactory results can only be expected when these components are optimized to the same extent.

Import of file systems

Method of working

In order to mount a file system on the server, in addition to the NFS server process, the *mount daemon*, which executes the MOUNT protocol, must also be active. Figure 10.2 gives a schematic representation of the individual steps in the execution of a mount procedure.

The program *mountd*, together with *nfsd*, is started when the system is brought up. In the mount procedure, the *mount* command on the client computer makes contact with the mount daemon in order to obtain the first file handle for the root directory of the file system to be mounted. The mount daemon hands the path name of the desired file system, found by the client using the system call *getfh()*, over to the operating system. The latter generates and returns a file handle which is forwarded by the mount

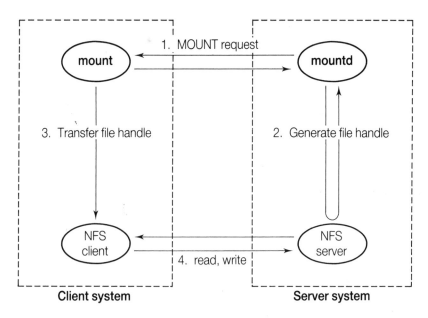

Figure 10.2   Execution of a mount procedure.

daemon to the *mount* command. This file handle is handed over to the NFS client in the operating system together with other entries, including the address of the server computer and other operational parameters, by the system call *mount ()*. The NFS client can now generate NFS protocol requests to the server.

The commands *mount* and *umount*

As previously mentioned, NFS file systems are also mounted with the *mount* command. Normally, the *mount* command may be summarized as follows:

/etc/mount [−r] *specialfile directory*

In UNIX versions with VFS or FSS, the *mount* command is modified to include entries for the type of file system in question, so that other objects may be specified in place of special files. When NFS is used, a computer and path name must be given at this point. The new synopsis, initially for SVR3, in which the type of the file system to be mounted is given with the −*f* option, is:

```
/etc/mount −f NFS[,options] hostname:pathname directory
```

BSD versions automatically recognize that a construct of the form 'hostname:pathname' has been given in place of a special file and assume the file system type NFS. Thus, the − t option is optional:

```
/etc/mount −t nfs −o options hostname:pathname
                                        directory
```

The syntax of the SVR4 command is a combination of the two:

```
/etc/mount −F nfs −o options hostname:pathname
                                        directory
```

In addition to the server and path name, options entries that affect the way in which the client operates with this particular file system are available in both versions. Table 10.1 shows the options that exist on both system variants.

On BSD systems, the option *retry* may be used to determine the number of attempts to be made to communicate with the *mountd* computer before abortion. There is also a −*bg* option whereby, after a first unsuccessful attempt, the command automatically moves to the background and executes subsequent attempts from there. This option is important at system start-up, when the subsequent running of the system should not hang in wait for the mounting of inactive server file systems. The default setting of the *mount* command is such that only one attempt is made, but with a retransmission time of 20 seconds. In addition to *retry* and −*bg*, there are a number of other system-specific options: for example, to influence the NFS file attribute cache, to switch on secure RPC, and so on.

In both types of system, the command:

```
/etc/umount directory
```

may be used to unmount a file system. Here too, BSD systems have additional options for selective unmounting of file systems on specific servers, and so on. The − *a* option is most important: it permits the *umount* command, via broadcast to all mount daemons, to delete all entries for the given client. This function is usually executed as a precaution on system start-up, to remove any entries remaining after a system failure.

Figure 10.3 shows the execution of a mount and unmount procedure as would be executed manually on a BSD system. The network administrator may use the command *showmount* (which we shall go into later) to determine which file systems on the server are accessible.

Table **10.1**   Options for the *mount* command.

Option	Effect
soft	Aborts the NFS operation currently active when the server does not answer after the repetition counter has run out. The program involved receives an error message. Usually, the RPC request is repeated until the server replies (a so-called *hard* mount).
ro	Read-only mount, which should be used if the server file system is write protected.
rsize = *n*	Sets the maximum transfer size for read operations to *n* bytes. This prevents the client from requesting too large packets from the server, which, for example, cannot be processed in the UDP implementation or by the Ethernet controller.
wsize = *n*	Sets the maximum transfer size for write operations to *n* bytes. Both transfer sizes should be integers divisible by 1024 and smaller than 8 kbytes.
timeO = *n*	Sets the timer for the retransmission of RPC requests in units of 1/10 second. Slow servers may be unnecessarily loaded by a hurried (redundant) retransmission of a request (default is 7/10 second) from the client. When abnormally high retransmission rates occur (see *nfsstat*), checks should be made to see if increasing the waiting time by using this option produces an improvement.
retrans = *n*	Sets the number of retransmissions of an RPC request in *soft mount* until the operation is terminated.
intr	Programs waiting for an NFS operation to terminate may be interrupted.
port = *n*	Entry of the port number of the NFS server, if this is not 2049. NFS servers running in parallel with the normal NFS servers on a system (for example, the automounter, which we shall discuss later) must use a different UDP port number.

Automatic operation on system start-up and shutdown

There are large differences between System V and BSD systems, particularly in respect of the way in which the system is started up and shut down. For automatic mounting on system start-up of all file systems subsequently required, entries must be made in various files. This is mainly done by hand, although on some systems it is a graphical or menu-driven process (for example, on System V Release 4.2). We shall only look at this property briefly, without going too far into the system-specific details. In this regard, we note yet again that the greatest differences between UNIX versions

```
$ hostname
train2
$ /etc/showmount -e train1
export list for train1:
/usr              train2
$ /etc/mount -t NFS train1:/usr /train1
$ /etc/mount
/dev/sd0a on / type 4.2 (rw)
/dev/sd0g on /usr type 4.2 (rw)
/dev/sd0h on /home type 4.2 (rw)
/dev/sd1a on /home2 type 4.2 (rw)
train1:/usr on /train1 type nfs (rw)
/dev/sr0 on /cdrom type 4.2 (ro,noauto)
$ /etc/showmount -a train1
train2:/usr
$ /etc/umount /train1
```

Figure 10.3   Mount dialogue (BSD system).

from different manufacturers lie in the system management area; thus, the functions described here may be implemented differently, or not at all, on some systems.

In both BSD and SVR3 systems, the names of the files to be mounted on system start-up are entered in the file */etc/fstab*, and in SVR4 in the file */etc/vfstab*, although the syntax used is not quite identical in the two cases. In a BSD or SVR4 system, the file system mounted in Figure 10.3 would be declared as:

```
train1:/usr /train1 nfs rw,nosuid 0 0
```

The *nfs* entry specifies the file system type; *rw* says that the system should be readable and writable. This may be followed by several *mount* command options separated by commas. The last two values refer to the file system management: they should both always be 0 for NFS.

In SVR3, the entry has the following syntax:

```
train1:/usr /train1 NFS,soft
```

Clearly, the file system type may again be followed by *mount* command options. Entries in */etc/fstab* are recommended since they make the required file systems available automatically on system start-up. As a prerequisite, the server computers chosen should be active. Here, the *−bg* option on BSD systems is helpful, since system start-up is not delayed by repetitions and the servers are automatically mounted after activation. Without this option, if the process breaks down within the predetermined time interval, the mounting must be carried out manually.

File systems may only be unmounted if none of the files they contain has been opened by a process. The same also holds for NFS. If the server is not active at the time of unmounting and thus the mount daemon is unobtainable, delays may arise. At this point, we mention the *mountall* command on System V and the −*a* option on BSD systems, which both execute an automatic mounting of all the file systems entered in */etc/fstab* (*/etc/vfstab*).

On BSD systems, a *umount* with the −*a* option is usually executed after stopping all user processes.

On System V, the program *fuser* is used to determine whether a file system contains open files. Before file systems are unmounted, programs with open files must be forcibly killed (with the −*K* option).

Export of file systems

Mount daemon

The mount daemon *mountd* presents itself to the port mapper, like any other RPC service, and waits for incoming requests. It has other functions in addition to the issuing of file handles. On the one hand, it has access to the so-called export list, and on the other, it stores the host and path names of all mount processes. In what follows, we shall consider these additional functions of the mount daemon in more detail.

Mount point

When a file system is mounted on a specific directory, that directory becomes a *mount point*. The directory used by a client as a mount point may lie anywhere in the server's local file tree, and may itself be in a file system mounted over NFS.

In the server file system, mounted subfile systems are invisible to the client and must be explicitly mounted on the client computer. This restriction prevents the creation of endless mount loops or inefficient mount chains.

Automatic export of file systems

The file */etc/exports* is very important for network management, since it contains specifications of whether and by whom a file system may be mounted over NFS. The syntax of the entries is as follows:

```
pathname [systemname|networkgroup| options] ...
```

Every given file system path name is associated with a list of the client computers or network groups (see later) authorized to mount that file system. If no entry follows a path name, the file system is accessible to all computers. When a path name is specified in */etc/exports*, it should be noted that old versions of the mount daemon can only export whole directories; thus, the path name given must represent the first (root) directory of a file system. The mount daemon checks this using the inode number. This restriction has been removed for the first time in SunOS Version 4.0 and SVR4.

Within the exported file system, any other directory may be selected as the beginning of a subtree. For example, */usr* is usually an individual physical file system containing the directory */usr/bin*. Entry of */usr/bin* in */etc/exports* would have no effect since */usr* must be first exported as a whole, after which the client may mount */usr/bin*. The reason for this lies in the implementation. Without knowing the root of a file system, the server cannot determine whether a file accessed using a file handle is above or below the exported point; this check is needed in order to reject illegal access to unexported parts of a file system.

Entries in *etc/exports* may contain a number of other options:

- *ro*   The file system can only be mounted for reading.
- *rw = host:host*   The file system may be mounted for writing by the given computers; if no computer names are entered all clients may write to the file system.
- *access = host:host*   The file system can only be mounted by the computers named in the list.
- *anon = uid*   Anonymous or non-authenticated users accessing this file system are mapped onto the given user ID.
- *root = host:host*   The given computer is granted superuser access.

Other options exist on some systems.

Network groups

Computer names are defined in the file */etc/hosts*. Network groups are newly created specially for NFS management and are specified in the file */etc/netgroup*. A *network group* consists of a group name and a list associating computer, user and domain names. Every list element is

```
all development office training
development (mitsouko,,eng) (aramis,,eng) (balahe,,eng)
office (joop,bogi,off)
training (train1,trainer,train) (train2,trainer,train)
```

Figure 10.4   Example of the file */etc/netgroup*.

```
/usr all
/usr/src development train2
/usr1 anteus fidji dior
```

Figure 10.5   Example of the file */etc/exports*.

composed of the following three parts, where an empty field stands for 'undefined':

$$([systemname], [username], [domainname])$$

Network group elements are used for unambiguous definition of objects, for example, user x on computer y in domain z. The definition of domains and their functions is described in detail in Chapter 11.

The entry of the user name is required for the definition of user groups but is initially unimportant to the mount process. We discuss the use of network groups in the */etc/passwd* file in more detail in Chapter 11.

As shown in Figure 10.4, the definition of a network group may also contain references to other network groups. This provides for the generation of recursive structures which are easier to manage.

In the file */etc/exports*, it is very easy to define groups of computers from the same domain. Figure 10.5 shows the listing of the network group defined above. Here, the file system */usr1* is only reserved for selected computers, while the other file systems are accessible by several groups. Naturally, computer and network group names may also be mixed, as can be seen in the second line.

showmount and *rwall*

Figure 10.3 showed an application of the command */etc/showmount*, which communicates with the mount daemon. We may use the $-e$ option of this command to interrogate the contents of a */etc/exports* file. Other

```
$ rwall 'showmount'
Server train2 has to be rebooted,
please logoff immediately.
$
```

Figure 10.6 Use of *rwall*.

options are −*a* for a list of all mount entries and −*d* for a list of all active
mounted file systems. The mount daemon stores this information in the
file */etc/rmtab* and thus preserves it between two system starts. The
showmount command usually talks to the local mount daemon, but it also
understands the entry of a computer name and in this case directs the
enquiry to the appropriate mount daemon. Thus, it is possible to find out
about the lists on other servers.

The computer names provided by *showmount* may, for example, be
used by *rwall*. The network administrator uses this command to send a
message to the terminals of all users of a given host, as in the local *wall*
command. The options of *rwall* allow the entry of host names and network
groups. If, for example, it is decided to take down an NFS server, all client
computers should be informed, as shown in Figure 10.6.

The *showmount* command uses the MOUNT protocol for its mount
daemon enquiries. The *rwall* command and the corresponding *rwalld*
process use their own RPC-based protocol.

Export of directories in System V Release 4

In SVR4, the procedure for managing the exporting of file systems
underwent a fundamental change. The reason for this was to unify the
administration of RFS and NFS, which are both supported in SVR4.
The functions and options were substantially unchanged; however, the
commands and the configuration files are new.

Sharing

In SVR4, the editing of */etc/exports* is replaced by the *share* and
unshare commands, which manipulate the file */etc/dfs/sharetab*, which
is also accessed by the mount daemon. The syntax of both commands is
similar to that of the mount command:

   share −o nfs [−o options] [−d description] pathname

The options are the same as those used when exporting files (for example,

```
$ share −F nfs/usr
$ dfshares −F nfs
RESOURCE     SERVER ACCESS    TRANSPORT
mozart:/usr mozart -          -
$ dfmounts santix
RESOURCE     SERVER PATHNAME CLIENTS
-            santix /home2    mozart
$ unshare /usr
```

Figure 10.7   SVR4 – NFS administrative commands.

soft, *ro*, and so on), and the path name specifies the directory to be exported. The *unshare* command deletes the entries. The *share* command does not generate a permanently exported path; in other words, when the system is restarted, all entries in the *sharetab* disappear again. However, it is possible to make *share* command entries in the file */etc/dfs/dfstab* that are automatically executed when the system is started. The *shareall* command may be used to make all *dfstab* entries operational, while *unshareall* does the opposite and temporarily turns all the existing *sharetab* entries off. Figure 10.7 illustrates the use of the commands described here.

Status information

In SVR4, the *showmount* command is replaced by the commands *dfshares* and *dfmounts*. The *dfshares* command provides the same information as *showmount* with the −*e* option, both locally and for other computers. The *dfmounts* command provides a list of the clients of an NFS server, similar to *showmount* with the option −*a*. Figure 10.7 gives examples of the screen output for both commands.

Export of directories in SunOS 4

exportfs

The command *exportfs* essentially covers the same functions as the *share* and *unshare* commands in SVR4 and avoids the cumbersome and error-prone editing of the */etc/exports* file. Figure 10.8 illustrates some of the functions of *exportfs*.

   In the first example, the directory */usr* is exported, the option *ro* only allowing the client read access. The *exportfs* command without parameters lists all the local directories currently exported. The option −*u* may be used to remove exported directories from the export list. The *exportfs* command can also be used to export all entries in */etc/exports*.

```
# exportfs —o ro/usr
# exportfs
/home
/user —ro
# exportfs —u/home
# exportfs
/usr —ro
#
```

Figure 10.8 Use of *exportfs*.

Diagnosis of RPC and NFS problems

rpcinfo

The port mapper (implemented by the program *portmap*) is one of the most important members of the chain of stations that a request must pass through between the client and the server; connections to the server are impossible without it. The program *rpcinfo* deals not only with the local port mapper, but also directly with the port mappers of other computers. It may be used to display the contents of the port/program number tables and can even activate individual servers for test purposes. Thus, it can provide considerable help in the diagnosis of RPC problems. The call:

```
rpcinfo —p [hostname]
```

provides the user with a list of the RPC programs registered with the port mapper (see Figure 10.9).

The *rpcinfo* used in SVR4 also works in conjunction with the RPC bind protocol and gives a somewhat different output if it is called without the −*p* option (with −*p* it uses the old port mapper protocol) (see Figure 10.10).

If a requested RPC service is not listed here, the corresponding server must be restarted. This may be the case when the port mapper is only started up after this server or when the original registration of the server has been lost owing to a crash of the port mapper. If the port mapper cannot be contacted, an error message is issued, which in certain cases provides further information about the source of the error. Error messages such as rpcinfo: can't contact port mapper: RPC: Remote system error - 125 are usually indications of a fundamental problem. In this case, it should be checked whether any contact at all

```
$ rpcinfo -p
program vers proto port
100004    2    udp   1027   ypserv
100004    2    tcp   1025   ypserv
100004    1    udp   1027   ypserv
100004    1    tcp   1025   ypserv
100017    1    tcp   1032   rexd
100012    1    udp   1082   sprayd
100008    1    udp   1084   walld
100005    1    udp   1086   mountd
100002    1    udp   1088   rusersd
100002    2    udp   1088   rusersd
100001    1    udp   1091   rstatd
100001    2    udp   1091   rstatd
100001    3    udp   1091   rstatd
100003    2    udp   2049   nfs
$
```

Figure 10.9   Output from *rpcinfo*.

with the server computer is possible, for example, using the program *ping*.
rpcinfo may also be used to access specific individual RPC
programs. The call:

```
rpcinfo -u localhost mountd
```

checks the functional integrity of the local mount daemon. Depending on
whether the RPC program in question is offered over UDP or TCP, the −*u*
or −*t* option must be used. To test the server, *rpcinfo* sends a request
to procedure 0 of the corresponding program and waits for an answer. If
everything is in order, the following message appears, as for the previous
example:

```
program 100005 version 1 ready and waiting
```

Otherwise an error message is given with a reference. An *rpcinfo* test call
may be summarized as follows:

```
/etc/rpcinfo -[u|t] systemname program [versionnumber]
```

The RPC program may be specified as both a program number and (as in
our example) a program name. The mapping of symbolic program names to

```
$ rpcinfo -p
program  vers  netid       address              service     owner
100000   3     udp         0.0.0.0.0.111        rpcbind     superuser
100000   2     udp         0.0.0.0.0.1          rpcbind     superuser
100000   3     tcp         0.0.0.0.0.111        rpcbind     superuser
100000   2     tcp         0.0.0.0.0.111        rpcbind     superuser
100000   3     ticotsord   mozart.rpc           rpcbind     superuser
100000   3     ticots      mozart.rpc           rpcbind     superuser
100000   3     ticlts      mozart.rpc           rpcbind     superuser
100008   1     ticlts      \003\000\000\000     walld       superuser
100008   1     ticots      \003\000\000\000     walld       superuser
100008   1     ticotsord   \003\000\000\000     walld       superuser
100002   1     ticlts      \007\000\000\000     rusersd     superuser
100002   1     ticots      \004\000\000\000     rusersd     superuser
100002   1     ticotsord   \004\000\000\000     rusersd     superuser
100002   1     tcp         0.0.0.0.4.4          rusersd     superuser
100012   1     ticlts      \020\000\000\000     sprayd      superuser
100012   1     ticots      \005\000\000\000     sprayd      superuser
100012   1     ticotsord   \005\000\000\000     sprayd      superuser
100003   2     ticlts      mozart.nfsd          nfs         superuser
200012   1     ticlts      mozart.nfsd          -           superuser
100003   2     udp         0.0.0.0.8.1          nfs         superuser
100008   1     tcp         0.0.0.0.4.3          walld       superuser
200012   1     udp         0.0.0.0.8.1          -           superuser
100008   1     udp         0.0.0.0.4.3          walld       superuser
100002   1     udp         0.0.0.0.4.4          rusersd     superuser
100002   2     ticlts      \007\000\000\000     rusersd     superuser
100002   2     ticots      \004\000\000\000     rusersd     superuser
100002   2     ticotsord   \004\000\000\000     rusersd     superuser
100012   1     tcp         0.0.0.0.4.5          sprayd      superuser
100012   1     udp         0.0.0.0.4.6          sprayd      superuser
100002   2     tcp         0.0.0.0.4.4          rusersd     superuser
100021   1     ticlts      \000\000\000         nlockmgr    superuser
100021   1     ticots      \007\000\000\000     nlockmgr    superuser
100021   1     ticotsord   \007\000\000\000     nlockmgr    superuser
100021   1     tcp         0.0.0.0.4.8          nlockmgr    superuser
100021   1     udp         0.0.0.0.4.8          nlockmgr    superuser
100021   3     ticlts      \000\000\000         nlockmgr    superuser
100021   3     ticots      \007\000\000\000     nlockmgr    superuser
100021   3     ticotsord   \007\000\000\000     nlockmgr    superuser
100026   1     udp         0.0.0.0.4.9          bootparam   superuser
```

Figure 10.10   Output from SVR4 *rpcinfo*.

100021	3	tcp	0.0.0.0.4.8	nlockmgr	superuser
100002	3	udp	0.0.0.0.4.4	rusersd	superuser
100021	3	udp	0.0.0.0.4.8	nlockmgr	superuser
100020	1	ticlts	mozart.lockd	llockmgr	superuser
100020	1	ticots	mozart.lockd	llockmgr	superuser
150001	1	udp	0.0.0.0.3.34	pcnfsd	superuser
100020	1	ticotsord	mozart.lockd	llockmgr	superuser
100020	1	tcp	0.0.0.0.4.9	llockmgr	superuser
100020	1	udp	0.0.0.0.4.10	llockmgr	superuser
100021	2	ticlts	\000\000\000	nlockmgr	superuser
100021	2	ticots	\007\000\000\000	nlockmgr	superuser
100021	2	ticotsord	\007\000\000\000	nlockmgr	superuser
100021	2	tcp	0.0.0.0.4.8	nlockmgr	superuser
100021	2	udp	0.0.0.0.4.8	nlockmgr	superuser
100024	1	ticlts	mozart.statd	status	superuser
100024	1	ticots	mozart.statd	status	superuser
100024	1	ticotsord	mozart.statd	status	superuser
100024	1	tcp	0.0.0.0.4.44	status	superuser
100024	1	udp	0.0.0.0.4.67	status	superuser
100005	1	ticlts	\254\000\000\000	mountd	superuser
100005	1	udp	0.0.0.0.4.93	mou td	superuser
100005	1	ticots	\221\000\000\000	mountd	superuser
100005	1	ticotsord	\012\000\000\000	mountd	superuser
100005	1	tcp	0.0.0.0.4.93	mountd	superuser

Figure 10.10   (*cont.*)

program numbers is made in the file */etc/rpc*. This information is shown
on the port mapper listing after the port number. We note moreover that
some RPC programs, such as NFS, already use a version of their protocol
higher than version 1 and in this case the number of the desired version
must be given after the program name.

In the most recent versions of *rpcinfo* in SunOS 4.0 and SVR4,
all RPC servers of a program may be simultaneously tested by broadcast,
using the −*b* option.   Of course, a broadcast only functions for UDP-
based services. In addition, the SVR4 *rpcinfo* supports a number of other
options, such as the explicit entry of a port number and the deletion of
an individual entry together with the extensions of the RPC bind service
including universal address entries and transport protocol types.

One more piece of advice: there may be many reasons why an RPC
program cannot be reached. Debugging should be carried out gradually step
by step, checking all RPC stations on a message route one after the other,
possibly using commands from the TCP/IP area such as *ping*, *netstat*,
and so on.

```
$ nfsstat
Server rpc:
calls         badcalls nullrecv badlen    xdrcall
8637          0        0         0         0

Server nfs:
calls         badcalls
8632          0
null          getattr  setattr  root      lookup
1  0%         25  0%   1  0%    0  0%     8177 94%
readlink      read     wrcache  write     create
0  0%         4  0%    0  0%    1  0%     2  0%
remove        rename   link     symlink   mkdir
1  0%         0  0%    1  0%    0  0%     1  0%
rmdir         readdir  fsstat
1  0%         413  4%  4  0%

Client rpc:
calls         badcalls retrans  badxid    timeout
8631          1        0        0         0
wait          newcred
0             0

Client nfs:
calls         badcalls nclget   nclsleep
8631          0        8631     0
null          getattr  setattr  root      lookup
0  0%         25  0%   1  0%    0  0%     8177 94%
readlink      read     wrcache  write     create
0  0%         4  0%    0  0%    1  0%     2  0%
remove        rename   link     symlink   mkdir
1  0%         0  0%    1  0%    0  0%     1  0%
rmdir         readdir  fsstat
1  0%         413  4%  4  0%
$
```

Figure 10.11   Output from *nfsstat*.

nfsstat

In debugging, statistics about the number and type of RPC requests to the
NFS server, the calls of the NFS client and other NFS-related processes
in the operating system kernel may be extremely helpful. The command
nfsstat exists for this purpose and calling it produces the output shown
in Figure 10.11 as standard. Normally, both client and server statistics

are shown, but the options $-c$ and $-s$ limit the output to statistics for one client or one server. The $-z$ option sets all internal system statistical counters to 0 and may only be used by the network administrator. The options $-r$ and $-n$ are used to show only the RPC or the NFS statistics.

RPC statistics provide very important information for diagnosis of problems. They provide information about possible problems at the transport level. The counter *badcalls* contains the total number of all defective RPC messages; *nullrecv* and *badlen* refer to empty or short RPC messages; *xdrcall* stands for errors in decoding call parameters. The counter *wait* is increased when no UDP communication end points are free to send, and *badxid* counts the number of received messages that were not answers to immediately preceding RPC requests. The *timeout* and *retrans* entries in the client are of particular importance. If errors are indicated here, one of the NFS servers connected to the client is either too slow or it is losing UDP packets. In this case, it is advisable (see *mount* command) to increase the RPC request retransmission waiting time for this server or, in certain circumstances, to decrease the size of read or write operations, to avoid overflow of one's own, or the server's, receive buffer. (There are no problems in experimenting here until the optimal setting is found – there is no need to be afraid of damage.)

nfsping

The *nfsping* command is a small auxiliary command in SVR4.2 used to test the availability of the local daemons needed for the operation of NFS, in other words, *nfsd, biod, statd, rpcbind, lockd, bootparamd, mountd* and *pcnfsd*.

Lock manager

Background

UNIX systems offer the facility to lock file regions for a period of time against read or write accesses. Such locking prevents several programs from making simultaneous alterations or read accesses while the data is inconsistent because of modifications. The available *file* and *record locking* operations are among other things implemented in the System V call *fcntl*.

Since NFS was developed on a BSD-based system where record locking was not defined, file locking was impossible in the earliest versions of NFS (up to 3.2). This function was first introduced when the demand for compatible interfaces for NFS and a complete mapping of the local file system semantics became vociferous. Naturally, file locking in a network is a good deal more complicated than in a local file system and the implementation of such a function is correspondingly harder.

Realization

The most important point is that file locking is handled not by the NFS protocol but as an additional RPC service parallel to it. This corresponds to one of the RPC philosophies that requires a 'particular protocol for a particular task'. Secondly, as already mentioned, NFS is a stateless protocol and there is no way that a function such as file locking may be resident there.

The NFS *locking service* is one of the most complicated services within NFS; it consists of several protocols and server programs. The philosophy behind Sun's implementation in SunOS makes the matter rather more complicated, since the tables to store locks are not implemented in the operating system but in a separate process, the lock daemon, `lockd`. This means that the SunOS operating system must communicate with the lock daemon, even for local locks. For this, it uses an RPC protocol over UDP called the *Kernel Lock Manager* (KLM) protocol. Every lock operation is first notified to the `lockd` process, which then decides whether the lock operation should be sent to a further `lockd` or whether it is a matter of a local operation.

The RPC protocol for communication between remote lock daemons goes under the name of the *Network Lock Manager* (NLM) protocol. Lock daemons may be both NLM clients and servers. There are various versions of NLM: when a computer is to be used as NFS server for PC-NFS and MS-DOS 3.1, compatible locking is required – at least Version 3 is needed.

The form of implementation chosen by Sun, at least for local lock operations as against kernel-based implementations as in System V, implies a clear loss of performance. In NFS implementations for System V, there is also the problem of consistency between the internal and external system lock tables in the lock daemon. Thus, some manufacturers have introduced modifications to the implementation of the locking service or have developed their own RPC protocols for communication between lock daemons and the operating system kernel. Not for these reasons alone the locking service has become a problem child for some manufacturers. The quality of the implementation of the lock daemon and the other associated processes has from the beginning left much to be desired. Even in the latest version of System V there are faults in the NFS-based lock support. Unfortunately, locking is now an essential requirement for commercial applications, so that an acceptable solution must soon be found for this.

Status monitor

One of the most important points in the lock operation is the question of how long the participating computers are active. We shall consider an example to illustrate this. Let us assume that a process on computer A has locked a region in a file in a file system mounted over NFS on computer B. If B now receives a request for the same region from computer C, there are

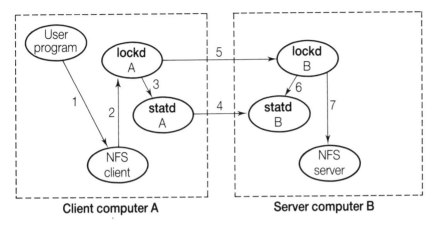

Figure 10.12   Execution of a lock procedure.

two possibilities: either B waits (under certain circumstances for ever) until the end of A's process, or it checks whether A is hanging in the network (crashed). If this is the case, the locking process no longer exists and the region is immediately released to C (via B). The so-called *status monitor* *statd* exists to monitor the activity of computers.

Figure 10.12 shows the execution of a lock operation in the network. Let us examine the function of the status monitor with an example:

(1) A user program on computer A generates a request to the system to lock a region of a file.

(2) The lock daemon on computer A receives a request from the NFS client module in the system to lock a file in computer B.

(3) A's lock daemon registers itself with A's local status monitor via an RPC procedure. The RPC request contains as parameters a call-back procedure in the lock daemon and the host name of the computer to be monitored (B).

(4) A's status monitor turns to B's status monitor, which stores the host name of the requesting computer A as a file name in the directory /etc/sm.

(5) After the monitoring has started, using an RPC request, the lock daemon A transfers the desired lock to the lock daemon on computer B.

(6) Lock daemon B permits the monitoring of computer A.

(7)   Finally, it locks the file.

If computer B with status monitor and lock daemon crashes, after a subsequent restart, status monitor B processes the stored list of host names and informs status monitor A of the restart. The latter informs lock daemon A which reclaims the previous lock in lock daemon B.

As this example shows, the monitoring does not involve the regular exchange of messages but feedback when the crashed status monitor is restarted.

System failure

As in other NFS services, so too for network-wide locking, the first commandment is transparency to local file system semantics. When a server crashes, after restart, the lock service attempts to reproduce the status as it was before the crash, so that the application running on the client should notice nothing of the interruption other than a time delay. Of course, this is only possible and sensible when a server crashes; failure of a client computer would also destroy the context of the application. In this case, the server can and must release the lock of a process that has ceased to exist. In both cases, the partner involved knows nothing of the interruption until the computer that crashed is restarted, and under certain circumstances this may lead to long delays.

After system start-up, before the lock manager passes over to normal operation, it waits for a short time called the *grace period*. During this time interval, client computers have the possibility of reinstalling locks in place before a possible crash. New locks may only be requested after this waiting period. As a standard, the grace period is 45 seconds, but it may be changed on activation of `lockd`.

If it is impossible for the client to reinstall a lock after a server is restarted, the client's lock daemon sends the process in question a newly defined signal for the lock service, SIGLOST. The SIGLOST signal behaves like other UNIX signals: the process may either take notice of it and institute recovery measures or ignore it (normally, the process is then itself terminated). This process may seem somewhat infuriating, but the alternative would be to work with possibly corrupted data.

Restrictions

Set against the locking implemented in System V, locking over the NFS lock service has only a few restrictions:

(1)   The lock daemon does not seek to identify *deadlocks*; thus, two programs may potentially lock each other out. In System V and XENIX, local deadlocks are recognized, but a network-wide

protection of this type would be associated with disproportionate expense.

(2) The reference implementation on BSD-based systems supports only *advisory* locking: only cooperating programs, which check whether locks are present before the access, experience the existence of any locking. Mandatory locking is not a function of the lock service but must be implemented in the operating system in the NFS file system code of the client computer. In this case, the operating system ensures that a locked file region cannot be accidentally accessed.

NFS-based services

Automounter

SunOS 4.x and SVR4 provide another higher-level service that is implemented using NFS, namely, the *automounter* (Callaghan and Lyon, 1989). There is also a public domain implementation of the automounter. This makes it possible to mount file systems on other computers only when required and transparently to the user. This prevents the permanent mounting of a large number of (often unrequired) file systems on workstations, which can lead to problems if the server breaks down. This also leads to a simplification of the management of the file system import configuration.

The automounter is one of the few commercially available examples of the species of 'NFS special servers' that are implemented as user programs and not as part of the operating system kernel. Sadly, in general, the facilities offered by the NFS protocol are still too little understood and used. Other uses for special servers include jukeboxes for optical disks and archiving systems.

Mode of operation

We shall use an example to give a closer insight into the functional description of the automounter. Imagine that on your workstation there is a directory */src* containing several subdirectories for further file trees. In fact, these file trees are not local but are stored on servers in the network. Accessing a file in one of the subdirectories, for example, */src/test/test.c*, leads to the automatic mounting of the file system *test* by NFS and the execution of the operation (for example, reading of *test.c*) as though the file system were always in its place. After some time, when there has been no further access to the file tree, */src/test* is automatically unmounted without further ado.

The automounter makes very clever use of various functions of the UNIX operating system and of NFS. It represents a local NFS server that is treated by the operating system like any other NFS server on a computer. The automounter NFS server manages a virtual file system, which is mounted in a directory */src* using the *mount* command. If a user accesses a file */src/test/test.c* in this directory, the operating system must first search through the path name. Thus, in order to find a directory *test* in */src* an NFS LOOKUP request is sent by the operating system to the automounter NFS server. If the underlying file system is not yet mounted, the automounter creates a mount point in a temporary directory */tmp_mnt* and mounts the actual file system from the remote server there. The trick is that the automounter simulates a symbolic link from the target directory */src/test* to the temporary mount point and returns a file handle for a symbolic link in the result of the *lookup* call. The operating system then follows the symbolic link to the target point */tmp_mnt/test/test.c* using a *readlink* call to the automounter NFS server. If the symbolic link is unused for more than five minutes (standard setting), the automounter attempts to unmount the file system again. This mode of operation of the automounter is known as *indirect mapping*. In *direct mapping*, the automounter NFS server is mounted at various points, from which it provides access to a specific individual file system.

Configuration

The mapping of automount points to NFS server computers and to file systems on them may be carried out in local files or in YP maps. The network administrator may use YP maps to specify a fixed mapping for whole groups of computers (for example, directories for the on-line manual or a source code hierarchy). This flexible configuration means that the possible uses of the automounter are manifold.

The definition of the automounter configuration of a computer begins in the so-called *master map* in which pointers to other *maps* that define certain subareas in greater detail are specified. Here too, the configuration facilities are probably best described using an example. Let us suppose that there is a central NFS server in which the login directories of all users in the network are stored. The directories must now be mounted on the users' workstations; this involves the uniform specification of the local directory */users*. The entries in the master map might now be:

```
/users /etc/users.map−rw,soft
/−     /etc/direct.map soft
```

The *users.map* in the given master map is an indirect map which may contain the entries:

```
andrea    santix:/home2/andrea
gabi      santix:/home2/gabi
santi     santix:/home2/santi
sjr       santix:/home2/sjr
reinhard santix:/home2/reinhard
```

The first field of the map denotes the subdirectory to be mounted within the */users* directory (for example, */users/santi*). This map could also be stored in the NIS, for example, as *users.map* so that it could be accessed by several computers but would only need to be managed once. The automounter recognizes NIS maps in the master map from the fact that the map entry does not begin with a / character. Our *users.map* may be simplified further:

```
* santix/home2:&
```

The * identifies every subdirectory of */users*. The & is used as an abbreviation for the name identified in the first column; for example, user andrea has login directory in */home2/andrea* on the computer santix. Of course, this map only works when all users have their login directory on the same server. The : enables the automounter to recognize shared subdirectories and to select an optimal mount strategy, such that the shared directory need only be mounted once to achieve several mounts.

Finally, we give an example of a direct map, where a server directory has to be mounted at a specific point on request:

```
/docs  -ro     santix:/home2/docs
```

In any map the usual NFS mount options may be entered between the first columns and the server entry; in this case, they overwrite the options defined in the master map.

The automounter also admits a number of other astonishing configuration possibilities, which we shall not discuss further here.

REX

In order to execute programs on other computers, the command *rsh* is usually used. This command creates a new runtime environment on the other computers. Sometimes one only requires to run a program on another computer where the data to be processed is stored locally. When *rsh* is used, this data must (as far as possible) be transferred to the other computer in a pipe or via *rcp*. In some cases, this restriction makes it impractical to use *rsh*. Another problem arises because *rsh* does not export the local environment variables of the calling process to the server computer and so the run- time environment there is not identical to that locally. Often tedious additional typing of parameters is necessary.

The use of NFS brings with it new possibilities for file access. It is no longer necessary to copy files to other computers; instead, processes may be permitted direct access. The data remains in the same computer, and the processing takes place where the necessary resources or a particular program are located. The support needed for such a mode of operation is provided by the *Remote Execution Service* (REX).

on and rexd

The *on* command is the client program of the REX service. It works alongside the *rexd* daemon as server. The syntax for *on* is as follows:

    on [−i] [−n] systemname command [parameter]

The *on* command sends further information with the command to be executed and its parameters to the *rexd* computer. This provides for an identical run-time environment with the following steps:

- Creation of a process with the same user and group IDs.
- Transfer of the environment variables.
- The current directory of the *on* process is mounted in a temporary directory on the server using NFS, if it is not already mounted elsewhere.
- If it is desired to run an interactive program, such as a screen editor, (option −*i*), the current options of the local terminal driver are exported. In this case, as in *telnet* and *rlogin*, a pseudo terminal is also used.

The *on* command and the *rexd* daemon communicate using RPC requests and use TCP as the transport protocol. Figure 10.13 shows the creation of a local file and the output of its contents to the screen using a *cat* initiated on the server computer. In this way, it is possible for application programs that are only present in specific computers in the network to process data throughout the network, without the user copying the data and without starting a session on this computer.

NFS specialities

Time daemon

Some UNIX programs take run-time decisions based on the time entries in a file. For example, the development tool *make* compares the modification

---

```
$ hostname
aramis
$ cat >fred
That is a text line.
^D
$ rsh mitsouko cat fred
cat:   cannot open fred
$ on mitsouko cat fred
That is a text line.
$
```

Figure 10.13   Execution of the *on* command.

times of source texts with those of the programs to be generated from
them; if the source file consists of younger data, a new compilation and
linking process is started. When a new file is generated over NFS access,
the current time of the server, and not that of the client, is entered in
the file attribute in the file system catalogue (inode). Since the system
clocks of the client and the server almost certainly have different settings,
this systematic comparison of client and server time entries may lead to
unexpected behaviour, unless particular steps are taken to synchronize the
two clocks.

    This is not the only reason why the *timed* daemon (which is also
supplied with NFS) has existed since 4.3BSD. The time daemons on all
computers in the network exchange messages among themselves in order to
synchronize the system clocks of the computers to within a few milliseconds.
To do this, they use the system call *adjtime* which slows or accelerates its
own system clock in order to gradually effect the desired time adjustment.
Regrettably, *adjtime* is not implemented in most versions of System V and
so *timed* loses its meaning. The only countermeasure on these computers
is to adjust the system clocks manually as exactly as possible.

pcnfsd

The program *pcnfsd* is an RPC server that was specially developed for
joint working with PC-NFS, the NFS version for MS-DOS computers. Its
tasks are the assignment of access rights to PCs and the allocation of a
spool service. Some of the details of this program are the following. On
MS-DOS computers, user and group IDs, which under NFS must be sent
as a component part of every RPC request, are not present. Thus, before
mounting an NFS file system on their PC, PC-NFS users must execute a
sort of login, during which they supply a login name and a password. These

two values are transferred by an RPC client integrated into PC-NFS to the *pcnfsd* computer, which returns the corresponding user and group IDs. These IDs are then used by all NFS requests.

PC-NFS also allows printer output to be redirected from the PC to the UNIX computer. Here, print requests in the PC are stored as files in a spool area mounted over NFS. To start the printing, a print request is sent to *pcnfsd*, which hands the file over to the UNIX spool system.

On some systems, *pcnfsd* is delivered with NFS, but it is also provided in source code with PC-NFS and must in the latter case be ported to the UNIX computer used as the NFS server.

spray and *sprayd*

The program *spray* and the corresponding server *sprayd*, like the program *ping*, are used to test the functional integrity of a computer; in addition to ICMP, they also use RPC requests. The program *spray* sends a number of consecutive RPC requests to the *sprayd* computer, without waiting for acknowledgements. Normally, a total of 100 000 bytes is transmitted. In addition, the actual number of RPC requests received and the duration of the whole process in the server are queried. The client may use these numbers to determine how many RPC requests were lost, and the number of packets and bytes per second that the server computer is capable of processing.

Using the $-i$ option, the same test procedure may be executed using ICMP echo requests. Here, the throughput is determined in the send and the receive direction. Other *spray* options relate to the number of packets to be sent and their size and length.

fsirand

The program *fsirand* is used to preset the generation numbers in the inodes and the file system ID of an NFS server file system to random numbers. In BSD systems, *fsirand* should be executed on every file system before the system is brought into operation as an NFS server and in every newly installed file system that is to be exported over NFS.

Quotas in the operation of NFS

Quotas are features of BSD systems that allow the network administrator to limit the disk space assigned to individual user IDs. Thus, every file system contains a so-called quota file in its root directory with entries giving the maximum number of file blocks assignable to specific user IDs. Commands are available that permit the user and the network administrator, respectively, to interrogate and modify the contents of the quota file.

Quotas are only defined in the Berkeley fast-file system. Since the NFS server process uses the file system interface in the same way as any other process, it is also subject to the file access restrictions determined by quotas for a specific user ID.

An RPC protocol called *remote quota* (RQUOTA) with program number 100011 and server *rquotad* is used to interrogate the quotas in file systems on NFS server computers. The RPC procedures contained in it supply the same information as a local *quotactl* system call. The RQUOTA service is needed because the local superuser login name does not have access to the quota file over NFS (see *nobody* login name), and furthermore access to the quota information of currently unmounted file systems is impossible.

11

Network Information Service

- Background

- Mode of operation

- Implementation

- Administrative commands

- Future

In what follows, we are concerned with the Network Information Services that are provided by the ONC. Since they represent very extensive and powerful services we have devoted a whole chapter to this topic.

Because NIS was previously known as Yellow Pages, the associated protocol was also known as the *Yellow Pages* protocol (YP) and has not been renamed since. NIS, like the NFS, MOUNT, port mapper and RPC bind protocols, is an RPC service of the application layer. As the name Yellow Pages indicates, YP provides a directory service.

Background

As we mentioned in the section on RPC under the heading of 'Authentication' (Chapter 9) the RPC authentication variant AUTH_UNIX/AUTH_SYS is based on the same numerical user and group IDs used in the UNIX system. User and group IDs are processes that execute the access to objects for the users using the user name assigned during the login procedure. Thus, a prerequisite for the orderly granting of a right to access a file is, for example, that the NFS client and server have identical mappings from the user ID to the user name, since the NFS server relies on the user and group IDs presented by the NFS client (this is the main reason why authentication using the *AUTH_UNIX/AUTH_SYS* procedure is not particularly secure). The user ID is mapped to the user name on UNIX systems via the file */etc/passwd*. Since each UNIX system in the network manages its own */etc/passwd* file, we must reckon with overlaps, resulting in the mapping of a single user ID to two different user names on different systems, if the two separate systems are uncoordinated. If the specification in Table 11.1 were in force and the processor *work* also had access over NFS to *home*, then the user *santi* could access files belonging to the user *christa*. The reverse would also be possible, because the NFS server would be unable to distinguish between RPC requests from the two users.

The YP protocol and the implementation of the NIS service with its servers and clients offers the possibility of managing the database and thus the mappings in a central location in the network (the master server), thereby attempting to rule out overlaps of the user IDs. However, as before,

Table 11.1   Example of overlapping user IDs in different computers.

Computer	User ID	User name
work	santi	123
home	christa	123

programs running on other computers must have access to the information held centrally by NIS. This is catered for by client functions in the form of NIS library routines and some NIS utilities.

In addition, it is possible to use an existing service such as NIS for information other than the distribution of user and group IDs. Fortunately, NIS is flexible and the network administrator may also use it for any other tables.

When properly used, NIS certainly simplifies the NFS management. However, the installation and maintenance of a network-wide NIS system requires a certain amount of discipline. In particular, the linking in to the operation of NFS on existing computers is comparatively demanding. Thus, many networks (principally small ones) do not use NIS at all. However, because the networks always increase in size, the cost of management without using NIS becomes unjustifiable at some stage. At the least, the problem of colliding user IDs must be resolved in some way (under certain circumstances, manually) since, otherwise, reliable operation of NFS cannot be guaranteed.

Mode of operation

NIS is a distributed system: it operates with several servers on different intercommunicating computers in the network. One of the servers is designated master server by the network administrator; the master server possesses the original version of a table. In order to be fail-safe, and possibly to spread the load, other slave servers are started up on other computers. If the contents of the tables are altered, the slave servers are brought up to date with the latest version by the master server.

The information in the servers is organized in *maps*, which are each valid only within an administrative area (or *domain*). Thus, it is possible to distinguish between several domains in the same network, for example, different departments within a company. Because there is no feedback between the DNS and NIS systems, the NIS domains are not necessarily identical with the DNS domains and may actually be organized in a different way.

Every NIS map contains data records consisting of an *index key* and the corresponding *information record* (usually an ASCII character string). To illustrate this, we shall consider an example from the */etc/passwd* file where the index is cleverly constructed from the user name. A query with the key *santi* would produce the data record:

```
santi:xjieQuhd:123:100:Michael Santifaller:/usr/santi:
```

As this example also shows, data records in the *passwd* map and in most other NIS maps are in the same format as the corresponding line of the original file. This means that programs that previously accessed the */etc* files directly remain virtually unchanged. In addition to the */etc/passwd* and */etc/group* files needed to assign access rights in NFS operation, for technical administrative reasons, the following files are available on most NFS systems as NIS maps:

- */etc/passwd*
- */etc/group*
- */etc/hosts*
- */etc/ethers*
- */etc/networks*
- */etc/rpc*
- */etc/services*
- */etc/protocols*
- */etc/netgroup*
- */usr/lib/aliases*

In the case of some of the files, the purposes of which we have already discussed, a central management structure seems to be possible. The information in a file such as */etc/hosts* is equally valid for all computers in the network and NIS guarantees that the latest version is available throughout the network.

Implementation

NIS is used to distribute important information in the network. Because many UNIX programs would not function (properly) without access to this data, access to an NIS server must be guaranteed at all times. This is a well-known problem in distributed data processing, where the increasing relocation of services outside one's own computer onto another computer in the network gives rise to an increasing dependence on the availability of these services. This problem is primarily resolved by *replicating* the services; in other words, in our case, a number of NIS servers are usually activated at the same time. All servers have their own database and can thus answer queries independently of other NIS servers. Replication also has the advantage that it results in a certain distribution of the load across the individual servers, which has a positive effect on the performance pattern of the NIS of the system as a whole, since clients can distribute themselves across the active servers.

The other side of the coin, as far as replication is concerned, is the maintenance of the consistency of the shared database when changes occur, since clients should obtain the same answer to the same question from each of the replicated NIS servers. The complexity of the replication is essentially determined by two factors: firstly, the frequency of changes to the database and, secondly, the requirements regarding the maximum period for which inconsistencies may exist among the replicas.

A very simple replication procedure was chosen for the implementation of NIS (which, in practice, does not necessarily mean that the management of the operational NIS system is trivial). In this procedure, one NIS server is designated master server, one or more servers are designated slave servers, and the master ensures that the slaves have the latest version of the database (in other words, of the maps). Maps are usually distributed immediately after they are changed; for safety, the versions of the maps are checked at regular intervals and, if necessary, a further distribution is triggered. We shall discuss the details of this distribution procedure later in this chapter.

Between the alteration of a map on the master server and its distribution to the slave servers, there is a window of inconsistency in which clients would obtain different results if they were to access different NIS servers at the same time. The size of the window depends on various factors such as the number of slave servers and the size of the map. Thus, the replication procedure used by NIS is referred to as a procedure with *weak consistency*. The opposite to this would be *strong consistency*, which would guarantee that the distributed database would at no time reach an inconsistent state. The requirements on the degree of consistency for a distributed system must be determined when drawing up the specification, since, naturally, high consistency affects the complexity of the design and its implementation. In the case of NIS, where the data in maps is relatively static (in other words, it usually changes at intervals of hours or days), the procedure chosen here is fully satisfactory.

RPC procedures

NIS clients use an RPC protocol to access the NIS server. There are already several versions of the NIS protocol; however, for reasons of backwards compatibility, all versions will be supported by the server from now on (this is possible using the version number contained in the RPC protocol; it also illustrates the point of the version number). The YP protocol contains procedures for searching for NIS servers in the network, interrogating data records using a key, transferring whole maps and interrogating management information.

The NIS service is also associated with the YPBIND protocol, whose function we shall learn about later, together with other RPC services that support the NIS management (for example, transferring maps between master and slave servers), which we shall not describe in detail here. YPBIND supports NIS clients in their search for an NIS server in the network.

Administrative domains

The concept of *domains* is introduced to simplify the management of a large NFS network. Thus, a domain consists of a group of computers that belong together for technical administrative purposes (for example, belonging to the same department, the same network section or the like).

There is no relationship between an NFS domain and an Internet domain, although the same intention, namely the subdivision of the network, underlies both.

The *domain name* may be up to 255 characters long and is entered into the computer via the command *domainname*, usually at system start-up. Entry of a domain name is essential to the functioning of the YP subsystem, since maps are only valid within a domain. Thus, the YP client must be able to determine which domain it is in, in order to access the YP server responsible for this domain.

Configuration

Master and slave servers

After installation of NFS and YP on the computer, the YP subsystem must be configured. There is usually an array of utilities for this, which facilitate the work. On some systems, a menu-driven shell is also available.

Before the YP subsystem is configured (if this has not already been done), a domain name must be chosen and a computer selected as master server. Every map within the domain is assigned to a master server. Usually, all maps of a domain have the same master server, although this is not mandatory. The network administrator could set up individual maps on a specific server (computer). However, whenever such special configurations are required, the network administrator must be able to cope without the utilities that are otherwise present.

The remaining computers may be configured with slave servers. When choosing NIS server computers, one should ensure that the computers chosen have the greatest possible availability. Otherwise, it may happen that, after the failure of all the servers, it is impossible to log in to the system, since even the login process accesses information in the *passwd* map. When NIS servers are running on several computers, it is very unlikely that not a single server is active. If a YP server is configured on every computer in the network, we know that the local YP server at least is always active; however, in the case of large networks, the cost of distributing maps then increases considerably and the advantage achieved is outweighed by the expense. In NFS networks with diskless workstations, the argument at this point is somewhat different: these workstations do not need a local YP server since NFS and YP servers usually run on the same server computer, and if the server computer crashes, operation is in principle no longer possible. Basically, the following rule holds: the more YP servers there are, the greater the protection against failure. In addition, practice teaches us that computers that are not designated as servers are less likely to crash than to be shut down or reconfigured.

Depending on the system, the files and network management commands belonging to the YP subsystem are found in the files */usr/etc/yp* or */etc/yp*. From SunOS 4.0 or System V.4, the files are held in the */var* directory. The installation of the YP subsystem usually involves the use of the shell script *ypinit*, which has two options: $-m$ to install a master server and $-s$ to install a slave server. It automatically sets up the required directories and transforms the local files in */etc* into maps in the case of a master server or fetches the maps from the master in the case of a slave server. The computer names of the slave servers are stored in a separate map called *ypservers*. Figure 11.1 shows the installation of a master server.

ypserv

The NIS server program *ypserv* implements the YP protocol and, like all other services, must register itself with the port mapper. When the system is started, *ypserv* is usually activated with other RPC servers such as the NFS system. In the case of queries, *ypserv* searches for the corresponding maps in the previously mentioned YP directory and in subdirectories of that directory named after domains, for example, */usr/etc/yp/domainname*. This means that the YP server can serve several domains simultaneously. These domain directories contain files with the map data. Because maps in the subdirectories are automatically served by the server, the network administrator can easily install his own maps by storing a map file there (see Figure 11.2).

makedbm

Maps are held in a special database format generated by the command *makedbm*. The dbm library routines used by *makedbm* are contained in *libdbm.a* or *libndbm.a* on most UNIX systems. The routines in the library implement a simple database with a single variable-length key. For fast access to the data, the key is stored in a hash table; unfortunately, it is not possible to pass through the database in order of increasing keys, for example, when one wishes to inspect the overall content. The *makedbm* utility generates such a database map, which basically consists of two

```
# ypinit −m
Installing the yp database will require that you answer a
few questions.  Questions will all be asked at the beginning
of the procedure.

Do you want this procedure to quit
on non-fatal errors?  [y/n:  n] y

At this point, we have to construct a list of the hosts
which will run yp servers.  train1 is in the list of yp
server hosts.  Please continue to add the names for the
other hosts, one per line.
When you are done with the list, type a <ctl D>.
next host to add: train1
next host to add: train2
next host to add: ^D

The current list of yp servers looks like this:
train1
train2


Is this correct?  [y/n:  y] y
There will be no further questions.  The remainder of the
procedure should take 5 to 10 minutes.

Building /etc/yp/ixtrain/ypservers...
/etc/yp/makedbm /tmp/yp3390 /etc/yp/ixtrain/ypservers
Running /etc/yp /Makefile...
updated passwd
updated group
updated services
updated protocols


train1 has been set up as a yp master server without any
errors.  If there are running slave yp servers, run yppush
now for any databases which have been changed.  If there are
no running slaves, run ypinit on those hosts which are
to be slave servers.
```

Figure 11.1   Output from *ypinit*.

```
$ makedbm −u /var/yp/ixos/group.bygid
YP_LAST_MODIFIED 0625443567
YP_MASTER_NAME aramis
100 santix::100:
12 daemon::12:root,daemon
6 mail::6:root
5 uucp::5:uucp
4 adm::4:root,adm,daemon
3 sys::3:root,bin,sys,adm
2 bin::2:root,bin,daemon
1 other::1:
0 root::0:root
$ makedbm −santix/telephone
Christa 321506-10
Michael 321506-11
Reinhard 321506-12
$ ypmatch telephone Christa
Christa 321506-10
$
```

Figure 11.2   Management of an NIS map with *makedbm*.

files. One file, ending in .*pag*, holds the data records; the second data file, which ends in .*dir*, holds the hash codes and access references.

A map usually consists of a number of data records, each with a key with which to search for individual entries. In addition to the data records, each map contains two internal entries. The key *YP_LAST_MODIFIED* may be used to query the generation number, while *YP_MASTER_NAME* queries the name of the master server for the map. Thus, every *makedbm* data input record consists of a line with a key and the associated data, where all characters up to a tab or a space character are interpreted as a key. The special entries for generation number and master server are generated automatically by *makedbm*, although they may be modified at will with command line options. The normal input files such as */etc/passwd* may be brought to the *makedbm* input format using *awk* scripts. The YP directory contains a *makefile* that provides all the information needed to generate the standard maps. It is also used by *ypinit* and when altering maps (see 'Administrative commands' section to follow). Thus, the creation of private maps should be recorded in this makefile, so that they may be managed and distributed in the proper manner. Existing maps may be displayed using the *makedbm* −*u* option (see Figure 11.2).

Since the dbm routines only support one key per data record, it is usual to generate several maps with different *indices* from the data in the same file. For example, for */etc/group*, in addition to a map *group.byname* in which the group names act as keys, a map called *group.bygid* is generated, which contains the group IDs as keys. Figure 11.2 shows the last version. The YP client should use one or other of these maps, depending on whether it is searching for the group name or for a group ID. The same is true of */etc/passwd* and most other maps.

The *makefile* for the YP configuration automatically generates the various maps with all indices; the existence of different indices is usually hidden to the YP user. However, some administrative commands require the explicit entry of the correct version of a map; thus, one should be familiar with the concept. Another example of this follows.

Figure 11.2 also shows the creation of a private map. In this example, the map *telephone* comprising a list of telephone numbers is created using *makedbm*; this becomes valid in this domain after it is stored in the directory *santix* and can then be interrogated immediately using *ypcat* or *ypmatch*. The *makedbm* utility automatically uses the name of the local system as the master for the new map. Of course, the whole of the above procedure must take place in the YP directory; it is also advisable to store the new map in the general YP *makefile*.

Access to maps

Once the NIS service is active, only the maps for */etc/hosts*, */etc/networks*, */etc/ethers*, */etc/services*, */etc/protocols* and */etc/rpc* are accessed. The files themselves must exist, as before, and contain at least all the information needed to start the system (in other words, for the time before NIS became active). In particular, the entries in */etc/hosts* with the addresses of the network interfaces must be present when the system is started.

The definition of network groups is read solely from NIS. Network groups may be addressed via the files */etc/passwd*, */etc/group*, */etc/exports*, */etc/hosts.equiv* and *$HOME/.rhosts*.

Indirect access from programs

Maps replace or supplement a range of files in the system. As soon as NIS is in operation, the files cannot and should not be accessed; only the NIS server should be used. Consequently, both a large number of the UNIX commands and a reasonable number of other programs that access the above files in some way require modification. These include important commands such as *login*, *ps*, *ls* and all TCP/IP commands. The modifications must be made in such a way that, as before, the commands also function without NIS systems and can read the appropriate files when necessary in the case of outages of the NIS subsystem. The mechanisms used for this are described in the section 'Associating files and maps'.

Program interfaces

Access to the files contained in /etc is usually via the routines in the C library such as *getpwuid()*, *getgrnam()*, *gethostbyname()*, *getprotoent()*, and so on. These routines are modified on systems supporting NIS so that they may have recourse to the NIS servers when the NIS subsystem is active. All programs that use these routines need therefore only be relinked for operation with NIS.

The above routines use the YP RPC calls, for which prepared stubs are stored on most systems in the *libyp*. These routines, which are described under *ypclnt* in the manual, contain interfaces for access to NIS maps and to the YPBIND service.

User interfaces

Two commands are available for use in shell scripts or for the display of maps on the screen, namely, *ypcat* and *ypmatch*. These output a map in full or in records. Both commands have the following options:

- $-d$ Name of another administrative domain.
- $-k$ Output of the key value before the data record.
- $-x$ Output of the conversion table for map names, which, for example, converts the entry *passwd* into *passwd.byname*. The name alone is known as a *nickname*.
- $-t$ Suppression of nickname conversion.

Figure 11.3 shows the use of both commands on the screen. First, the map name conversion table (nickname table) is output, followed by the *group* map (actually *group.byname*). The two subsequent examples illustrate the concept with several maps for different keys. The call to *ypmatch* searches for the entry for the group *santix* in a map, where, initially, the nickname for the group map is again recognized. Then the same record is interrogated again, this time using the group ID key; in this case, the map indicated according to this criterion must be used (*group.bygid*). The data record returned is the same in both cases because the same data is contained in both maps.

Associating files and maps

Since the files /etc/group and /etc/passwd are held in YP for all computers in the network, they could actually be deleted from the local file system. But, even in a fail-safe system such as YP, it may happen

```
$ ypcat -x
Use "passwd" for map "passwd.byname"
Use "group" for map "group.byname"
Use "networks" for map "networks.byaddr"
Use "hosts" for map "hosts.byaddr"
Use "protocols" for map "protocols.bynumber"
Use "services" for map "services.byname"
Use "aliases" for map "mail.aliases"
Use "ethers" for map "ethers.byname"
$ ypcat group
daemon::12:root,daemon
other::1:
uucp::5:uucp
root::0:root
mail::6:root
santix::100:
sys::3:root,bin,sys,adm
bin::2:root,bin,daemon
adm::4:root,adm,daemon
$ ypmatch santix group
santix::100:
$ ypmatch 100 group.bygid
santix::100:
$
```

Figure 11.3   Screen dialogue with *ypcat* and *ypmatch*.

that not a single YP server is obtainable. However, since the access to the information in the password file is essential for entry to the system, in such a case no one would be able to log in to the system to eliminate the cause of failure. Moreover, the network administrator must also be able to make computer-specific entries, such as the location of the Login directory for a login name or the closure of individual login names. For this reason, both files are retained and their syntax is extended in such a way that they may be combined with the information in the maps.

A YP entry begins with a '+' symbol at the beginning of a line. An '@' symbol after the '+' means that this refers to a network group. A minus sign evidently has the opposite effect: a user or group entry identified in this way is ignored by the NIS routines. An '@' means that a network group is referred to here. In */etc/passwd* and */etc/group*, the above may be followed by fields separated by a colon, where an entry in a field means that

```
root:2zFsHfeqselC.:0:3:0000-Admin(0000):/:
sysadm::0:0:general system administration:/usr/admin:
powerdown:pxHL.g5d.2wSQ:0:0:power down machine:/usr/admin:
+christa:
+santi:::::/usr/santi:
+@training:NOLOGIN:
-fred:
+:::Guest
```

Figure 11.4 Password file with NIS extensions.

the value entered locally replaces the value in the map.

In the example in Figure 11.4, the entry *christa* is taken, without alteration, from YP, and *santi* is given a new Login directory. The members of the network group *training* can no longer log in to the system since their password entries have been invalidated. All other users are allocated the entry Guest in the GECOS field. User *fred* is not allowed to log in.

The '+@' syntax is used in */etc/hosts.equiv* and *$HOME/.rhosts* as well as in */etc/passwd*. Here, there is also a −@ entry, which may be used to define unambiguous network group combinations.

Administrative commands

Modification of maps

In the course of operation, it will from time to time be necessary to supplement, modify or delete entries in the maps. For this, the alterations must be implemented in the master file on the server computer and a *make* activated in the YP directory. The entries in the makefile generate new map files (using *makedbm*) and distribute them automatically to the slave servers.

yppasswd

Changing the password of a login name means a change in the file */etc/passwd*. In YP operation, the alteration must be undertaken on the master server. The *yppasswd* command replaces the UNIX command *passwd* on NFS systems with YP subsystems: here, every user may change his password directly in the map. On the master server computer, there must be an active *yppasswdd* daemon, which makes the changes in the master file and distributes the updated map to the slave servers.

The behaviour of *yppasswd* is almost identical to that of the normal *passwd* command, although the old and the new passwords are transmitted in a single RPC message. Since the new password is only accepted when the old one is correctly entered, errors are first noticed in the *yppasswdd* server.

ypupdate

The ypupdate service was introduced with SVR4 and SunOS 4.0; it may be used to modify NIS maps of processes outside the master server and provides for limited dynamic alteration of the NIS. The centrepiece of the service is the *ypupdated* daemon which is started on the master server. It accepts calls which are executed by clients using the *ypupdate* library routine and starts a makefile called *updaters* in the YP directory. The command sequences in this file check whether the client is authorized to alter the map and, if appropriate, execute the alteration. They then authorize the distribution of the altered map to the slave servers. Because alteration of maps places high demands on security, it is recommended that only AUTH_DES should be used as the authentication protocol for this service, although AUTH_UNIX/AUTH_SYS is also supported.

Distribution of maps

It is very important to transfer an altered map to all slave servers most promptly, since the YP servers are freely selectable by the YP clients. Map inconsistencies may lead to reactions that appear inexplicable to the user, and it usually takes some time before the cause is discovered. The names of all slave servers are stored in the map *ypservers*. When a new slave server is installed in the network, it must be included in this map, since otherwise it is not included in the distribution of altered maps. Slave servers that are not active at the time of the distribution will not receive the alteration. Thus, it is advisable to fetch the maps periodically from the master server oneself. The network administrator may instigate regular distribution of the current maps from the master server via *cron* and the shell scripts */etc/yp/ypxfr1pdy*, */etc/yp/ypxfr1phr* and */etc/yp/ypxfr2pdy*.

The maps are fetched by the program *ypxfr* on the slave server. The program *yppush* is used by the master server to initiate the sending of maps; the program ensures that all slave servers receive altered maps via *ypxfr* and checks that the transfer was successful.

Map diagnosis

The command *yppoll* supplies the version number of a map together with the administrative domain it supports and the name of the master server.

This information is important, for example, if inconsistencies between two servers are found. Note here that the full map name (for example, *passwd.byname*) should be given and not the nickname.

NIS server binding

ypbind

In the previous sections, we explained why several YP servers should run in the network. When an application program requires information from a map, it must first find out which YP server it should turn to (it should seek an active YP server). This search would be carried out for all programs that access YP each time a program is activated and would put a load on the network and on the other computers in it. Thus, an extra service has been inserted between the YP client and the YP server, the so-called YP binder. The YP binder carries out a one-off search on behalf of the YP client of a computer to find the Internet address of an active server in the network and then stores this address.

The *ypbind* daemon must be active on every computer on which YP is activated, since the YP client can only address requests for the address of a YP server to the local *ypbind*. If *ypbind* has stored the address of a server, it returns it immediately to the YP client; if it does not have such an address it begins to search for a YP server using the YPBIND RPC protocol.

The port mapper's broadcast function is used for this purpose. Figure 11.5 shows a schematic representation of such a search procedure. For every request from a YP client for a valid YP server address, *ypbind* checks that the YP server at the stored Internet address is in fact still active. (The corresponding computer may have been shut down in the meantime.) If the YP server is no longer active, a search is automatically made for another active YP server and the following message is displayed on the console of the client computer:

```
yp:  server not responding for domain yzx; still trying
```

This message is regularly repeated and terminates when a search is finally successful with:

```
yp:  server for domain xyz OK
```

Checking the YP server has the knock-on effect of distributing the load in the YP subsystem. If an overloaded YP server does not answer within the expected time interval, the YP binder instigates a change to another YP server. The additional load is transferred to the first YP server that replies to the broadcast of the YP binder; that is, the YP server that

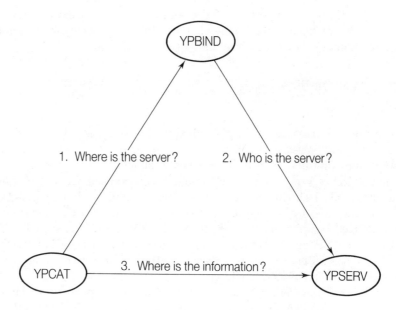

Figure 11.5 Execution of the YPBIND process.

is the least loaded and most efficient computer.

The *ypbind* daemon can support several domains simultaneously and can store a separate server address for each different domain. For most commands, the current domain is used when there is no entry.

Activation of *ypbind* is not initially followed by further actions: the program just waits for requests. It only begins the search for a YP server on receiving the very first request; thus, when a command with YP access is first used there may be a short delay. Annoyingly, it is only then that one notices whether at least one server is active; when no servers are active one may have some time to wait. Normally, this contact is established on the first attempt to log in to the computer, thus creating a very irritating situation. In fact, it is necessary to log in to */etc/passwd* under a local management login name and sort the problem out from there, since the login program is doggedly waiting for the reply from *ypbind* and access remains blocked. In this case, only one thing helps: switching off the computer, starting it up again and immediately entering a local management login name.

ypwhich

The *ypwhich* command communicates directly with *ypbind* and thus permits queries of the Internet address stored by *ypbind*. It outputs the name of the computer whose *ypserv* is used for requests by the YP client. If a local YP server is active, one's own computer name will usually appear, since this *ypserv* is the quickest to answer. Otherwise the name of a computer in the network appears here. By giving a computer name as an argument, it is possible to find out which master server is responsible for a given slave server.

Other options permit queries of the YP master server relating to individual maps or entry of other domains. The *ypwhich* command may be used by all users.

ypset

The setting stored in *ypbind* may be altered from the outside. The command *ypset*, which is only accessible by the network administrator, is used for this.

If a computer name or an Internet address is given when calling *ypset*, *ypbind* is instructed to use this computer as its YP server in the future (see Figure 11.6). However, *ypbind* only checks this address when a client submits a request. In the case of error, another server in the network is then sought.

Other options allow another domain to be given or *ypbind* to be configured on another computer. Note here that if a computer name is given, this name must be converted into the Internet address. However, in certain circumstances this is only possible if the YP server is reachable. Thus, direct entry of the Internet address is the best way in the case of error.

```
$ hostname
train2
$ ypwhich
train2
$ ypwhich train2
train1
$ ypset train1
$ ypwhich
train1
$ ypset train2
$ ypwhich
train2
$
```

Figure 11.6   Use of *ypwhich* and *ypset*.

Future

Although the NIS system has been tried and tested over many years, it is not uncontroversial, and rightly so; its suitability as a general naming service is limited not only by its close dependence on the specifics of UNIX but also by the fact that it is relatively static and changes can only be made by the NIS manager. In this respect, *ypupdated* offers only a minor improvement. In addition, the assignment of access rights by the attached UNIX systems (in the version of NFS described here, using AUTH_UNIX/AUTH_SYS) is insufficient for secure operation of a network. Moreover, the implementation of NIS contains serious security loopholes, which, for understandable reasons, we shall not go into here.

However, better procedures, such as those of secure NFS or the OSF/DCE DFS, which uses the DCE RPC together with the DCE security system based on Kerberos (Miller *et al.*, 1987), are already in use: secure NFS is a component of SVR4; OFS/DCE contains a service called *user registry*, which provides functions similar to the NIS password and group maps and is already integrated with the OSF/DCE security services.

The static nature of NIS has its origins in the prevalent ideas about distributed systems in the early 1980s:

- The networks operated with UNIX systems were relatively small and thus still manageable at an acceptable cost.

- The need to exchange information between a large number of systems or organizations was relatively small; thus, networks were divided into domains, which could essentially be operated and managed independently of each other.

- Services in the network were provided and managed from a central point; thus, there was no need for a dynamic assignment to the services using a directory service or for data protection in the management of the name space.

- Open systems were not used in critical areas of companies; thus, data protection was not an important requirement.

However, with the increasing success of open systems in commercial data processing, the main emphases have changed somewhat in recent years.

NIS+

Driven by the competition to ONC with the release of OSF/DCE, SunSoft decided to undertake a fundamental revision of ONC. The result, ONC+, also contains an improved version of NIS, called NIS+. The improvements in the architecture of NIS+ essentially relate to three areas:

- the structure of the global name space, which is hierarchical;
- the structure of the data records within the maps, which may be more complex than in NIS;
- the support for data protection functions for authentication and authorization.

This extension makes it possible to use NIS+ as a general directory service for distributed environments.

As far as the implementation is concerned, the following improvements have been made:

- partitioning of the information managed within the service across individual servers, which makes the service more scalable;
- replication of information with simultaneously greater consistency, which results in higher availability and reliability;
- a more complete set of administrative functions for managing the infrastructure and the directory database.

Despite all these improvements, NIS+ remains compatible with NIS, although old NIS clients are unable to use some of the new NIS+ functions directly.

Name space

The structure of the NIS+ name space is similar to that of the DNS, which we have already discussed. Every node of the tree-like structure is a domain that can be individually managed. A domain may contain other subdomains. Individual domains are addressed via path names, such as *suns.development.santix*, in the way with which we are familiar from DNS, although, of course, NIS+ and DNS names are in no way related.

Object model

The NIS+ database consists of objects of the following classes:

- Directory. These objects contain pointers to other objects together with information about the systems that manage these domains.
- Table. These objects define a table pattern in the NIS+ database and point to entries.
- Group. These objects contain names of users (principals), which are collected together in groups and can be authenticated.
- Link. These objects point to other objects.

- Entry. These objects contain the data records for a table.

- Private. These objects are used as place holders for object classes with a non-standard definition.

Every object class contains a number of standard attributes such as object identification, name, domain, owner, group, access rights and lifetime. In addition, each class has its own class-specific attributes.

These object classes may be used to construct a complete directory service. The concept of table classes with their pointers is interesting; these may be used to map NIS maps onto the new object-oriented, hierarchically structured model of NIS+. Other directory services such as X.500 and the OSF/DCE cell directory service (CDS) do not include the concept of tables; in these, the children of a node in the tree form a type of table. However, it would also be possible to implement this hierarchical model in NIS+ using the entry objects.

Authorization model

The NIS+ authorization model is similar to that of the UNIX file system. There are four different classes of user for each object (owner, group owner, all and all users that cannot be authenticated), to whom four access rights may be granted (read, modify, create and destroy).

Within table objects an extended model is used, which enables one to protect individual entries and whole columns of a table. The levels of protection have a nested priority: table above entry above column.

Interfaces

Of course, there are a number of interfaces for accessing NIS+ objects. These include library routines and commands. All the YP commands that we have discussed are supported in compatibility mode.

12

Operation of NFS

- Organizational viewpoint

- Performance and throughput

- Diagnosis

- File system organization

This chapter includes fundamental advice for operating and configuring NFS in the network.

Organizational viewpoint

The operation of a network and the networking of computers with NFS is not a trivial matter and requires a certain preparation and regular attention from a trained person, the network administrator, during the operation.

Neglect of management, particularly in the NIS subsystem area, soon leads to disorganization of the files, which requires some effort to sort out. Thus, it is most important for the organization as a whole that there should be a single person or a group of people who are responsible for the management of the whole network and whose duties include the allocation of user IDs.

Performance and throughput

The most important factor as far as the performance of NFS is concerned is the NFS server and the access to it, since, in the nature of things, this is the pivot and central point of each data transfer. If the operating system is not perfectly adapted to the hardware and the server disk controller or Ethernet controller cannot cope with some or all of the load, there arises a chain, whose weakest link becomes the crucial factor, and the achievable data throughput falls to values that may be far less than those expected.

The possible reasons for performance problems include:

- Network bandwidth. An overloaded network or overloaded network elements such as routers are a frequent cause of poor data throughput as a result of repeats and propagation time delays.

- Client network interface. The problems range from faults in the connection to the overflow of receive buffers during read access, because the server delivers the data faster than the network interface can accept it, giving rise to a repetition of the RPC request.

- Server network interface. As in the client, the server input buffer may also overflow, leading to repetitions of RPC requests.

- Server resources, including CPU, main memory, and disk throughput together with system tables, NFS daemons and the like. System statistics may be used to determine whether these resources are sufficient for the required load.

As in the local case, one prerequisite for good NFS performance is an even distribution of the load across the disks connected to the server (or the partitions of these disks).

NFS accelerator

A product known as Prestoserve™ from the company Legato Systems Inc. has been on the market for some time; this product, which consists of a hardware and a software component, gives rise to astonishing performance improvements for NFS servers. Prestoserve is based on the following functional principle. The performance capability of an NFS server is essentially determined by the rate at which it can read and write data blocks from and to its hard disk. Since the server guarantees to the client that the data blocks written to are physically located on the disk on the return from an NFS write request, writing is a particularly critical factor.

Prestoserve gets round this crucial point by copying the data into interim storage (RAM) and simulating physical write operations via a corresponding disk driver; a true transfer of the data only takes place later. The fact that the interim storage has its own battery and is not affected by restarts of the server means that the storage is semi-permanent and provides sufficient data security against power outages or breakdown of the server.

Diagnosis

As a rule, on smaller networks, it is possible to get away with the commands and diagnostic programs supplied with the TCP/IP and NFS software. In larger networks, in which perfect operation also has financial and organizational dimensions, it is advisable to use an Ethernet monitor to monitor the network in respect of transmission quality and loading, since faults or bottlenecks are mostly compensated for by the software and thus may remain unnoticed for long periods. However, in the long term, they may lead to a perceptible deterioration in the overall operation.

For monitoring, we recommend the use of one of the many SNMP management stations now on the market. This may be used for permanent monitoring of all clients and servers attached to the network, and additional information can be called up should faults occur. Suitable software packages (for example, from NetMetrix) are also available for monitoring and analysing NFS and TCP/IP traffic and relationships between the traffic on the attached systems.

File system organization

NFS may be used to establish a variety of client–server combinations. The most important reasons for using NFS are to facilitate systems management, to decrease the cost of additional hardware and to secure consistency of the data, which may be achieved by central storage. In practice, this means that NFS client–server relationships are of three main types:

(1) Centralized organization, in which one or more servers provide disk storage for the entire network, whose stations are either diskless or have only a limited storage capacity. This form of organization has advantages in terms of systems management (for example, central backup of all the data is possible) and sometimes also in terms of cost (the costs of procuring the individual stations fall correspondingly). In addition, it gives the impression of an overall system involving all the computers in the network, in that within such a configuration a user may use any station and will always find the same directory structure.

(2) Dedicated organization, in which NFS servers manage a particular data set, for example, source code or application programs. In this case, the systems have sufficient local disk storage for user data.

(3) Hybrid organization, in which a system represents a part of a file tree of another system, and conversely. This permits access to shared data, although the individual systems actually operate independently of each other.

Clearly, this third procedure has the greatest disadvantages, since it only provides for a true independence under certain conditions; applications and utilities that expect data from a certain directory cease to operate if the corresponding NFS server is inactive. As the number of active NFS relationships of this type increases, so too does the probability of being directly affected by the failure of other systems. For example, if you have mounted a file system on a colleague's workstation and this person likes to switch off his workstation when leaving the office, you may experience all kinds of disturbances. One simple example of an otherwise harmless utility that will cause a problem in a situation of this type is the UNIX command *df*, which, when executed, hangs while it waits for a response from a server that is switched off. Some UNIX systems display the amount of free disk space on mounted servers during the login procedure; if a server is not active, you will not be able to log into the system until the server becomes active again.

This simple example makes it clear that care must be taken when designing an NFS network. It may be sensible to consider using an automounter, as this automatically adjusts the number of active NFS mounts to the required minimum.

In addition to simplifying the systems management and saving costs, any centralization, as in the first two cases, also brings with it a dependence on the availability of the server. The failure of the latter usually affects a large number of client systems, which cannot operate independently. In critical environments, it is advisable to use shadow disks or a disk subsystem in the RAID (Redundant Array of Inexpensive Disks) technology. Such configurations are usually provided for dedicated systems.

13

Programmer interfaces

- Socket interface

- TLI and XTI

- RPC/XDR programming

This chapter describes the interfaces to TCP/IP and RPC/XDR that enable UNIX programmers to develop their own distributed applications.

Socket interface

Background

For the first time in UNIX systems, 4.2BSD introduced a group of programmer interfaces specifically designed for communication between processes, the so-called *socket interface* (named after the first system call of the group). At that time, sockets were revolutionary, since they were constructed as generic communication interfaces: in addition to TCP and UDP, they may also be used for local interprocess communication in the so-called *UNIX domain*. Moreover, they allow access at the IP level.

Initially, sockets served only two different communication domains (transport systems): Internet (TCP/IP) and UNIX. In 4.3BSD, the *Xerox Network System* (XNS) protocols were added. Many applications using the socket interfaces were developed and today they are found in almost all TCP/IP implementations. Important technologies such as the first versions of NFS, the X window system from MIT and DCE RPC from OSF use the socket interface.

While socket interfaces have not been standardized by any institution, they are however a *de facto* industry standard. This is largely because they are easy to understand and are accommodated completely harmoniously in the UNIX environment. A variant of the socket interface known as WinSock was included among the interfaces of the *Windows Open Service Architecture* by Microsoft and other companies and has now become an established standard in the PC world.

System calls

One of the main design criteria for socket interfaces was their seamless integration into existing UNIX system interfaces. We may add that this criterion was fulfilled without giving up any of the flexibility with which very different network architectures are served. The symmetry of the interfaces used in server and client programs is initially striking. Except for limited compulsory differences, the same sequence of system calls is executed on connection set-up by the client and on connection acceptance by the server (see Table 13.1).

One particular advantage of the integration of TCP/IP in UNIX is the fact that TCP, like UNIX pipes, is not record- but stream-oriented. Since the standard system calls *read* and *write* are sufficient for almost all

Table 13.1   Socket interfaces in client and server programs.

Phase	Active		Passive
Open end point		socket	
Designate end point		bind	
Connection set-up (TCP)	connect		listen
			accept
Send data		write, send	
		sendto, sendmsg	
Receive data		read, recv	
		recvfrom, recvmsg	
Close connection (TCP)		shutdown	
Shut down end point		close	
Miscellaneous		getpeername, getsockname	
		getsockopt, setsockopt	
Accept input from		select	
multiple sources			

input and output under TCP, existing programs may be run in a networked environment without problems (see *rsh*, Chapter 5).

UDP-based communication is somewhat different from the predominant data-stream model in UNIX and although it may theoretically be executed using standard system calls, it is advisable to use the interfaces that are specially provided for this. Thus, as a rule, UDP is only used for cases, such as efficient query services, when broadcast functions are required and when there exists a separate application-specific interface (such as RPC) above the UDP socket interface.

Although the BSD system call *select()* listed above is not a special interface for data communications, it is often used in communication-oriented applications. It permits simultaneous waiting for data from several data sources, for example, terminal input and TCP data traffic.

In BSD-based systems, sockets are a component of the standard C library */lib/libc.a*. In most versions of System V, the socket interfaces are not true system calls, but are emulated by library routines and are contained in other libraries such as */usr/lib/libsocket.a* or */usr/lib/libinet.a*, which must be explicitly specified, usually with other libraries, when linking programs. The same is true of the additional library routines described later in the chapter.

Header files and address structures

In order to use sockets, programs must include several header files. As shown in Figure 13.1, one begins with *sys/socket.h* and *netinet/in.h* which

```
#include <sys/types.h>  /* needed by others */
#include <sys/socket.h> /* socket types and flags */
#include <netinet/in.h> /* Internet declarations */

#include <netdb.h>      /* get...by... services */
```

Figure 13.1   Typical header files for a socket program.

contain the most important data structures and parameters for use with sockets and TCP/IP. Since both these files use special type declarations, the file *sys/types.h* must be included beforehand.

Library routines are very often used to read information from the configuration files from */etc* or YP maps. These routines return pointers to structures defined in *netdb.h*.

BSD systems support several different protocol families including TCP/IP, UNIX and XNS. The socket system calls are designed to work with different address structures. The first entry of every address structure is a field that specifies the address type. The example in Figure 13.2 shows the Internet-specific structure *struct_sockaddr_in*. The TCP/IP programmer enters the value of AF_INET in the *sin_family* field for the protocols of the TCP/IP family. The fields *sin_port* and *sin_addr* contain the port number and the Internet address, given in the network format, which defines the byte sequence in binary integers. There are also corresponding routines for conversion from local into network format, which we shall not go into.

```
/*
 * Internet address (a structure for historical reasons)
 */
struct in_addr { u_long s_addr; };

/*
 * Socket address, Internet style.
 */
struct sockaddr_in {
    short   sin_family;
    u_short sin_port;
    struct  in_addr sin_addr;
    char    sin_zero[8];
};
```

Figure 13.2   Declaration of the Internet address.

Table 13.2 Other frequently used system and library calls.

bcopy	bcmp	lbzero	
htonl	htons	ntohl	ntohs
gethostname	sethostname		
gethostent	gethostbyname	gethostbyaddr	
getnetent	getnetbyname	getnetbyaddr	
getservent	getservbyname	getservbyport	
getprotoent	getprotobyname	getprotobynumber	
inet_addr	inet_network	inet_ntoa	
inet_makeaddr	inet_lnaof	inet_netof	
rcmd	rresvport	ruserok	rexec
res_mkquery	res_send	res_init	
dn_comp	dn_expand		

For historical reasons, the address *sin_addr* is itself a structure, although there would be room for it in an *unsigned long*. The complete *sockaddr_in* structure is padded to 16 bytes in the *sin_zero* field.

Other library routines

In addition to the socket interfaces, there are a number of other library routines that support the programmer at the development stage. These routines (see Table 13.2) are used in so many programs that they have practically become a component part of the socket interface. The most important routines include copying, comparison and deletion of data regions (*bcopy*, *bcmp*, *bzero*), which have been replaced in System V by the so-called *memory*. Equally crucial are the routines to convert *short*s and *long*s from network into host format, and vice versa (*ntohs*, *ntohl*, *htons*, *htonl*). The *gethostname* routine is used in many programs to determine the name of one's own computer. The *get* routines read and fetch entries in the configuration files from /etc or YP maps; the *inet_* routines form and convert Internet addresses. The *rcmd* and *rexec* routines are interfaces to the *rshd* and *rexecd* servers. The *res_* and *dn_* routines are interfaces for the DNS resolver.

Programming examples

The following programming examples for sockets and TLI/XTI essentially concern variants of the same task.

The example involves a client and a server, where the function of the server is defined in such a way that it waits for incoming messages at a port number specified previously in the command line, and then returns these messages to the sender. From the start, the client reads entries from the standard input channel until EOF is detected. It sends these individually to a server specified by entering a number on the command line and outputs the response from the latter to the standard output channel.

In the examples, no value is placed on particularly elegant programming style, the main aim being to demonstrate the interface. Of course, the commercial programs you develop will have better comments, be implemented using higher-level library services and have better error handling facilities.

Simple TCP client

The first example, shown in Figures 13.3 and 13.4, involves a simple TCP-based client.

```
/*
 * Simple TCP socket client
 */
#include <stdio.h>
#include <sys/types.h>
#include <sys/socket.h>
#include <netinet/in.h>
#include <netdb.h>

short portno; /* server port number */
char *hostname; /* server host name */

main(argc, argv)
int argc;
char **argv;
{
int sock, i; /* socket descriptor and return value */
char *cp, buffer[512]; /* input buffer, parameter */
struct sockaddr_in addr; /* own (client) address */
struct hostent *hp; /*server address */

/*
 * Check the command line parameter
 */
if (argc < 4) {
  fprintf(stderr, "Usage:  client -p port host\n");
  exit(1);
}
```

Figure 13.3 TCP socket client.

```
/*
 * Retrieval of server port number and host name
 */
while (--argc) {
  cp = *++argv;
  if (*cp == '-' && (cp+1) == 'p') {
    portno = atoi(*++argv);
    argc--;
  } else
    hostname = *argv;
}
/*
 * Open own transport end point
 * AF_INET = TCP/IP protocol
 * SOCK_STREAM = connection-oriented transport
 * 0 = default for SOCK_STREAM and AF_INET (TCP)
 */
if ((sock = socket(AF_INET, SOCK_STREAM, 0)) < 0 ) {
  perror ("socket");
  exit(1);
}
/*
 * Fill in the local transport address,
 * 0 for port number = system chooses free number
 * 0 for IP address = local system
 * entries are given in network byte order
 */
addr.sin_family = AF_INET;
addr.sin_port = htons(0);
addr.sin_addr.s_addr = hton1(0L);
i = sizeof addr;
/*
 * Allocation of the address of the local transport end point
 */
if (bind(sock, &addr, i) < 0) {
  perror("bind");
  exit(1);
}
/*
 * Determine the server IP address from the host name
 */
if (hostname && (hp = gethostbyname(hostname))) {
```

Figure 13.3   (cont.)

```
      /* Copy the server IP address */
      memcpy((char *) &addr.sin_addr, (char *)hp->h_addr,
             (size_t) hp->h_length);
      /* Recovery of the server port number */
      addr.sin_port = htons(portno);
   } else {
      fprintf(stderr, "Unknown host:  % s\n", hostname);
      exit(1);
   }

   /* Establishment of the TCP connection */
   if (connect(sock, &addr, i) < 0) {
      perror("connect");
      exit(1);
   }

   /* Processing loop */
   /* Read standard input channel */
   while ((i = read(0, buffer, sizeof buffer)) != 0) {
      if (i < 0) {
         perror("read stdin");
         exit(1);
      /* Write to the server */
      } else if (write(sock, buffer, i) != i) {
         perror("write sock");
         exit(1);
      /* Read from the server */
      } else if ((i = read(sock, buffer, sizeof buffer))
               ==i) {
         /* Write to the standard output channel */
         if (write(1, buffer, i) < 0) {
            perror("write stdout");
            exit(1);
         }
      } else {
         perror("read sock");
         exit(1);
      }
   }

   /* Close the TCP connection */
   shutdown(sock, 2);

   /* End of program */
   exit(0);
}
```

Figure 13.3   (*cont.*)

```
/*
 * Simple TCP socket server
 */
#include <stdio.h>
#include <sys/types.h>
#include <sys/socket.h>
#include <netinet/in.h>

short portno;

main(argc, argv)
int argc;
char **argv;
{
int sock, sock2, i;
char *cp, buffer[512];
struct sockaddr_in addr;

if (argc > 2) {
  cp = *++argv;
  if (*cp == '-' && *(cp+1) == 'p')
    portno = atoi(*++argv);
} else {
  fprintf(stderr, "Usage:  server -p <portno>\n");
  exit(1);
}

if ((sock = socket(AF_INET, SOCK_STREAM, 0)) < 0) {
  perror("socket");
  exit(1);
}

addr.sin_family = AF_INET;
addr.sin_port = htons(portno);
addr.sin_addr.s_addr = hton1(0L);
i = sizeof addr;

if (bind(sock, &addr, i) < 0) {
  perror("bind");
  exit(1);
}
/*
 * TCP end point is switched into passive mode
 * 5 is the maximum number of simultaneous incoming
 * connection requests
 */
listen(sock, 5);
```

Figure 13.4   TCP socket server.

```
/*
 * Acceptance of a connection:
 * note that a separate file descriptor (sock2) is opened
 * for the new connection
 */
if ((sock2 = accept(sock, &addr, &i)) < 0) {
  perror("accept");
  exit(1);
}
while ((i=read(sock2, buffer, sizeof buffer)) != 0) {
  if (i < 0) {
    perror("read socket");
    exit(1);
  } else if (write(sock2, buffer, i) != i) {
    perror("write socket");
    exit(1);
  }
}
exit(0);
}
```

Figure 13.4   (*cont.*)

TLI and XTI

The Transport Level Interface (TLI) was first supplied with System V
Release 3 and STREAMS. It follows the *ISO transport service definition*
specified in IS 8072-1986 (connection-oriented) and IS 8072/Add.1-1986
(connectionless) very closely. The Extended Transport Interface (XTI)
denotes an improved form developed by X/Open, in which the interfaces to
TLI are scarcely altered. It is likely that XTI will also penetrate the *Portable
Operating Standard System Interface on UNIX* (POSIX) as a standard.

TLI/XTI was conceived as a generic interface to arbitrary transport
protocols and as such can also serve TCP/IP. In ONC/RPC 4.0, the RPC
implementation, which was originally based on the socket interface was
replaced by a TLI-based implementation. Since then, it has been possible
to operate NFS and its auxiliary functions over protocols other than TCP
and UDP at a relatively low cost.

Many of the names of the TLI/XTI interfaces (see Table 13.3) are
very similar to those of the socket interfaces. However, TLI/XTI interfaces
are more expensive to use than the socket interfaces, because they have a
higher level of abstraction.

Table **13.3**   Overview of XTI/TLI library interfaces.

t_accept	t_alloc	t_bind
t_close	t_connect	t_error
t_free	t_getinfo	t_getstate
t_listen	t_look	t_open
t_optmgmt	t_rcv	t_rcvconnect
t_rcvdis	t_rcvrel	t_rcvudata
t_rcvuderr	t_snd	t_snddis
t_sndrel	t_sndudata	t_sync
t_unbind		

TLI has a synchronous and an asynchronous mode of operation. The application may either wait for an event to occur or be informed of an event by a signal (in which case it must find out the reason for the event). Only a synchronous interface is specified for XTI.

In STREAMS-based TLI/XTI implementations, part of the interface operation is handled within the UNIX system kernel in a special STREAMS module called *timod*, which must be pushed onto the current protocol stack before TLI/XTI is used. The interface between the protocol modules and *timod* is officially called the Transport Provider Interface (TPI). Any protocol stacks may be used below this interface.

Another STREAMS module called *tirdwr* is required for *read* and *write* operations over network connections. This module converts the read and write requests into STREAMS protocol elements. Without *tirdwr*, one has to use, for example, the TLI calls *t_snd* and *t_rcv*, which do not access UNIX file descriptors directly and only interwork with a STREAMS interface. In connection with the TLI example shown in Figures 13.5 and 13.6, we note that in the STREAMS-TCP/IP implementation used here, it is assumed that the network addresses are passed on in the same format as in the socket interface, although this is not true for all implementations.

```
/*
 * Simple TCP TLI client
 */
#include <tiuser.h>
#include <fcntl.h>
#include <stdio.h>
#include <sys/types.h>
#include <sys/socket.h>
#include <netinet/in.h>
#include <netdb.h>
```

Figure **13.5**   TCP TLI client.

```
#define ADDRTYPE struct sockaddr_in *
short portno;
char *hostname;

main(argc, argv)
int argc;
char **argv;
{
int fd, i;
char *cp, buffer[512];
struct t_bind *bind;
struct t_call *call;
struct t_info info;
struct hostent *hp;

if (argc < 4) {
  fprintf(stderr, "Usage:  tliclient -p port host\n");
  exit(1);
}

while (--argc) {
  cp = *++argv;
  if (*cp == '-' && *(cp+1) == 'p') {
    portno = atoi(*++argv);
    argc--;
  } else
    hostname = *argv;
}

/* Open the TCP end point */
if ((fd=t_open("/dev/tcp", O_RDWR, &info)) < 0) {
  t_error("t_open");
  exit(1);
}

/* Optional output of TLI information about the transport system
used */
#ifdef VERBOSE
fprintf(stderr,
  "addr %ld, options %ld, tsdu % ld, etsdu %ld, \
    connect %ld, discon %ld, servtype %ld\n",
      info.addr, info.options, info.tsdu, info.etsdu,
        info.connect, info.discon, info.servtype);
#endif

/* Allocation of the end point address, t_alloc allocates storage
space for this */
```

Figure 13.5 (*cont.*)

```
if ((bind = (struct t_bind *)t_alloc(fd, T_BIND, T_ADDR)) == NULL)
{
  t_error("t_alloc bind");
  exit(1);
}
if (t_bind(fd, NULL, bind) < 0) {
  t_error("t_bind");
  exit(1);
}
/* Determination of the server address, reservation of storage
space using t_alloc */
if ((call = (struct t_call *)t_alloc(fd, T_CALL, T_ADDR)) == NULL)
{
  t_error("t_alloc call");
  exit(1);
}
if (hostname && (hp=gethostbyname(hostname))) {
  call->addr.len = info.addr;
  memcpy((char *)&((ADDRTYPE)call->addr.buf)->sin_addr,
         (char *)hp->h_addr, hp->h_length);
    ((ADDRTYPE)call->addr.buf)->sin_port = htons(portno);
    ((ADDRTYPE)call->addr.buf)->sin_family = AF_INET;
} else {
  fprintf(stderr, "Unknown hostname:  %s\n", hostname);
  exit(1);
}
/* Connection establishment */
if (t_connect(fd, call, NULL) < 0) {
  t_error("t_connect");
  exit(1);
}
/* Processing loop */
while ((i = read(0, buffer, sizeof buffer)) != 0) {
  if (i < 0) {
    perror("read stdin");
    exit(1);
  /* Write to the server */
  } else if (t_snd(fd, buffer, i, 0) != i) {
    t_error("t_snd");
    exit(1);
  /* Read from the server */
  } else if ((i = t_rcv(fd, buffer, sizeof buffer, 0)) == i) {
```

Figure 13.5 *(cont.)*

```
        /* Write to the standard output channel */
        if (write(1, buffer, i) < 0) {
          perror("write stdout");
          exit(1);
        }
    } else {
        t_error("t_rcv");
        exit(1);
    }
}
t_snddis(fd, NULL);
exit(0);
}
```

Figure 13.5   (*cont.*)

```
/*
 * Simple TCP TLI server
 */
#include <stdio.h>
#include <fcntl.h>
#include <tiuser.h>
#include <sys/types.h>
#include <sys/socket.h>
#include <netinet/in.h>

#define ADDRTYPE struct sockaddr_in *

short portno;

extern int t_errno;

main(argc, argv)
int argc;
char **argv;
{
int fd, fd2, i, flags;
char *cp, buffer[512];
struct t_bind *bind;
struct t_call *call;
struct t_info info;

if (argc > 2) {
  cp = *++argv;
```

Figure 13.6   TCP TLI server.

```
    if (*cp == '-' && *(cp+1) == 'p')
      portno = atoi(*++argv);
  } else {
    fprintf (stderr, "Usage:  tliserver -p <portno>\n");
    exit(1);
  }
}

if ((fd = t_open("/dev/tcp", O_RDWR, &info)) < 0) {
  t_error("t_open");
  exit(1);
}

if ((bind = (struct t_bind *)t_alloc(fd, T_BIND, T_ADDR)) == NULL)
{
  t_error("t_alloc bind");
  exit(1);
}

bind->qlen = 5; /*Simultaneous connection requests, cf. listen */
bind->addr.len = sizeof (struct sockaddr_in);
((ADDRTYPE)bind->addr.buf)->sin_family = AF_INET;
((ADDRTYPE)bind->addr.buf)->sin_addr.s_addr =0L;
((ADDRTYPE)bind->addr.buf)->sin_port = htons(portno);

if (t_bind(fd, bind, bind) < 0) {
  t_error("t_bind");
  exit(1);
}

if ((call = (struct t_call *)t_alloc(fd, T_CALL, T_ADDR)) == NULL)
{
  t_error("t_alloc call");
  exit(1);
}

t_listen(fd, call);

/* Unlike sockets, the new file descriptor has to be created
separately here */
if ((fd2 = t_open("/dev/tcp", O_RDWR, NULL)) < 0) {
  t_error("t_open");
  exit(1);
}

if (t_bind(fd2, NULL, NULL) < 0) {
  t_error("t_bind2");
  t_close(fd);
  exit(1);
}
```

Figure 13.6   (*cont.*)

```
      if (t_accept(fd, fd2, call) < 0) {
        /* Check for special error case:  abortion by partner */
        if (t_errno == TLOOK && t_look(fd2) == T_DISCONNECT) {
          if (t_rcvdis(fd2, NULL) < 0)
            t_error("t_rcvdis");
        } else
          t_error("t_accept");
        t_close(fd);
        t_close(fd2);
        exit(1);
      }

      while ((i = t_rcv(fd2, buffer, sizeof buffer, &flags)) != 0) {
        if (i < 0) {
          /* Check for special error case:  abortion by partner */
          if (t_errno == TLOOK && t_look(fd2) == T_DISCONNECT) {
            if (t_rcvdis(fd2, NULL) < 0)
              t_error("t_rcvdis");
          } else
            t_error("t_rcv");
          break;
        } else if (t_snd(fd2, buffer, i, 0) != i) {
          t_error("t_snd");
          exit(1);
        }
      }
    }
    t_close(fd);
    t_close(fd2);
    exit(0);
  }
```

Figure 13.6   (*cont.*)

RPC/XDR programming

Libraries

UNIX systems with NFS usually contain a program interface for C to RPC
and XDR. A programmer may use these C subroutines to implement his
own RPC services.

On systems of the BSD line, the RPC/XDR routines are mostly
already contained in the standard C library */lib/libc.a*; thus, the linking
of RPC programs does not require further entries. Under System V,
the RPC/XDR libraries are mostly integrated separately, being found

under names such as */usr/lib/librpc.a*. Since the RPC/XDR routines usually require interfaces to TCP/IP and the socket interface, a network interface library must also be given (for example, */usr/lib/libinet.a* or */usr/lib/libsocket.a*).

XDR routines

Before we consider a sample program, we shall give a brief overview of the routines available in the libraries and their structure.

The routines in the XDR library (see Table 13.4) handle the basic C components and additional internal functions.

Table 13.4 Overview of the XDR library interfaces.

xdr_array	xdr_bool	xdr_bytes
xdr_destroy	xdr_double	xdr_enum
xdr_float	xdr_getpos	xdr_inline
xdr_int	xdr_long	xdr_opaque
xdr_reference	xdr_setpos	xdr_short
xdr_string	xdr_u_int	xdr_u_long
xdr_u_short	xdr_union	xdr_void
xdr_wrapstring	xdrmem_create	xdrrec_create
xdrrec_endofrecord	xdrrec_eof	xdrrec_skiprecord
xdrstdio_create		

RPC routines

The RPC routines listed in Table 13.5 provide the user with an interface consisting of several layers of varying complexity. Thus, they allow the user to have a variably strong impact, but require differing depths of knowledge of the functional description of RPC and XDR.

The topmost layer is designed for the application programmer who only generates RPC programs with limited functionality. Complex data structures and access rights are not handled. This layer includes the routines *rpc_reg()*, *rpc_call()* and *svc_run()*. The UDP transport protocol is used as standard. This layer makes use of the level below, where it is possible to access interface parameters directly, to construct RPC messages (for example, for authentication) and to select the transport protocol used.

This level includes routines with prefix *clnt_* on the client side and prefix *svc_* on the server side. The topmost and middle layers may be combined in a program.

The underlying basic routines are used by all layers. Programmers will scarcely ever have to access this level themselves. The RPC protocol, the port mapper dialogue and several fundamental objects are implemented

Table 13.5 Overview of the RPC library interfaces.

registerrpc	callrpc	svc_run
rpc_broadcast	rpc_call	rpc_reg
clnt_freeres	clnt_geterr	clnt_pcreateerror
clnt_perrno	clnt_perror	clnt_sperrno
clnt_sperror	clnt_raw_create	clnt_tcp_create
clnt_udp_create	clnt_create	clnt_dg_create
clnt_vc_create	clnt_spcreateerror	clnt_destroy
clnt_tli_create	clnt_tp_create	
svc_destroy	svc_freeargs	svc_getargs
svc_getrpccaller	svc_getreqset	svc_reg
svc_sendreply	svc_unreg	svc_create
svc_dg_create	svc_fd_create	svc_raw_create
svc_tli_create	svc_tp_create	svc_vc_create
svcerr_auth	svcerr_decode	svcerr_noproc
svcerr_noprog	svcerr_progvers	svcerr_systemerr
svcerr_weakauth		
rpcb_getmaps	rpcb_getaddr	rpcb_rmtcall
rpcb_set	rpcb_unset	rpcb_gettime
auth_destroy	authnone_create	authsys_create
authsys_create_default	authdes_seccreate	authdes_getucred
xdr_accepted_reply	xdr_authunix_parms	xdr_callhdr
xdr_callmsg	xdr_opaque_auth	xdr_pmap
xdr_pmaplist	xdr_rejected_reply	xdr_replymsg
xprt_register	xprt_unregister	

at this level. The prefix *rpcb_* stands for RPC bind (previously, the same routines with prefix *rpcb* were available for access to the port mapper), *auth_* stands for authentication and routines beginning with *xdr_* implement XDR objects.

Example of an RPC program

Client program

We shall use the next two examples to show how easy it is to develop an RPC program. The first example of an RPC program is called DAYPROG and has version number DAYVERS. It consists of a client and a server program, where the server program is executed as a single RPC procedure DAYPROC, which returns the current date as a result. The client program

```
/* day.h - Header file for the day service */

#define DAYPROG          1000000000
#define DAYVERS          1
#define DAYPROC          1
```

Figure 13.7   Parameters of the day service in the *day.h* file.

outputs this date to the terminal. The program, version and procedure numbers are specified in the file *day.h* (see Figure 13.7) and are included in both the server and the client.

Program numbers may be freely chosen, although Sun's specifications on reserved program number areas should be observed (see RPC protocol (Sun Microsystems, 1988a, 1988b)). The file *day.c* (see Figure 13.8) contains the client program.

```
/* day.c - Client program for the day service */

#include <stdio.h>
#include <rpc/rpc.h>
#include "day.h"

main(argc, argv)
int argc;
char **argv;
{
  int day;
  /* Check whether computer name entered */
  if (argc < 2) {
      fprintf(stderr, "Call:  day computer name\n");
      exit(1);
  }
  /* Execution of the RPC request */
  if (rpc_call(*++argv, DAYPROG, DAYVERS, DAYPROC,
              xdr_void, 0, xdr_int, &day, "udp") !  = 0) {
      fprintf(stderr, "Error in rpc_call\n");
      exit(1);
  }
  /* Output of results and termination */
  printf("Today is day %d of the month\n", day);
  exit(0);
}
```

Figure 13.8   Client program.

The routine *rpc_call ()* carries out all actions required for the internal execution of the RPC request, including opening a communication end point, communication with the port mapper and the server, retransmission in the case of failure and conversion of parameters and results.

Server

Figure 13.9 shows the definition of an RPC user service consisting of the following steps:

- Specification of a program, version and procedure number.
- Specification of the input parameter type, in our case *void*.
- Specification of the return value type, in our case *int*.
- Transfer of the address of the function *day ()* to *rpc_reg ()*.
- Call to *svc_run*.

```
/*
 * dayd.c - Server program for the day service
 */
#include <stdio.h>
#include <rpc/rpc.h>
#include "day.h"

day()
{ long t;
  struct tm *tmp;

  /* Determination of the day number */
  time(&t);
  tmp = localtime(&t);
  return (char *)&tmp->tm_mday;
}

main()
{ /* Registration of the service */
  rpc_reg(DAYPROG, DAYVERS, DAYPROC,
                day, xdr_void, xdr_int, "udp");
  /* Start of the (infinite) server loop */
  svc_run();
}  /* main */
```

Figure 13.9 Server program.

The routine *rpc_reg()* registers the required procedure, both internally and with the port mapper. In *svc_run*, the server then waits for incoming RPC requests and automatically activates the procedure *day()* after converting the procedure parameters into the local format. The server does not return from *svc_run()*. If it is desired to halt this process, a separate procedure must be defined or the server must be stopped with an external signal.

rpcgen

When defining more complicated protocols with many new data types (which is often the case), the lower layers of the RPC/XDR library should be used. The RPC program generator *rpcgen* is a tool to support the programmer; it automatically generates RPC/XDR programs from a definition file.

Figure 13.10 again shows the file *day.x*, which defines the day service. By convention *rpcgen* definition files have the suffix *.x*. From the definition file, the generator generates XDR routines and header files containing the declarations of DAYPROG, DAYVERS and DAYPROC, as required. Parameters and results are defined in the XDR language, which was discussed in Chapter 9.

In addition, a server program skeleton and, from NFS Version 4.0, a client program skeleton may be generated. These program skeletons only require programmers to add code for the actions of the individual RPC procedures and thus save them (at least in part) from having to learn the specifications for RPC or XDR programmer interfaces by heart.

If special functions such as verification of access rights or broadcast are used, some knowledge of the interfaces is required, since the RPC program generator is out of its depth here. It is also very easy to extend the program skeletons produced by the generator in the above respects.

```
/*
 * day.x - Definition of the day service
 */
program DAYPROG {
  version DAYVERS {
    int DAYPROC(void) = 1;
  } = 1;
} = 1000000000;
```

Figure 13.10   Definition of the day service using *rpcgen*.

Summary

Nowadays, only RPC/XDR should be used to create networked applications. The advantages of this approach over classical programming using, for example, socket interfaces, include the following:

- The RPC concept enables easier and more structured design of protocols.
- The data conversion required in a heterogeneous network is automatic and implicit.
- The higher levels of abstraction of the RPC/XDR interfaces make programs created with them more independent of the underlying network protocols and programmer interfaces.

Until System V Release 4, the RPC mechanism described here was still contained in the (separate) NFS package.

Glossary

/etc Directory on UNIX systems in which programs for configuration and management are stored.

ACK Acknowledgement.

administrative domain Group of computers that for technical administrative purposes belong together.

advisory Principle of file region locking, where processes only experience the existence of locked regions by first-hand checking.

alias Pseudonym.

application User program that supplies the user with information and/or processes data.

ARP Address Resolution Protocol.

ARPA Advanced Research Project Agency.

ASN.1/BER Abstract Syntax Notation One/Basic Encoding Rules.

authentication Presentation to the server of some form of proof that the client has authorized access to the service facility or to the information it provides. On UNIX systems, the user and group IDs are used.

awk Programmable UNIX text filter command.

BBN Bolt, Beranek & Newman.

BCD Binary-Coded Decimal.

BER Basic Encoding Rules.

Berkeley Fast File System Optimized and particularly fast file system in BSD systems.

BIND Berkeley Internet Name Domain.

bitmap String of bit values, for example, to represent images.

block Unit of data.

BOOTP Bootstrap protocol.

broadcast A message sent to all the stations in the network.

BSD Berkeley System Distribution.

cache Rapidly accessible buffer area for temporary interim storage of information, sometimes associated with algorithms that use behaviour analysis to predict access to certain areas of data and in certain cases store this data in interim storage beforehand.

CAE Common Application Environment.

CCITT Comité Consultatif International Téléphonique et Télégraphique.

client User or customer of a service. Sometimes this also designates a role pattern in the relationship between two cooperating processes, where the client takes the active, requesting role.

cluster Combination of several objects into an outwardly indivisible homogeneous unit.

CMIP Common Management Information Protocol.

CMIS Common Management Information Service definition.

CMOT Common Management Information Service over TCP.

command Program executable by a user.

communication end point Logically, an addressable object from which and to which data may be sent. Physically, a collection of related table entries and data structures that define an input/output point for network access in the operating system.

congestion window Volume of data that may be in transmission at a given time.

connectathon Meeting of NFS developers to enable their implementations to communicate with one another.

cookie Unknown data object that can only be evaluated by its creator.

CRC Cyclic Redundancy Check.

cron UNIX daemon for the time-controlled automatic execution of command procedures.

CSMA/CD Carrier Sense Multiple Access with Collision Detection.

cut and paste Extract data from one place and transfer it to another.

daemon UNIX jargon for a user program that is usually loaded on system start, runs in the background until system termination and executes jobs.

DARPA Defense Advanced Research Project Agency.

data corruption Alteration of data due to external effects.

datagram A self-contained message.

DCE Distributed Computing Environment.

DEC Digital Equipment Corporation.

DF Don't Fragment.

DIN Deutsches Institut für Normung.

DNS Domain Name Service.

DOD Department of Defense.

driver A program module in the operating system that is responsible for service and control of a peripheral building block.

EGP   Exterior Gateway Protocol.

environment variables   Keyword parameters, in the form of ASCII characters, which are inherited on UNIX systems when processes are divided.

EUNET   European UNIX Network.

expedited   Preferentially forwarded information.

fan-out unit   Interface multiplexer on LAN networks.

file system   This is normally a collection of data and the corresponding administrative information on a storage medium. In a certain context, it also refers to the implementation of methods of access to data and administrative information.

FIN   Final.

flag   Variable with truth value true or false (1 or 0).

fragment   Piece of an IP message.

fragmentation   Process of fragment generation.

front end   Stand-alone computer that executes the data transfer protocols for the host.

FSS   File System Switch.

FTP   File Transfer Protocol.

GECOS   General Electric Computer Operating System.

GECOS field   Field in a data record of the file */etc/passwd* on UNIX systems. In the early days of UNIX, this field was reserved for the GECOS operating system. Today, its meaning is unspecified and it is used to hold various information (for example, the name of the user, and so on).

hash code   A pointer to a data record, which may be determined using a function of the data or its key.

HDLC   High-level Data Link Control.

host   Computer on which applications may be executed.

IAB   Internet Activities Board.

ICMP   Internet Control Message Protocol.

ID   Identification.

identification   Unambiguous designation, mostly numerical.

IEEE   Institute of Electrical and Electronics Engineers.

IEN   Internet Engineering Note.

IMP   Internet Message Processor.

inode (index node)   Catalogue entry for storing file attributes on UNIX file systems.

IP   Internet Protocol.

ISO   International Organization for Standardization.

KLM   Kernel Lock Manager.

LAN   Local Area Network.

layer   Functional unit.

library   Collection of program modules in a file.

link   Reference to the same physical file by several file names.

LLC   Logical Link Control.

lock   Locked data area.

login   Terminal session.

login   UNIX command to open a terminal session.

Login directory   Directory that becomes the current directory on opening a terminal session.

loopback   Reflect back.

ls   UNIX command to list file names.

LU6.2   Logical Unit 6.2.

MAC   Media Access Control.

mailbox   Object in which electronic mail may be stored.

make   UNIX development tool for configuration management in software projects.

makefile   Command file for the UNIX development tool *make*.

mandatory locking   Instruction to the operating system to check for the existence of a locked area on file access by processes.

master   Privileged instance of an object (for example, a server) that is capable of taking control of the other objects of the same class.

memory management   This includes, for example, the conversion of virtual program addresses into real storage addresses, access protection on memory pages, and so on.

MF   More Fragments.

MIB   Management Information Base.

MIL-STD   Military Standard.

module   A self-contained part of a program, which may be used in specific interfaces.

MSL   Maximum Segment Lifetime.

MTU   Maximum Transfer Unit.

multicast   Message to a group of stations in the network (see also **broadcast**).

multivendor show   Demonstration by several manufacturers.

NCP   Network Control Program.

NCS   Network Computing System.

network administrator   Person responsible for the administration of the network and the relevant networked components of the connected systems (may be identical with the network manager).

NFS   Network File System.

NIC   Network Information Centre.

NIS   Network Information Service.

NLM   Network Lock Manager. Network Loadable Module (Novell NetWare).

node   A computer that serves several network connections simultaneously. This may be a host, a gateway, a router or a bridge.

NVT   Network Virtual Terminal.

ONC   Open Network Computing.

option   Possible setting, functional switch.

OSF   Open Software Foundation.

OSI   Open Systems Interconnection.

paging   Function of memory management, to read in individual program pages from the memory medium and store them in the main memory and vice versa.

path name   Strings of a name separated by slashes, which denote an object in the file system.

POSIX   Portable Operating System Interface on UNIX.

protocol   Agreement between two communicating entities regarding the type and format of message exchange between them.

protocol header   Area preceding data with information for the partner of a protocol layer participating in the data transmission.

ps   UNIX command to list active processes.

pseudo terminal   Virtual device in the operating system, which communicates with a program instead of a terminal.

PSH   Push.

RAID   Redundant Array of Independent Disks.

RARP   Reverse Address Resolution Protocol.

regular expression   Description of a search pattern in text lines.

result   The information obtained during the execution of a program, or a returned value.

REX   Remote Execution Service.

RFC   Request For Comment.

RFS   Remote File Sharing.

RFT   Request For Technology.

RIP   Routing Information Protocol.

route   Path through several connected networks.

RPC Remote Procedure Call.

RR Resource Record.

RST Reset.

RTO Retransmission Timeout.

RTT Round Trip Time.

run-time environment The attributes and parameters determining the execution of a process (for example, user and group IDs, current directory, run-time variables, and so on).

script File with commands that is processed by a command interpreter.

segment Message block in TCP.

server Partner providing service in the relationship between two cooperating processes.

slave Entity that cannot act independently. The master–slave role pattern should not necessarily be compared with the client–server role pattern (see also **master**).

sliding window In data-transmission protocols, a principle applied to optimize the data throughput, using parallel send and acknowledgement of data units. Here, the available buffer capacity designated by the receiver for the receipt of data is viewed as a window relative to transmitted but unacknowledged data units, which increases or decreases in size in the course of transmission.

SLIP Serial Line IP.

SMB Server Message Block.

SMTP Simple Mail Transfer Protocol.

SNAP Subnetwork Access Protocol.

SNMP Simple Network Management Protocol.

SQL Structured Query Language.

SRI Stanford Research Institute.

SRTT Smoothed Round Trip Time.

stderr Standard error channel for error messages in UNIX processes.

stdin Standard input channel in UNIX processes.

stdout Standard output channel in UNIX processes.

subsystem Self-contained system that may be installed and activated as a whole.

SVID System V Interface Definition.

SYN Synchronize.

System V UNIX variant developed and sold by AT&T; its continuing development takes the form of ongoing releases. The current version is System V Release 4, released in December 1989.

TCP Transmission Control Protocol.

terminal identifier   Terminal type identifier used for the *termcap* or *terminfo* control character database.

test suite   A collection of programs to check the functional capability of a system.

TFTP   Trivial File Transfer Protocol.

three-way handshake   Three-way message exchange on connection set-up.

time sharing   Technique for multiple use of a computer installation, where the operating system allocates each user part of the computing facility over a time slice.

timer   Time-controlled alarm function.

TLI   Transport Level Interface.

TPI   Transport Provider Interface.

trailer   A protocol header stored after the data.

TTL   Time To Live.

UCLA   University of California, Los Angeles.

UCSB   University of California, Santa Barbara.

UDP   User Datagram Protocol.

URG   Urgent.

user program   Program that runs not in the privileged part of the operating system but outside the operating system kernel.

UUCP   UNIX-to-UNIX copy.

validation   Check that the functionality conforms with the specification.

VFS   Virtual File System.

WYSIWYG   What You See Is What You Get.

XDR   External Data Representation.

XNS   Xerox Network System.

XPG   X/Open Portability Guide.

XTI   X/Open Transport Interface.

YP   Yellow Pages.

Contact addresses

Contact address of the IAB:

Jon Postel
Deputy Internet Architect
USC Information Sciences Institute
4676 Admiralty Way
Marina del Rey
CA 90292-6695
USA
1-213-822-1511
Email: Postel@ISI.EDU

Address of the publisher of RFCs:

Jon Postel
RFC Editor
USC Information Sciences Institute
4676 Admiralty Way
Marina del Rey
CA 90292-6695
USA
1-213-822-1511
Email: Postel@ISI.EDU

Official Internet numbers are issued by:

Joyce K. Reynolds
Internet Assigned Numbers Authority
USC Information Sciences Institute
4676 Admiralty Way
Marina del Rey
CA 90292-6695
USA
1-213-822-1511
Email: JKRey@ISI.EDU

Address of the NIC for information about RFCs:

SRI International
DDN Network Information Centre
333 Ravenswood Avenue
Menlo Park
CA 94025
USA
1-800-235-3155, 1-415-859-3695
Email:NIC@SRI-NIC.ARPA

Old and new RFCs are accessible by FTP and email on the host nisc.sri.com.

FTP users should log in with user name anonymous giving their email address (for example, santi@santix.de) as password. The RFCs and various other information can be found there in the various accessible subdirectories.

Electronic mail users should send email to the mailserver @nisc.sri.com; the subject field should be left free. Instructions to the mailserver should follow in the text of the letter.

- The instruction rfc-index should be used to obtain a list of all RFCs published to date.
- The entry rfcxxxx.txt is an instruction to send the the text of RFC xxxx, where xxxx is a number specified by the requester.

A mail message may contain several instructions. RFCs are also issued from time to time on CD-ROMs. Readers should enquire in specialist shops such as computer book stores or distribution centres.

Bibliography

Callaghan B. and Lyon T. (1989). *The Automounter Proceedings of the 1989 Winter USENIX Technical Conf.*, San Diego

Case J.D. *et al.* (1990). *Simple Network Management Protocol (SNMP)*. RFC 1157

Cerf V. (1988). *IAB Recommendations for the Development of Internet Network Management Standards*. RFC 1052

Cerf V. and Kahn R. (1974). A protocol for packet-network interconnection. *IEEE Trans. Comm.*, Com-22(5)

Croft B. and Gilmore J. (1985). *Bootstrap Protocol (BOOTP)*. RFC 951

DEC, Intel and Xerox (1982). *The Ethernet – A Local Area Network Data Link Layer and Physical Layer Specifications.*

Deering S. (1989). *Host Extensions for IP Multicasting*. RFC 1112

DOD (1983a). *DOD, Military Standard Internet Protocol*. MIL-STD 1777

DOD (1983b). *DOD, Military Standard Transmission Control Protocol*. MIL-STD 1778

Everhart C.F. *et al.* (1990). *New DNS RR encodings*. RFC 1183

Finlayson R. (1984). *Bootstrap Loading Using TFTP*. RFC 906

Finlayson R. *et al.* (1984). *A Reverse Address Resolution Protocol*. RFC 903

Hedrick C. (1988). *Routing Information Protocol*. RFC 1058

Hornig C. (1984). *A Standard for the Transmission of IP Datagrams over Ethernet Networks*. RFC 894

IEEE (1983, 1984, 1985, 1986). *Standard IEEE 802 Local Area Networks*. IEEE Publication Service

IEEE (1985). *IEEE Standard for Binary Floating-point Arithmetic*. ANSI/IEEE Standard 754

ISO (1987a). *Information Processing Systems – Open Systems Interconnection – Specification of Abstract Syntax Notation One (ASN.1)*. International Standard 8824

ISO (1987b). *Information Processing Systems – Open Systems Interconnection – Specification of Basic Encoding Rules for Abstract Syntax Notation One (ASN.1)*. International Standard 8825

ISO/IEC 8072 (1986). *Information Processing Systems – Open Systems Interconnection – Transport Service Definition*. International Standard 8072 *Addendum 1: Connectionless-mode Transmission*. IS 8072/AD 1

ISO/IEC 9595. *Information Processing Systems – Open Systems Interconnection – Management Information Service Definition.*

ISO/IEC 9596-1 (1991). *Information Technology – Open Systems Interconnection – Common Management Information Protocol Specification – Part 1: Specification,*

Edition 2. CCITT Recommendation X.711

Jacobson V. (1990). *Compressing TCP/IP Headers for Low-speed Serial Links.* RFC 1144

Juszczak C. (1989). Improving the performance and correctness of an NFS server. In *Proc. 1989 Winter USENIX Technical Conf.*, San Diego

Kent S.T. (1984). *Security Options for IP.* DOD

Kirton P. (1984). *EGP Gateway under Berkeley UNIX 4.2.* RFC 911

Korb J. (1983). *A Standard for the Transmission of IP Datagrams over Public Data Networks.* RFC 877

Leffler J.S. and Karels M.J. (1984). *Trailer Encapsulations.* RFC 893

Lougheed K. and Rekhter Y. (1991). *Border Gateway Protocol 3.* RFC 1267

Malis A., Robinson D. and Ullmann R. (1992). *Multiprotocol interconnect on X.25 and ISDN in the packet mode.* RFC 1356

McCloghrie K. and Rose M.T. (1990a). *Structure and Identification of Management Information for TCP/IP-based Internets.* RFC 1155

McCloghrie K. and Rose M.T. (1990b). *Management Information Base for Network Management of TCP/IP-based Internets.* RFC 1156

McManis C. and Jang S. (1991). *Solaris ONC: Network Information Service Plus (NIS+) – A White Paper.* Sun Microsystems, Inc., Mountain View

Miller S.P. *et al.* (1987). *Kerberos Authentication and Authorization System.* Project Athena Technical Plan Section E.2.1

Mills D.L. (1983). *DCN Local Network Protocols.* RFC 891

Mills D.L. (1984). *Exterior Gateway Protocol Formal Specification.* RFC 904

Mockapetris P. (1987a). *Domain Names – Concepts and Facilities.* RFC 1034

Mockapetris P. (1987b). *Domain Names – Implementation and Specification.* RFC 1035

Mockapetris P. (1989). *DNS Encoding of Network Names and Other Types.* RFC 1101

Mogul J. and Deering S. (1990). *MTU Discovery Path.* RFC 1191

Mogul J. and Postel J. (1985). *Internet Standard Subnetting Procedure.* RFC 950

Mogul J. *et al.* (1988). *IP MTU Discovery Options.* RFC 1063

Moy J. (1992). *OSPF version 2.* RFC 1247

OSI (1984). *Information Processing Systems – Open Systems Interconnection: Basic Reference Model.* ISO/IEC Standard 7498

Plummer D.C. (1982). *An Ethernet Address Resolution Protocol.* RFC 826

Postel J. (1980). *User Datagram Protocol.* RFC 768

Postel J. (1981a). *Internet Protocol.* RFC 791

Postel J. (1981b). *Internet Control Message Protocol.* RFC 792

Postel J. (1981c). *Transmission Control Protocol.* RFC 793

Postel J. (1982). *Simple Mail Transfer Protocol.* RFC 821

Postel J. and Reynolds J. (1983). *TELNET Protocol Specification.* RFC 854

Postel J. and Reynolds J. (1985). *File Transfer Protocol (FTP).* RFC 959

Postel J. and Reynolds J. (1988). *A Standard for the Transmission of IP Datagrams over IEEE 802 Networks.* RFC 1042

Reynolds J. and Postel J. (1992). *Assigned Numbers.* RFC 1340

Romkey J. (1988). *A Non-standard for Transmission of IP Datagrams over Serial*

Lines: SLIP. RFC 1055

Rose M.T. and Class D.E. (1987). *ISO Transport Services on Top of the TCP: Version 3.* RFC 1006

Rose M.T. and McCloghrie K. (1991). *Management Information Base for Network Management of TCP/IP-based Internets: MIB-II.* RFC 1213

Rosen E.C. (1982). *BBN Exterior Gateway Protocol (EGP).* RFC 827

St Johns M. (1988). *Draft Revised IP Security Option.* RFC 1038

Sämonson L.J. and Rosen E.C. (1984). *'STUB' Exterior Gateway Protocol.* RFC 888

Schneider H.J., ed. (1983). *Lexikon der Informatik und Datenbearbeitung.* Vienna: Oldenbourg

Simpson W.A. (1992). *Point-to-Point Protocol (PPP) for the transmission of multi-protocol datagrams.* RFC 1331

Sollins K.R. (1981). *The TFTP Protocol (Revision 2).* RFC 783

Stahl M. (1987). *Domain Administrators Guide.* RFC 1032

Sun Microsystems, Inc. (1987). *XDR: External Data Representation Standard.* RFC 1014

Sun Microsystems, Inc. (1988a). *RPC: Remote Procedure Call Protocol Specification.* RFC 1050

Sun Microsystems, Inc. (1988b). *RPC Version 2: Remote Procedure Call Protocol Specification.* RFC 1057

Sun Microsystems, Inc. (1989). *NFS: Network File System Protocol Specification.* RFC 1094

Sun Microsystems, Inc. (1993). *Federated Services – White Paper.*

Unix Software Operation (1990). *UNIX SYSTEM V/386 RELEASE 4 – Network User's and Administrator's Guide.* Englewood Cliffs, NJ: Prentice Hall.

Unix System Laboratories (1992). *UNIX SYSTEM V RELEASE 4 – User's Reference Manual/System Administrator's Reference Manual.* Englewood Cliffs, NJ: Prentice Hall. 1095

Warrier U. *et al.* (1990). *Common Management Information Services and Protocol for the Internet (CMOT) and CMIP.* RFC 1189

X/Open. *X/Open Portability Guide III.* Prentice Hall.

More extensive literature

Bloomer J. (1991). *Power Programming with RPC.* Sebastopol, CA: O'Reilly and Associates

Corner D. (1991). *Interworking with TCP/IP. Vols 1–3.* Englewood Cliffs, NJ: Prentice Hall

Madron T.W. (1992). *Network Security in the '90s.* New York: John Wiley and Sons, Inc.

Hunt C. (1992). *TCP/IP Network Administration.* Sebastopol, CA: O'Reilly and Associates

Stern H. (1991). *Managing NFS and NIS.* Sebastopol, CA: O'Reilly and Associates

Washburn K. and Evans J.T. (1993). *TCP/IP – Running a Successful Network.* Wokingham: Addison-Wesley

Index